D0640879

THE PRESS
AND THE ORIGINS OF
THE COLD WAR,
1944–1947

LOUIS LIEBOVICH

THE PRESS
AND THE ORIGINS
OF
THE COLD WAR,
1944–1947

PRAEGER

New York
Westport, Connecticut
London

PN4738 .L53 1988

Liebovich, Louis.

The press and the origins of
the cold war, 1944-1947
#17354216

Library of Congress Cataloging-in-Publication Data

Liebovich, Louis.
    The press and the origins of the cold war, 1944–1947 / Louis
Liebovich.
        p.   cm.
    Bibliography: p.
    Includes index.
    ISBN 0–275–92999–X (alk. paper)
    1. Government and the press—United States. 2. Press and
politics. 3. World politics—1945– 4. United States—Foreign
relations—Soviet Union. 5. Soviet Union—Foreign relations—United
States. I. Title.
PN4738.L53 1988
070.4'49327—dc19   87–38478

Copyright © 1988 by Louis Liebovich

All rights reserved. No portion of this book may
be reproduced, by any process or technique, without
the express written consent of the publisher.

Library of Congress Catalog Card Number: 87–38478

ISBN: 0–275–92999–X

First published in 1988

Praeger Publishers, One Madison Avenue, New York, NY 10010
A division of Greenwood Press, Inc.

Printed in the United States of America

The paper used in this book complies with the
Permanent Paper Standard issued by the National
Information Standards Organization (Z39.48–1984).

10 9 8 7 6 5 4 3 2 1

Augustana College Library
Rock Island Illinois 61201

For Shirley

Contents

Acknowledgments

I would like to extend a note of appreciation to the many persons who assisted in the preparation of this book. I am especially indebted to James L. Baughman, associate professor of mass communication, University of Wisconsin, and to Gene Gilmore, associate professor of journalism (emeritus), University of Illinois, for their tireless efforts in the review of this manuscript. I would also like to thank Thomas McCormick, John Cooper, and Edward Coffman, professors of history, University of Wisconsin, and John McNelly, professor of communications, and Stephen Vaughn, associate professor of communications, University of Wisconsin, for their help in the compilation of this study. Thanks also to William Solomon, University of Illinois, and William Weiss, associate professor at the University of Wisconsin, Whitewater.

A special note of appreciation is also extended to retired educator Lloyd Spear and to graduate students Richard Fruto, Rahul Jacob, Sharon Raksnis, John Burge, and Douglas Isbell for their help. This manuscript also would not be possible without the aid of the researchers at the Harry S Truman Library, Independence, Missouri, and the University of South Carolina's Caroliniana Library, Columbia, South Carolina.

THE PRESS
AND THE ORIGINS OF
THE COLD WAR,
1944–1947

Chapter 1
Introduction

During the years 1944 to 1947, occupying armies and bargaining diplomats fashioned a new political and military alignment that reshaped the international framework throughout the globe. The Axis dream of a New World Order disappeared with the end of World War II in the summer of 1945. Europe, the core of world diplomacy for hundreds of years, largely receded as a center of world power. Germany lay prostrate and occupied by foreign armies, and Great Britain was economically crippled by the costly burdens of war. In Asia the United States accepted the task of rebuilding a defeated Japan, while China, finally free of foreign domination, was divided by civil war.

From the wreckage two nations arose to dominate the diplomatic and military arenas, the United States and the Soviet Union. The latter suffered the loss of 20 million citizens during World War II, far more than any other nation. Millions were displaced, and major industry and transportation routes throughout Eastern Europe were devastated. Although the United States sustained the loss of approximately 390,000 soldiers, the contiguous forty-eight states remained untouched by bombings or invading armies throughout the war.

The leaders of the United States, the Soviet Union, and Great Britain first attacked the problem of postwar conditions and settlements through diplomatic conferences, executive agreements, and initiation of a United Nations organization. When cooperation failed, East–West mutual antagonism followed. Consequently, a position of cooperation in early 1944 deteriorated to confrontation, hostility, and mutual suspicion by the summer of 1947. The Soviet Union initiated a policy of domination in Eastern Europe, and the United States countered with economic and military plans to align capitalist governments against the perceived communist threat.

This study will examine the role of four print news organizations in the United States during the years 1944 through 1947 in interpreting the burgeoning Cold War. This span begins when an Allied victory first seemed inevitable, continues through the end of the war and the beginning of Soviet–U.S. hostility, and ends with the declaration of the Truman Doctrine and the Marshall Plan, signaling a formal policy of ideological warfare.

The Truman declaration was designed to convince Congress to appropriate $400 million in loans to Greece and Turkey to push back encroaching communism, but the containment philosophy had wide-ranging implications that formally set in motion a Cold War policy in the United States. The Marshall Plan, fashioned to provide food and economic aid to war-torn European nations, established the United States as the key economic force in the rebuilding of Western Europe. The Soviet Union declined to become part of the Marshall Plan because Soviet leaders claimed the United States was dictating how the plan would be implemented. Together, these two foreign affairs approaches laid the framework for U.S. efforts to contain and later confront what policy makers considered communist subversion in Europe and later in Asia.

The four print organizations selected for this study are *Time* magazine, the *New York Herald Tribune*, the *Chicago Tribune*, and the *San Francisco Chronicle*.[1] Chosen for a geographical and philosophical balance, these represent a collection of major urban news groups, which disseminated foreign affairs news during a crucial international period in U.S. history. The newspapers represent some of the leading journals in heavily populated areas of the country at the time and, with the exception of the *Chronicle*, were among the highest-circulation newspapers of the time.[2]

The four were chosen for a variety of reasons. The *New York Herald Tribune* had a reputation as an internationalist newspaper with a pro-British point of view. Star columnist Walter Lippmann played a role in enunciating the foreign policy choices of the postwar era in his columns, which supported regional hegemony and opposed George Kennan's theories of containment. This philosophical duel between Kennan and Lippmann placed Lippmann and, consequently, the *Herald Tribune* at the forefront of the intellectual debate over foreign policy during the origins of the Cold War. Because of Lippmann's key role and because both the *Herald Tribune* and *The New York Times* followed thoughtful, insightful editorial policies, the former rather than the latter was chosen for this study. The choice proved difficult, but the study would be unbalanced if two newspapers were chosen from the same city.

The *Chicago Tribune* provided a strong midwestern ethnocentric voice for comparison. The *Chicago Tribune* pursued its isolationist attitudes through the war and postwar years with heavily conservative Republican tendencies. Though not necessarily a leader in providing foreign news coverage, the *Chicago Tribune* did offer a point of view widely divergent from the more cosmopolitan eastern news organizations. The Chicago newspaper, though antagonistic to the Roosevelt and Truman administrations, favored a contentious stance against the Soviet Union, similar to Truman's. This anticommunist sentiment, however, precluded any thought of costly expenditures for foreign aid or military buildups. In short, the *Chicago Tribune* provided a distinct type of foreign news coverage that reflected the fundamentalist attitude of many readers in the nation's heartland.

Finally, this study required a newspaper from the West Coast. Removed from the government and business influence of the East and the isolationist attitudes of the Midwest, the West Coast provided an altered regional attitude toward war and international affairs. During the war years, a certain hysteria about Japanese Americans existed, particularly in California. The influence of the aircraft industries and a general melting pot population offered support for an internationalist posture. The *Chronicle* supported a moderate, Republican position and a liberal social philosophy. The San Francisco-based newspaper was one of few journals to support the Nisei who were victimized by government relocation during the war. Slow to support anticommunist confrontational policies, the *Chronicle* offered a regional view of foreign affairs without the hysteria that accompanied the observations of some other West Coast newspapers. The author was able to contact a former editorial writer who wrote for the *Chronicle* during this time period, and he provided valuable insights into the inner workings of the newspaper. Also, the San Francisco Conference, where the final structure for the United Nations was established, received wide coverage by the *Chronicle*. The attention devoted to international affairs provided a compromise between the economic constraints of a smaller-circulation newspaper and a daily journal located in an internationally oriented city.

The choice of a West Coast newspaper was the most difficult because none of the newspapers in the region was regarded as a leading foreign affairs journal and because no newspaper had a large circulation. The *Chronicle* was not the most popular newspaper in the area at the time, but five newspapers split the Bay Area readership in more or less equal terms. Only on Sunday did the Hearst-owned *Examiner* far outdistance the field. Consequently, the *Chronicle* was chosen because of its efforts to weigh foreign affairs issues, because of its coverage of the San Francisco Conference, because it represented a West Coast point of view, and because of a valuable oral history source.

It is important that such newspapers as the *Herald Tribune* and the *Chronicle* be studied in such contexts. Such news organizations were geared to serious discussion of international events and political motivations, both on their editorial pages and in their news columns. The New York newspapers often originated news stories that were later picked up by media elsewhere in the country. Many of the lesser newspapers in the country assumed that their readers wished less detailed news about foreign affairs, while the elite newspapers were designed to serve a more cosmopolitan audience, many of whom were well educated or opinion leaders. Such periodicals influence readers and public opinion beyond the mere circulation numbers. Their news reports hold sway with other news organizations and opinion leaders. Thus, weighty observations in Walter Lippmann's column would bring pause for thought among the nation's elite in a way that would not likely occur in such larger circulation newspapers as the *New York Mirror* or the *New York News*. As Bernard C. Cohen states: "The image of the audience as especially interested in foreign affairs incorporates both the view that readers are the foreign policy elite, and the feeling that they are in unspecified ways unusual or distinguished though perhaps not expertly knowledgeable. . . . [The news persons] see their newspapers, and thus their own stories, as read by government people all the way up to the top levels."[3]

Inclusion of a news magazine in the study provides a source of more summarized and analytical news reporting than that of the daily newspapers, where news coverage was plagued by constant deadline pressure. A weekly publication also has a more nationally dispersed audience and has no regional news bias or innate interest in regionally oriented events, thus providing an entirely national and international scope of emphasis. *Time* magazine was selected because it was the most prestigious, established news weekly of the period with a higher circulation than the combined circulation of its two nearest competitors, *Newsweek* and *U.S. News*.[4] Thus, this study will account for a certain balance among types of media reporting. It does not represent a cross section of the media in the country at the time, but a sample of the most influential or diverse sources of journalistic observation.

II

Scholarly debate has swirled around the causes and nuances of the origins of the Cold War. It is necessary to review earlier observations before embarking upon this study. The first group of postwar historians, including Arthur Schlesinger, Jr., Herbert Feis, Louis Halle, and George Kennan, contended that Truman gave Stalin every opportunity to establish common goals and a direction for both countries. Stalin, they argued, responded by severing lines of communication and shutting the West out of Eastern Europe with the intention of extending Soviet influence throughout the world. As Kennan summarized, "What Stalin was really after was the expulsion of American influence from the Eurasian land mass generally, and its replacement by that of his own regime." Schlesinger added that conceding Eastern Europe to the Soviet Union and recognizing spheres of influence would recreate the old balance of power geopolitics, which would only lead to another world war.[5] They saw a potential power grab by Stalin extending to such areas as China, Turkey, Iran, Greece, and even such strongly democratic Western countries as France, where communists gained strong minorities in government through elections.

The earliest school of thought saw Stalin and Soviet communist leaders as untrustworthy and ambitious. U.S. policy was interpreted as reactive and defensive, while Soviet aims were aggressive. These historians saw a threat to both U.S. security and world peace. One such advocate John Spanier summarized, "Thus the cold war grew out of the interactions between traditional power politics and the nature of the Soviet regime."[6] While most of these scholars advocated a strong U.S. position in world affairs, Kennan felt the United States should concentrate on containing Soviet influence to Eastern Europe. U.S. might should only be exerted in important industrialized areas, and confrontation with the Soviet Union over lesser nations should be avoided, Kennan argued.

These scholars focused on evidence that tended to support official U.S. policy in the late 1940s and early 1950s. They emphasized Soviet secrecy, historical friction caused by revolutionary Soviet ideals, and the basic world aims of theoretical communism. Though there was disagreement over how strongly the United States should have reacted, these scholars clearly placed the onus on the Soviet Union. But they did not examine closely some identifiable overt acts by U.S. leaders nor the effects of public opinion and internal pressures in the United States.

With a deepening U.S. military involvement in Southeast Asia in the 1960s and the liberal backlash that developed in the United States, a second group of historians reached very different conclusions about the origins of the Cold War. This group varied considerably more in their contentions than did the first set of scholars. However, essentially they assigned a greater share, if not a major share, of the blame for the Cold War to U.S. aggression and historical capitalist aims.

The first major work generally recognized as revisionist was written by William Appleman Williams, who argued that Truman pursued a traditional capitalist path, seeking European markets for U.S. business. An anti-Soviet Europe offered an attractive trading partner, and the need for markets had formed the foundation of U.S. foreign policy since the 1890s, according to Williams.[7] He blamed the origins of the Cold War on historical U.S. aims and downplayed Soviet responsibility. Williams ignored a number of practical realities at the time. His continuity theory did not allow enough latitude for changing public perceptions, personalities of leaders, or the altered role of the United States in the world, according to David S. Patterson in his essay on revisionist thought.[8]

Nevertheless, other revisionists followed in Williams's footsteps, anchoring their postulations to perceived ambitious U.S. economic policies. Lloyd C. Gardner argued that Truman "wanted to teach the Russians that they had to play their part in the new order, and he wanted to do it by making it clear that America did not need Russian markets."[9] Gardner spent more time than Williams elucidating the personalities of U.S. leaders and offering insights into personal motivations, but the thrust of his conclusions and his probe of U.S. motivations followed Williams's work closely.

Early revisionists focused on traditional U.S. economic needs and tended to look toward long-term patterns of international relations. They then considered the postwar period as but a portion of a half century of unfolding policies. Michael Leigh in his essay on revisionism notes that Williams, for instance, saw U.S. policy makers as "more constrained by factors than personality." Paul Seabury pointed out that the search for markets as an explanation for Soviet–U.S. tension in the postwar era "makes little sense—such expectations have always been latent in the American business community."[10] While Seabury too quickly dismissed the "Open Door" theory, he did accurately reflect the key weakness in the Williams argument—the lack of emphasis on personalities, short-term trends, and Soviet ambitions and insecurity.

During the height of the war in Southeast Asia, New Left scholars carried the revisionist arguments further, describing Truman and his advisers as open advocates of aggressive policies. The more radical leftists such as Gabriel and Joyce Kolko and David Horowitz viewed the entire U.S. capitalist system as the moving force behind the Cold War. That is, the politics of the postwar era reflected the goals of an entire unbalanced system, not just the market orientation of business.[11]

At the same time, revisionists downplayed the Soviet Union's role in the Cold War even more than Williams or Gardner. Fred Warner Neal contended, "There is now beginning to be some limited recognition that the danger of Soviet military aggression never existed, that the fear so deeply embedded in a whole generation of Americans was based upon fantasy."[12] The later revisionists saw Stalin as a nationalist seeking only to protect Soviet interests. Gabriel and Joyce Kolko argued, for instance, that during the early period of the Cold War, Stalin had ample opportunity to push Soviet influence, but he chose not to. Finland assumed a nonmilitary posture and thus soothed Soviet insecurity, so Finland remained a democratic country. In Austria, too, the Soviet leadership did not impose its will.[13] Walter LaFeber noted that rising U.S. hostility and the Truman Doctrine came at a time when Soviet leadership had done the least in the postwar era to antagonize the United States.[14]

Inevitability plays a major role in the revisionist argument. Just as Williams saw capitalist markets as inevitable magnets for U.S. world ambition, the Kolkos saw the triumph of the Left as an inevitable political factor. As Warren Kimball argued, the Kolkos attributed everything to ideology and oversimplified to the point of ignoring much historiography.[15]

Not all revisionists cling to this ideological overview. Many focus on personality rather than ideology and maintain that Franklin Roosevelt's death in April 1945 and Truman's rise to the presidency brought a Cold Warrior to leadership and suspicions among Soviet leaders. Williams, the Kolkos, and Diane Shaver Clemens put forth ideological and economic themes. Others, such as Dana Fleming, Gar Alperovitz, and Horowitz, found fault with Truman's tough talk. Most historians, including revisionists, are cautious about such comparisons because Roosevelt died before his policies toward the Soviet Union could be tested in a postwar world. The focus in such analyses is on Truman and his tough talk at Potsdam and during a conference with Foreign Minister V. M. Molotov in Washington just after Roosevelt's death.[16]

The strengths of later revisionists were their abilities to cast aside the vision of the Soviet Union and world communism as simplistic monolithic threats. They were able to take into account nationalistic factors and a certain propensity among U.S. leaders to pursue ethnocentric, self-interested goals while generalizing about the renewed bolshevik threat. Many of these revisionists were tied to the activist 1960s and postulated themes that fit with the antigovernment mood of the times. In so doing, they sometimes ignored the public climate of the 1940s and tried to impose a 1960s frame of reference.[17]

III

This study will examine the line of logic followed by the designated newspapers and magazine and analyze how their observations relate to these three theories.

Although the literature concerning political and diplomatic events during this period is plentiful and wide ranging, few works of note have dealt specifically with the role of newspapers and news magazines during this period. James Aronson's *The Press and the Cold War* concerns Soviet–U.S. relations and domestic press reactions from 1945 through 1970. Aronson, a liberal journalist who suffered through the McCarthy era, concentrates on events in the 1950s, and he is primarily concerned with excoriating his former colleagues throughout the profession for not taking a more courageous stand against McCarthyism.[18] John L. Gaddis has written a number of books about foreign relations in the immediate postwar period, but he only touches on the role of the press within a wide-ranging scope of unfolding events.[19] Ralph B. Levering's books on U.S. opinion and the Soviet Union during this period are excellent, but again, newspapers are only one aspect within the entire public opinion spectrum in Levering's studies.[20] A few unpublished dissertations have dealt with topics similar to that of this book. For instance, Ronald S. Reinig's 1974 study at Syracuse University concerns Cold War attitudes in the United States in the mid–1940s as reflected in magazines. At St. John's University in 1957, Sister Mary Assumpta

Mazza composed a study of attitudes toward the Soviet Union in U.S. periodicals between 1942 and 1949.[21]

Besides the differing time period and news organization focuses, these studies are not comparable to this work in other ways. Most importantly, they do not offer mass communication interpretations for media behavior. They merely chart the reactions and statements of journalistic institutions, noting that liberal or conservative philosophies and outside influences on these news organizations contributed to the positions they assumed in regard to foreign affairs.

This study will explore the composition of the news organizations involved and offer insights into the individual characteristics of those institutions, as well as explain their commentary on the origins of the Cold War. Each newspaper or magazine reacted to the perceived Soviet threat, not only because of the ideological precepts of the journalistic organization and not only because of the ebb and flow of world affairs and national leadership, but also because of the changing nature of the staff and writers within the institution itself. The term, news organizations, refers to a collection of individual groups competing with each other at various levels. Generalizations about their characteristics do not allow for the nuances that can affect decision making from a human standpoint. This study, then, will not only concern itself with foreign relations in the period, 1944 to 1947, but will also be a case study of four news institutions' policies on handling crucial national and international issues at a given time in history.

A complete assortment of historical, contemporary, and ideological constraints acted on the editors and reporters of these four print media during the period of study. Traditional views of Soviet values, bolshevik ideals, the United States' role in the world, and images of such heavy-handed leaders as Josef Stalin affected coverage during this time. Identification of Stalin as a leftist version of Hitler certainly influenced media perceptions.[22] Franklin Delano Roosevelt's death in April 1945 and Harry S Truman's elevation to the presidency influenced the personal relationships between president and press and press confidence in U.S. leadership. Concurrently, the change in press secretaries from Stephen Early to Charles G. Ross, a former journalist with the *St. Louis Post-Dispatch*, brought about a changed relationship between White House and Washington press corps.[23] Finally, the press in Washington and their home offices had been conditioned to a certain patriotic fervor and acceptance of censorship during World War II. According to A. Merriman Smith, United Press White House correspondent, the censorship code during the war forbade unauthorized reporting of the president's whereabouts. He recalled:

As the war continued, Mr. Roosevelt did virtually what he pleased, in public and in private, and in the secure knowledge it would not be on the radio or in the newspapers. . . . This was all very fine, but the president began to put on and take off security like winter underwear. When he wanted it, he ordered it . . . True, the pressure of the Presidency is heavy and seclusion a welcome antidote, but Mr. Roosevelt made a fetish of his privacy during the war.[24]

This study, then, will attempt to answer questions about foreign affairs reporting, about decision making within news organizations, about Roosevelt's and Truman's influence over journalists during the specific period, about perceptions in the aforementioned print organizations concerning the Soviet Union, and about the role the news groups played in urging caution and considered steps in dealing with foreign relations leading to the origins of the Cold War. This study will not attempt to establish a causal relationship between foreign policy makers' decisions in response to news reporting and editorializing. Establishing such a relationship can only be speculative and tenuous at best. It is historically valuable to trace the reporting and journalistic decisions on foreign affairs issues during a given period to establish just what environment existed when crucial governmental leaders constructed diplomatic and political policy. It is also important to monitor the actions of news institutions, because such institutions constantly cling to a notion of watchdog responsibility over government. How did these three newspapers and *Time* magazine exercise their obligations to question U.S. foreign affairs policy decisions with regard to the Soviet Union?

Conversely, while the news organizations attempt to fulfill their roles as watchdogs, they are constrained by institutional factors that limit their effectiveness. Sociologist Herbert J. Gans points out that news firms do not hire staffs that are able to cover adequately all important in-depth issues in government. The antagonistic role of the press is restrained by the capitalist profit motive. The *Chronicle*, for instance, had neither a Moscow nor a Washington correspondent for most of the period of this study. None of the other larger news organizations sent teams of reporters to review the shifting attitudes in both Washington and Moscow, nor did they probe deeply to explore the context of major policy announcements, such as the Truman Doctrine. They were content to report what had been proposed and then wait for others, most notably Congress, to react.

At the same time these wealthy capitalist publishers were natural enemies of communism and Soviet ideology. They inherently viewed the Soviet Union as an enemy, especially when war-time allegiances were removed. The *Chicago Tribune* and the *Chronicle* at times confused Soviet goals and ambitions with domestic communist concerns in the United States. They lumped the aims of the U.S. Communist party with those of the Soviet Union and viewed left-wing labor organizations as tools of the Soviet Union.

Additionally, the three newspapers and *Time* had reporters who were source oriented, not wishing to stop the flow of information. A negative story by a Washington correspondent about President Truman could eliminate that reporter from the inner circle of discussion at the White House and, as Gans pointed out, reporters often become encased in the system. "Journalists rise to the top by being cautious," Gans concluded.[25]

This study will be divided into ten chapters. The first chapter will provide the historical backdrop for the period of study, tracing the development of the periodicals over time and the evolution of foreign affairs through 1943. The second chapter will introduce the press environment in the United States and the military and diplomatic situation in 1944. Chapter 3 will focus on press coverage of Soviet–U.S. relations in 1944. Chapter 4 will deal with the Yalta and San Francisco Conferences, while Chapter 5 will trace press perceptions of the change in presidents and the events leading up to and including the Potsdam Conference. Chapter 6 will examine diplomatic effects of the atomic bomb and the immediate aftermath of World War II. U.S. interest in civil strife in China and, most notably, press coverage of the Marshall Mission to China in 1945 and 1946 will provide the focus for Chapter 7. The final three chapters will explore the rapidly changing image of the Soviet Union in the United States, the press response and handling of the changing mood, and the reception of the four news institutions to the Truman Doctrine and the Marshall Plan in 1947.

NOTES

1. Though this analysis will concern itself with the four specific news operations, many other print accounts of unfolding events have been examined to provide a perspective on news treatment at the time. For example, other newspapers in Chicago, New York, and San Francisco were reviewed, as well as newspapers in Boston, Baltimore, New Orleans, and Los Angeles. For comparison, the author also reviewed other magazines and the radio scripts of broadcast commentators of the time. Though all three of these newspapers, to a large extent, supported Republican policies, candidates, and officeholders, this did not present a problem to the reliability of this study. Most newspapers subscribed to such a philosophy. Few supported Roosevelt editorially in his election bids. Historian Graham J. White points out that Roosevelt claimed that 85 percent of the major newspapers in the nation opposed him, but actually the number was closer to 60 percent. The percentage of large city dailies that subscribed to editorial philosophies parallel to the Democratic party was even smaller than the 40 percent, who supported Roosevelt. See Graham J. White, *FDR and the Press* (Chicago: University of Chicago Press, 1979), 72–79. The three newspapers varied in their editorial approaches, and though they were Republican in scope, they were not mirror images. Only the *Chicago Tribune* could have been described as a partisan sheet. Additionally, *Time*, the *Herald Tribune*, and the *Chronicle* all had been internationalist in their views of U.S. foreign policy before and during World War II. The *Chicago Tribune* had offered a more isolationist, nationalistic approach.

2. Circulation figures as of March 31, 1947, were as follows: *Chicago Tribune*, daily 1,058,627, Sunday 1,582,656; *The New York Times*, daily 555,932, Sunday 1,091,183; *New York Herald Tribune*, daily 352,154, Sunday, 729,363; *San Francisco*

Chronicle, daily 168,842, Sunday, 271,120. By comparison, figures for other newspapers in the cities were *New York Mirror,* daily 1,105,026, and Sunday, 2,169,873; *New York News,* daily 2,352,484, Sunday 4,765,721; *New York Post,* daily 272,272, Sunday, 314,156; *Chicago News,* daily 504,073, no Sunday; *Chicago Sun,* daily 321,187, Sunday, 467,716; *Chicago Times,* daily 472,879, Sunday, 545,438 (the latter two merged on August 5, 1947); *Chicago Herald-American,* daily 524,155, Sunday 1,111,791; *San Francisco Examiner,* daily 228,522, Sunday, 606,349; *San Francisco News,* daily 144,723, no Sunday; *San Francisco Call-Bulletin,* daily, 169,596, no Sunday; *Oakland Tribune,* daily, 167,305, Sunday, 161,002. See *Editor and Publisher Market Guide* (New York: Editor and Publisher Company, 1948), 40, 96, 269. For complete figures for several years' circulation at *The New York Times,* also see Meyer Berger, *The Story of the New York Times, 1851–1951* (New York: Simon and Schuster, 1970), 570.

3. Bernard C. Cohen, *The Press and Foreign Policy* (Princeton, N.J.: Princeton University Press, 1963), 108.

4. Circulation of *Time* in 1945 was 1,181,467 and 1,554,323 in 1947. *Newsweek's* circulation was 207,257 and 244,009. See J. Percy N. Johnson, ed., *N. W. Ayer and Son's Directory 1945* (Philadelphia: N. W. Ayers and Son, 1947), 1230–35.

5. George Kennan, *Russia and the West under Lenin and Stalin,* rev. ed. (Boston: Little, Brown, 1961), 367. Arthur Schlesinger, "Origins of the Cold War," in *America and the Origins of the Cold War, 1945–80,* 4th ed., ed. James V. Compton (New York: John Wiley and Sons, 1980), 9–12. See also Louis Halle, "The Cold War as History," in *America and the Origins of the Cold War,* ed. Compton, 36–45; Arthur Schlesinger, "The Origins of the Cold War," *Foreign Affairs* 46 (October 1967): 23–56; and Herbert Feis, *From Trust to Terror: The Onset of the Cold War* (Princeton, N.J.: Princeton University Press, 1970).

6. John Spanier, "American Foreign Policy Since World War II," in *America and the Origins of the Cold War,* ed. Compton, 25.

7. William Appleman Williams, *The Tragedy of American Diplomacy,* rev. ed. (New York: Dell, 1972).

8. David S. Patterson, "Recent Literature on Cold War Origins: An Essay Review," *Wisconsin Magazine of History* 55 (Summer 1972): 320–29.

9. Lloyd C. Gardner, *Architects of Illusion: Men and Ideas in American Foreign Policy, 1941–1949* (Chicago: Quadrangle, 1970), 58.

10. Michael Leigh, "Is There a Revisionist Thesis on the Origins of the Cold War?" *Political Science Quarterly* 89 (March 1974): 106; Paul Seabury, *The Rise and Decline of the Cold War* (New York: Basic, 1967).

11. See especially Geoffrey S. Smith, " 'Harry, We Hardly Know You': Revisionism, Politics, and Diplomacy, 1945–54," *American Political Science Review* 70 (1976): 564; David Horowitz, *Free World Colossus: A Critique of American Foreign Policy in the Cold War* (New York: Hill and Wang, 1971); Gar Alperovitz, ed., *Cold War Essays* (Garden City, N.J.: Anchor, 1970).

12. Fred Warner Neal, "The Cold War in Europe: 1945–1967," *Struggle Against History: U.S. Foreign Policy in an Age of Revolution,* ed. Neal D. Houghton (New York: Washington Square Press, 1968), 22.

13. See especially Gabriel Kolko, *The Politics of War: The World and United States Foreign Policy, 1943–45* (New York: Random House, 1968); Gabriel Kolko and Joyce

Kolko, *The Limits of Power: The World and United States Foreign Policy, 1945–1954* (New York: Harper and Row, 1972).

14. Walter LaFeber, *America, Russia, and the Cold War, 1945–1980*, 4th ed. (New York: John Wiley and Sons, 1980).

15. Warren Kimball, "The Cold War Warmed Over," *American History Review* 29 (October 1974): 1121.

16. Leigh, "Is There a Revisionist Thesis on the Origins of the Cold War?": 114–25.

17. Richard Kluger, *The Paper: The Life and Death of the New York Herald Tribune* (New York: Knopf, 1986); Robert Shaplen, "Denson's Revolution at the *Herald Tribune*," *Saturday Review* 44 (July 8, 1961): 36–38; and Oswald Garrison Villard, *The Disappearing Daily: Chapters in American Newspaper Evolution* (New York: Knopf, 1944), 93–102.

18. James Aronson, *The Press and the Origins of the Cold War* (Indianapolis, Ind.: Bobbs-Merrill, 1970).

19. See John L. Gaddis, *The United States and the Origins of the Cold War, 1941–1947* (New York: Columbia University Press, 1972).

20. Ralph B. Levering, *The Cold War, 1945–1972* (Arlington Heights, Ill.: Harland Davidson, 1982); Ralph B. Levering, *American Opinion and the Russian Alliance, 1939–1945* (Chapel Hill: University of North Carolina Press, 1976).

21. Ronald S. Reinig, "American Looking Outward: American Cold War Attitudes during the Crucial Years, 1945–1947, As Reflected in the American Magazine Medium," Ph.D. dissertation, Syracuse University, 1974; R. P. Mazza (Sister Mary Assumpta), "A Survey of Changing Attitudes Toward the Soviet Union as Reflected in American Periodicals, 1942–1949," Ph.D. dissertation, St. John's University, 1956.

22. See Les K. Adler and Thomas G. Paterson, " 'Red Fascism': The Merger of Nazi Germany and Soviet Russia in the American Image of Totalitarianism, 1930s–1950s," *American Historical Review* 75 (1970): 1046–64; Ralph K. White, "Hitler, Roosevelt and the Nature of War Propaganda," *Journal of Abnormal and Social Psychology* 44 (April 1949): 157–74.

23. See Ronald T. Farrar, *Reluctant Servant: The Story of Charles G. Ross* (Columbia: University of Missouri Press, 1969).

24. A. Merriman Smith, *Thank You, Mr. President: A White House Notebook* (New York: Harper and Brothers, 1946), 130.

25. Herbert J. Gans, *Deciding What's News: A Study of CBS Evening News, NBC Nightly News, Newsweek and Time* (New York: Pantheon, 1979), 283–99.

Chapter 2
Such Good Friends

In early 1943 Eddy Gilmore, Associated Press correspondent assigned to the Soviet Union, accompanied a friend to Spokane, Washington, for a brief respite from the rigors of reporting at the Eastern front. As a joke, Gilmore was introduced to a crowded nightclub as a Soviet officer who had been decorated for his sharpshooting on the Soviet–German front. The crowd applauded wildly. Spurred by the enthusiastic response, Gilmore delivered a ringing speech in broken English on the momentous relationship between the Soviet Union and the United States and the audience applauded even more enthusiastically.[1]

Americans, like those in the audience at the nightclub in Spokane, generally felt a warm sympathy and friendship toward the Soviet people, whose brethren were dying by the millions in the frozen war zones of the Soviet Union, and toward the Red Army, in general, which was singlehandedly turning back Hitler's forces in Eastern Europe. This feeling carried over to the Soviet government. A National Opinion Research Center poll in February 1942 found that 38 percent of respondents agreed that the Soviet Union could be trusted to cooperate with the United States after World War II, while 37 percent disagreed and 25 percent were undecided or had no opinion. By August 1943, 51 percent responded favorably, while 27 percent reacted negatively and 22 percent were undecided or had no opinion.[2] A *Fortune* magazine poll in 1943 found that 81 percent of Americans thought the United States should work with the Soviet Union as equal partners after the war.[3] *Life* magazine, which along with *Fortune* was owned by Time, Inc., published a special issue in March 1943, which praised the

Soviet people and particularly Soviet leadership.[4] *Time* carried a cover pic-
ture of Stalin to mark the first edition of the magazine in 1943 praising
Stalin as the "Man of the Year" in 1942. "Only Stalin knows how he
managed to make 1942 a better year for Russia than 1941," *Time* concluded.
"Russia was displaying greater strength than at any point in the war. The
genius who had won that overall battle [Stalingrad] was the man who runs
Russia."[5] Just three months earlier, in New York City, a group of the
United States' wealthiest capitalists met at the Banker's Club to hear Robert
A. Lovett, assistant secretary of war for air, praise the Soviet Union.[6]

If the mid-war images of the Soviet Union were initially favorable, then
those images were certainly fostered by Soviet leaders. From the first confused moments after the bombing of Pearl Harbor on December 7, 1941,
until the Normandy invasion in southern France on June 6, 1944, Soviet
leaders employed every diplomatic and public relations tactic at their dis-
posal to convince leaders of Great Britain and the United States of the
necessity of a second front invasion in Nazi-occupied Western Europe. A
belated move by the Soviet hierarchy came on May 23, 1943, when they
dissolved their international revolutionary agency, Comintern. The Comintern had not been active for years, but its dissolution helped to dissuade
the United States and Great Britain of its future potential. While this step
may not have had a great deal of impact in diplomatic circles, it drew
substantial positive reaction in news reports.[7]

During the early war years, feelings between the West and the Soviet
Union had thawed since the unfriendly years after the Russian revolution.
From 1921, when nearly all opposition to the Bolsheviks had been eliminated in the Soviet Union, until the 1940s, the Soviet Union built an industrialized nation primarily through internal sacrifices. As the only Marxist
government in the world, the Soviets stood alone, largely separated both
diplomatically and economically from the rest of the world.

In order to understand Soviet-U.S. relations at the close of 1943, one
must trace the course of events from 1917 through the middle of World
War II. These relations encompassed philosophical, economic, and diplomatic considerations.

For over a generation the Soviet Union held a certain fascination for
liberals in the West. During the years just prior to the Russian revolution,
these liberals found the primitive, monarchical Russian society the antithesis
of their decadent, bourgeois life style. They viewed the brutal excesses of
the Russian nobility with a certain horrified interest. Russia's feudal society
recalled the old ways of preindustrial Europe. Certainly, the harsh repression
meted out to the peasants and the uncaring ostentatiousness of the czarist
elite repulsed these Western ideologues, but as historian Christopher Lasch
pointed out, "It became a museum of preindustrial antiquities, in which
were preserved all the things that liberalism itself had wiped out wherever
it had the power to do so."[8] All that was needed was the egalitarian spirit

to transform this monarchical society into a democracy that hopefully would not be despoiled by the excesses of nineteenth-century-style capitalism. As Hollander noted, "The American conception of the proper role of the state, deriving from a broader Western European liberal tradition, is diametrically opposed to the Soviet-Marxist point of view." Americans could not understand how such a Marxist system could possibly survive.[9]

Despite the brutality of the Russian Revolution, which began spontaneously in March 1917, Americans greeted the ouster of the czar with a renewed hope of their vision for the Russian people. After two months of chaos Aleksandr Kerensky formed a provisional government and Soviet forces resumed fighting in World War I. But in October 1917 the weak Kerensky leadership was replaced by a radical bolshevik government under Vladimir Ilich Lenin, who had just returned to the Soviet Union after ten years of exile. As part of a movement away from ties to capitalist Europe, Lenin quickly moved to end the Soviet Union's participation in what he considered a war of imperialism. In March 1918 Germany and the Soviet Union signed the Treaty of Brest-Litovsk, ending the Soviet Union's role in the war. With the conclusion of the war eight months later and the subsequent signing of the Versailles Treaty, Western countries feared the threat of bolshevism and loathed the revolutionary movement in the Soviet Union, which had displayed its independence through Brest-Litovsk.[10]

On the other hand, Lenin faced a civil war that drained precious reserves already decimated by war, revolution, and the terms of Brest-Litovsk. The intervention of Allied forces in Siberia to aid the cause of the White Russian opposition to the Red regime, fostered a resentment that would fester for decades to come. The troops were withdrawn eighteen months later, and Americans quickly forgot the episode, but the Soviets never forgave what they considered an intrusion on their internal affairs. By the end of 1921 nearly all remnants of opposition had been driven from the Soviet Union and the Bolsheviks turned to the task of rebuilding a war-torn country, while establishing a communist system of governance. All of the traditional institutions of the country had to be converted to a Marxist philosophy—schools, universities, factories, farms; all required government supervision and organization. Additionally, Moscow became the seat of the communist international, Comintern. The Bolsheviks were not merely rebuilding a country but offering a revolutionary philosophy for export to every part of the world.[11]

Meanwhile U.S. intellectuals and political leaders developed a growing antipathy for the bolshevik hierarchy, viewing their revolutionary philosophy as naive, at best, and a dark cloud of anarchy hanging over the West, at worst. After the White opposition in Russia collapsed, U.S. leaders waited for the bolshevik system to fail of its own volition. Most felt a system based on what they conceived as anarchy could not meet the problems of day-to-day government. Many mainstream U.S. liberals, who lost much of their influence in the 1920s anyway, largely refused to accept the precepts of the radical, communist philosophy, and conservatives turned their backs on the Soviet Union with a shudder of horror mixed with dread.

When in 1924 the revolution's prime force, Lenin, died, Josef Stalin emerged as leader of the Soviet experiment and remained at the helm for the ensuing twenty-eight years. The exile of Stalin's chief rival, Leon Trotsky, combined with Stalin's iron-handed, autocratic methods further alienated Western opinion. At the same time the Soviet Union's historical inferiority complex fed by centuries of backward, feudal rule and a fear of invasion by her neighbors ingrained a suspicion of the colonial powers of Europe. Through a series of five-year plans begun in 1928, the Stalinist regime sought to raise the Soviet people to a model socialist, industrialized mass, free from the influences of capitalist powers. At the same time, sociologist Paul Hollander pointed out, the repressive Soviet regime under Stalin tended to lower the expectations of the average Soviet citizen. Small concessions, such as a discontinuance of rationing or a less harsh response to dissent, brought an outpouring of gratitude from the people.[12]

But in many ways the leaders of the Soviet Union still viewed the world in the same way as the czars. The Bolsheviks harbored the same historical expansionist desires. Russia had always wanted warm water ports to the south and a buffer zone against hostile nations to the east. Her fear of her neighbors led to alienation, but the remedy always lay in the acquisition of a sphere of influence in the Balkans, in Poland, and in Central Europe.

In the interwar period the United States assumed a detached diplomatic posture in its relations with the Soviet Union. At the same time, although the United States turned from Europe in general during the 1920s, a growing number of U.S. businessmen developed respect for the Soviet attempts to forge an independent, self-contained state. They abhorred the communist system and wished to avoid political entanglements in Europe, including the Soviet Union, but the Soviet market offered an enticing target for future trade development. Despite the clashing ideological values, the Soviet Union still could provide the United States with profitable trade. The passage of time, the lack of international communist activity, and the election of a Democratic president who hoped to rejuvenate the country economically contributed to an atmosphere in which the United States in 1933 finally extended diplomatic recognition to the Soviet regime.

Pressed to salve its own economic wounds, the United States found little time to realize the advantage of its newfound diplomatic relations with the Soviet Union. The idealistic five-year plans in the Soviet Union met with limited success as the inherent mechanical problems of a socialist system combined with a lack of industrial expertise to plague Stalin's attempts at modernization. A ruthless and paranoid leader, Stalin turned to repression in the middle 1930s, exiling millions of citizens to Siberia and executing millions of others. A bloody purge of the Red Army left the Soviet military bereft of competent leadership, a move that would hamper the Soviet effort in the impending World War II.

At the same time the Spanish Civil War with its polarized factions brought a new wave of sympathy and support among U.S. liberals for Stalin and the Soviet Union. The antifascist Popular Front in Spain found only the Soviet Union willing to support their cause actively with arms and other military supplies. Many in the United States conveniently ignored the brutal excesses of the Stalin purges and chose instead to concentrate their attention on the ideological conflict in Spain.[13]

The rise of fascism and right-wing philosophy in Europe worried Stalin and fed his mistrust of the West. The acquiescence in Western Europe to Hitler's increasingly bold military and political moves gnawed at the suspicious Soviet leader. In the summer of 1939 he moved to extend the Soviet Union's influence and to protect her flank against the increasingly powerful Nazi forces in Central Europe. The two ideological enemies, Nazi Germany and the communist Soviet Union, signed a Pact of Nonaggression, and on September 1, 1939, Hitler's military invaded Poland from the west. Two weeks later, Soviet troops invaded from the east, while a second military unit later in November crossed into Finland. The Soviet Union expanded to the west and north, while Germany expanded to the east and in the spring of 1940 to the west. By mid–1940 the Nazis had overrun almost all of Western Europe, including France. But when the Luftwaffe was unable to score an immediate success in the skies over England, Hitler in June 1941 turned against Stalin and invaded the Soviet Union, retracing the steps Napoleon had taken a century and a half before.

Five months later, Hitler declared war on the United States after his Axis ally, Japan, bombed Pearl Harbor, destroying much of the U.S. Pacific fleet. Thus, 1942 was a grim year for the Allies, as the Soviets dug in along the eastern front. The Germans drove deep into the Soviet Union, eventually taking Stalingrad in bitter house-to-house fighting before eventually being turned back. The United States sustained one defeat after another in the Pacific Theater. But the United States gradually rebuilt its Pacific fleet, and the massive German assault became an ever-widening retreat before the dreaded Soviet winter and the determined Red Army.

The Soviets continuously urged a cross-channel invasion of Western Europe to relieve the pressure on Soviet troops in the East. The British and Americans, feeling they did not have the military strength for an early invasion, instead chose to land troops in North Africa and cross the Mediterranean Sea into Italy. This difference over military tactics fanned Soviet suspicions that the West covertly sought to bleed the Soviet nation under the guise of Allied unity. Still, as 1943 came to a close, the U.S. public opinion of the Soviet people and their government reached new heights.

The communist revolutionary movement, the purges of the 1930s, the Pact of Nonaggression, and Stalin's duplicity gave way to a feeling of mutual respect and admiration through Red Army diplomacy. The Soviet leadership, eager for the channel invasion, deemphasized ideological differences between West and East. But the animosities lay submerged, not buried. The images had changed but only to suit the circumstance.[14]

II

The four news institutions in this study also developed over several decades prior to the last years of World War II. The epitome of capitalist enterprises, the four groups sprang from the ingenuity of a few enterprising men. The same men or families had been connected with the ownership of each news organization since the beginning of the century or the inception of the news organization.

The *San Francisco Chronicle* originated in 1865 as the *Daily Dramatic Chronicle*, a theatrical handout published by Charles and Michael de Young. In 1868 the newspaper was renamed the *Daily Morning Chronicle*. Michael de Young remained publisher for sixty years until he died in 1925. His son-in-law, George T. Cameron, became publisher and remained in that post until 1955.

In 1944, then, the *Chronicle* was eighty-nine years old but had had only two publishers. Cameron appointed Paul C. Smith, a protégé of Herbert Hoover, as editor in 1937. Hoover, who had been handily defeated by Roosevelt in 1932, traveled on a world tour with Smith in 1938, and so the *Chronicle*, while retaining a moderate, independent stature on issues, generally adopted a Republican point of view on political matters.[15]

In 1944 the *Chicago Tribune* was a conservative, ethnocentric major newspaper in the United States. The *Chicago Tribune*'s isolationist, pro-U.S. attitudes had been legendary for over a half century. The iron-handed publisher responsible for *Chicago Tribune* policy was Robert R. McCormick, the grandson of long-time publisher Joseph Medill. McCormick and his cousin, Joseph Medill Patterson, became joint publishers and editors in 1914, just fifteen years after their grandfather's death. The pair founded the *New York Daily News* in 1919, and Patterson concentrated his efforts there while McCormick became sole publisher of the *Chicago Tribune*. McCormick's father, Robert S. McCormick, had served as ambassador to Austria-Hungary, Russia, and France during the first decade of the twentieth century, and so the younger McCormick was privy to the inner workings of diplomacy and European politics.[16] McCormick, nevertheless, continued the Medill tradition of solid upper-class conservatism with a suspicion of all foreign influences, particularly those British. The *Chicago Tribune* also adhered to an inherently midwestern view of affairs, both foreign and domestic, distrusting eastern influences and a strong centralized government.

Similarly, the *New York Herald Tribune* originated as a family enterprise with its roots in the nineteenth century, but with a tradition of anglophilia, not anglophobia. The legendary Horace Greeley founded the *New York Tribune*, forerunner to the *Herald Tribune*, in 1841. Whitelaw Reid was appointed managing editor in 1869 and, upon Greeley's death in 1872, acquired control of the newspaper. Through his influence the *Herald Tribune* developed an internationalist, pro–British point of view—the voice of the sophisticated, metropolitan elite in the United States. Reid's son, Ogden, became publisher upon his father's death in 1912, and he and his wife, Helen, directed the newspaper until Ogden Reid died in January 1947.[17] In 1931, after the *New York World* closed its doors, the Reids wooed Walter Lippmann, *World* editorial editor, to the *Herald Tribune*. Despite his liberal leanings and the *Herald Tribune*'s conservative outlook, it was felt that Lippmann could work amicably with the *Herald Tribune* owners, and they hoped he would draw a fresh group of readers. The strategy succeeded, and Lippmann became one of the most popular and powerful columnists in the country.[18]

Also in New York, Briton Hadden and Henry Luce established *Time* magazine, the nation's first weekly news magazine, in 1923. From the beginning the pair openly acknowledged that *Time* would not be objective. The ultimate purpose of the magazine was to "keep men well-informed— that, first and last, is the only axe this magazine has to grind." *Time* had no editorial page. It was a magazine of subjective news and so, in total, an expression of opinion. No editorial page was needed. *Time*, the founders declared in their prospectus, would support positions that argued "a general distrust of . . . increasing interference by government, a prejudice against the rising cost of government, faith in the things which money cannot buy, an interest in the new, particularly in ideas."[19]

When Hadden died in 1929, Luce became the owner and publisher of *Time*, and throughout the 1930s he built the magazine into one of the most powerful forces in U.S. journalism. *Time* gave virtually no bylines and habitually quoted unidentified sources who were said to be on-the-scene observers. These unknown voices sounded suspiciously similar in tone to those of *Time* editors.[20] Unquestionably Republican in philosophy, *Time* nonetheless stressed an internationalist position.

During the late 1930s and early 1940s, the management of *Time* entered a state of flux. Luce stepped down as president and chief executive officer of the company to become editor-in-chief and chairman of the board. The change permitted Luce to concentrate more on setting the tone of the contents of *Time*. He retained those responsibilities for five years. Between 1943 and 1946 there were many turnovers at various levels of management. After twenty years of success, Luce reshaped his staff and the structure of his organization to meet the demands of a postwar economy.[21]

Thus, the news organizations looked on the Soviet Union in the interwar years with a wary eye. Throughout the years after the Russian revolution and preceding the conclusion of World War II, the four maintained positions ideologically opposed to that of the Soviet Union, while protesting any conciliatory moves by the United States.

Not all writers for all journals in the United States assumed antagonistic postures toward Soviet goals and ambitions, however. Many writers sent back glowing reports to the United States extolling the Soviet system and finding only encouraging signs in the Soviet collective experiment. Walter Duranty of *The New York Times* and Louis Fischer of *Nation* magazine were two prime examples of such writers. Duranty won the Pulitzer Prize in 1932 for his reporting on Soviet internal affairs, but studies by Marco Carynnyk and James W. Crowl indicate that Duranty not only incorrectly reported developments in the Soviet Union, but purposely distorted accounts because of sympathies for the Stalin regime.[22] Similarly, Fischer earned Soviet admiration and cooperation by filing supportive stories and praising socialism. Crowl observed: "Fischer wrote more about living conditions than about any other subject in 1931, and, unlike Duranty, based his writing on an endless investigation of those conditions. But whether he was checking stores for consumer goods, or visiting apartments, resthomes, or schools, Fischer overlooked the signs of hardship and indicated that a revolution in living conditions was underway."[23] Duranty's worst excesses came during the period from 1932 to 1934 when a drought caused widespread famine among Ukrainian peasants. Ralph Barnes of the *New York Herald Tribune* and several other U.S. reporters traveled through the area and sent to their newspapers stories of peasants starving. But Duranty and Fischer erroneously refuted such stories, arguing that problems with food production had been exaggerated.[24]

George Seldes of the *Chicago Tribune* provided an example of the other extreme in reporting. Seldes in the early 1920s found only repression and police state tactics in the Soviet Union. In a series of articles in 1923, Seldes castigated the Soviet system, finding the bolshevik regime uncharacteristically ruthless. Seldes had been sent by the *Chicago Tribune* editors to reinforce the *Chicago Tribune*'s utter distaste for communism, and Seldes fulfilled his assignment. Seldes himself found little trouble in approaching his topic in such a manner, and the tone of his stories reinforced that enthusiasm.[25]

Time's ideological inclinations were such that columnist Walter Winchell observed in February 1936 that *Time*'s attitude was fascist. Winchell, of course, greatly exaggerated and hardly qualified as a competent magazine critic, but the accusation touched off a bit of soul searching on the *Time* staff. Four Time, Inc., editors, Archibald MacLeish, Eric Hodgins, Wilder Hobson, and Dwight Macdonald, wrote Luce advising him that *Time*, though not fascist, was biased on ideological matters, especially those pertaining to the Spanish Civil War. MacLeish said he considered himself a liberal and found reports in the *Nation*, the *New Republic*, and the *New Masses* to be more revealing than those in *Time*. Luce, however, dismissed the complaints with a noncommittal, though restrained, response.[26]

The one instance when most U.S. publishers, editors, and writers tended to agree with a positive step taken by the U.S. government toward the Soviet Union came in 1933 when President Roosevelt extended diplomatic recognition to the U.S.S.R. Most newspapers felt it was time to acknowledge the other force in the world. The *Chicago Tribune*, of course, vehemently opposed such a move and never forgave Roosevelt for committing an act that the newspaper editors felt opened the door to bolshevism in the United States.

Each step Hitler took in Europe and each move Stalin made brought another shrill cry from McCormick, who urged a complete withdrawal from the affairs of Europe. The *Chicago Tribune* observed in a January 4, 1943, editorial that the United States' role after World War II should be defined as keeping Europeans from killing each other without the United States involving itself in European affairs.[27]

The other two newspapers, however, were internationalist throughout the prewar years and largely applauded Roosevelt's lend-lease policies in 1940. Once recognition had been extended to the Soviet Union, the *Chronicle* and the *Herald Tribune* grudgingly accepted the Soviet Union as a force in Europe. But neither McCormick nor Luce could accept the presence of the Soviet Union as palatable. Luce visited the U.S.S.R. in 1936 and took an instant dislike to the country.[28] Throughout the prewar years, both *Time* and the *Chicago Tribune* remained predisposed to dislike anything Soviet.

With the beginning of World War II and the announced signing of the Pact of Nonaggression, all four of the print organizations understandably turned against the Soviets in indignant outrage. After 1941 the outrage subsided. *Time* modified its stance, applying a more conciliatory tone, but Luce remained suspicious of Soviet intentions. He was among the first to urge the United States to oppose Soviet gains in Europe as the German Army fell to defeat in battle after battle.

If 1943 was marked by words of praise for the U.S.S.R. from U.S. editorial offices, it reflected only a confined sense of history. The publishers and editors of these news groups were not sympathetic to Soviet aims and policies. Were it not for Hitler and the Germany Army, the reader would have been hard pressed to locate published words of praise for the Stalinist regime in the early 1940s. Even under the best circumstances, the Soviet leadership and their motivations were greeted with suspicion by newspaper executives and owners. After the war these suspicions would either translate into hostility or would be further submerged. The deciding factors in the eyes of the news people would be the parallels that could be drawn between U.S. and Soviet interests. If those interests diverged greatly, enmity and not cooperation would be urged editorially. Soviet conciliation and compromise were needed to overcome these suspicions. Neither the extreme sacrifices of the Soviet people nor the paranoid personality of Josef Stalin made those responses seem likely.

The early and mid-war years were also times of mutual hostility between the four news groups and the Roosevelt administration. None of the four had supported Roosevelt in 1940. *Time* and Luce actively touted Wendell Willkie, while the *Chicago Tribune* applied every tactic available to its news and editorial-page editors to defeat Roosevelt's bid for a third term. The *Chronicle*, of course, was still close to Hoover and readily leaned toward Willkie, while the conservative *Herald Tribune* naturally endorsed the Republican. Roosevelt, while maintaining a friendly relationship with the working press throughout the 1930s, caustically criticized the Republican tendencies among newspaper owners nationwide. He spent a great deal of time and energy in expressing his unhappiness with *Time* and the *Chicago Tribune*. This was a time when the press of the country was separated philosophically from mainstream United States on political matters. Roosevelt enjoyed overwhelming popularity from newspaper readers, but little support among publishers.

Though Luce and Roosevelt were briefly on amicable terms after Pearl Harbor, the president particularly disliked the magazine editor. It was especially galling for Roosevelt when in 1942 Luce's wife, Clare, was elected to Congress. Two incidents underscored the Luce–F.D.R. antagonism. In 1943 Luce applied for press credentials to review the Pacific Theater. Roosevelt personally vetoed the request claiming that correspondents could go, but not publishers. Luce, stung by the rebuff, viewed it as a personal affront by Roosevelt.[29] The other incident occurred in November of 1941 when *Time* carried an article that attacked the president of Chile, Pedro Aguirre Cerda, as more concerned with his grape vineyard than the political crisis in Chile. Cerda died ten days later, and F.D.R. announced at a press conference that the U.S. government had offered apologies to Chile for *Time*'s words.

Thus, in 1943 the four news groups certainly represented a clique outside the political mainstream. A popular Democratic president had been returned to office twice by strong majority votes, but the four news organizations largely opposed his philosophy and the editors remained personally aloof from him.

Independent critics helped to place newspaper and magazine reporting in perspective, but the intense scrutiny emanating from journalism schools at scholarly institutions had not become general practice. Such schools of journalism were predominantly devoted to courses of practical instruction rather than review and research of daily publications. The key scholarly journal in the field, *Journalism Quarterly*, generally devoted its pages to innocuous reports and word-for-word reproductions of speeches by publishers at conventions.

As 1944 opened, a precarious relationship existed among U.S. leaders and these four news enterprises. Similarly, a tenuously friendly relationship existed between the Soviet Union and the editors and publishers in the

United States. It seemed during the final full year of war that these thin threads might snap, clouding the news reporting of the future. Yet, other leaders and different policies would emerge in the coming years, and the real question in foreign affairs would be what relationship would develop between the U.S. and Soviet governments and how would these news groups view that relationship.

NOTES

1. Eddy Gilmore, *Me and My Russian Wife* (New York: Greenwood Press, 1968), 140–41.

2. Hadley Cantril, *Public Opinion, 1935–1946* (Westport, Conn.: Greenwood Press, 1951), 370–71.

3. W. A. Swanberg, *Luce and His Empire* (New York: Charles Scribner's Sons, 1972), 211.

4. John L. Gaddis, *The United States and the Origins of the Cold War, 1941–1947* (New York: Columbia University Press, 1972), 38.

5. *Time* cover, 29 (January 3, 1943).

6. Ralph B. Levering, *American Opinion and the Russian Alliance, 1939–1945* (Chapel Hill: University of North Carolina Press, 1976), 100.

7. See Levering, *American Opinion and the Russian Alliance*, 111.

8. Christopher Lasch, *American Liberals and the Russian Revolution* (New York: Knopf, 1962).

9. Paul Hollander, *Soviet and American Society: A Comparison* (New York: Oxford University Press, 1973), 40.

10. See Hollander, *Soviet and American Society*; Melvin C. Wren, *The Course of Russian History*, 2d ed. (New York: Macmillan, 1964); and John E. C. Hill, *Lenin and the Russian Revolution* (New York: Penguin, 1971).

11. See Ernest Milton Halliday, *The Ignorant Armies: The Anglo-American Archangel Expedition, 1918–1919* (London: Weidenfeld and Nicolson, 1961); Morton Schwartz, *Soviet Perceptions of the United States* (Berkeley: University of California Press, 1978); and Donald W. Treadgold, *The Development of the U.S.S.R.: An Exchange of Views* (Seattle: University of Washington Press, 1964).

12. Hollander, *Soviet and American Society*, 391. See also Harriet Barland, *Soviet Literary Theory and Practice During the First Five-Year Plan, 1928–32* (New York: Greenwood Press, 1969); Peter G. Filene, *American Views of Soviet Russia, 1917–1965* (Homewood, Ill.: Dorsey, 1967); and Hadley Cantril, *Soviet Leaders and Mastery Over Man* (New Brunswick, N.J.: Rutgers University Press, 1960).

13. William L. O'Neill, *The Great Schism: Stalinism and the American Intellectuals, A Better World* (New York: Simon and Schuster, 1982), 13.

14. See Joseph Davies, *Mission to Moscow* (New York: Simon and Schuster, 1941); Robert A. Divine: *The Reluctant Belligerent: America's Entry into World War II* (New York: John Wiley and Sons, 1965); Herbert S. Dinerstein, *Fifty Years of Soviet Foreign Policy* (Baltimore: Johns Hopkins Press, 1968); and O'Neill, *The Great Schism*.

15. Richard Reinhardt, "Doesn't Everybody Hate the Chronicle?" *Columbia Journalism Review* 20 (January–February 1982): 25–32; Ben Bagdikian, "The *Chronicle* Chronicles," *San Francisco Magazine* (May 1982): 67–69; Templeton Peck telephone

interview, March 27, 1985; "Making History, Day by Day for Over a Century," *San Francisco Chronicle* in-house brochure, 1984.

16. Jerome E. Edwards, *The Foreign Policy of Col. McCormick's Tribune, 1929–1941* (Reno: University of Nevada Press, 1971), 5.

17. Robert Shaplen, "Denson's Revolution at the *Herald-Tribune*," *Saturday Review* 44 (July 8, 1961): 36–38; and Oswald Garrison Villard, *The Disappearing Daily: Chapters in American Newspaper Evolution* (New York: Knopf, 1944), 93–102.

18. See Ronald Steel, *Walter Lippmann and the American Century* (Boston: Little, Brown, 1980).

19. Robert T. Elson, *Time, Inc.: The Intimate History of a Publishing Enterprise, 1923–1941*, vol. 1 (New York: Atheneum, 1968), 8–9; Swanberg, *Luce and His Empire*, 53; and John Kobler, *Luce: His Time, Life and Fortune* (Garden City, N.J.: Doubleday, 1968), 45.

20. Elson, *Time, Inc.*, vol. 1, 29; Swanberg, *Luce and His Empire*, 204.

21. Robert T. Elson, *Time, Inc.: The Intimate History of a Publishing Enterprise, 1941–1960*, vol. 2 (New York: Atheneum, 1973), 378–79, 413.

22. See Marco Carynnyk, "The Famine the *Times* Couldn't Find," *Commentary* 77 (November 1983) 356–58; and James William Crowl, *Angels in Stalin's Paradise: Western Reporters in Soviet Russia, 1917 to 1937, a Case Study of Louis Fischer and Walter Duranty* (Washington, D.C.: University Press of America).

23. Crowl, *Angels in Stalin's Paradise*, 41.

24. Crowl, *Angels in Stalin's Paradise*, 154–73; Carynnyk, "The Famine the *Times* Couldn't Find," 356.

25. Crowl, *Angels in Stalin's Paradise*, 41.

26. Elson, *Time, Inc.*, vol. 1, 249–52.

27. "The Wish for Peace," *Chicago Tribune* editorial, January 4, 1943, 12.

28. Swanberg, *Luce and His Empire*, 209.

29. Elson, *Time, Inc.*, vol. 2, 480–81; Graham White, *F.D.R. and the Press* (Chicago: University of Chicago Press, 1981), 53.

Chapter 3
Wartime News, 1944

I

News from battlefronts dominated the pages of newspapers and news magazines throughout the year 1944 and, consequently, provided continued stimulus for pro-Soviet images in the minds of many Americans. This was the last full year of military conflict in the most destructive war in history, and so attention remained riveted on the job at hand—defeating the Axis forces and preventing enemy designs for world conquest. This single-minded purpose provided not only a common goal for mutual submersion of ideological differences between the Soviet Union and the United States, but also trained the attention of working U.S. journalists and their editors and publishers on the urgent news of the day—the men in battle. This interest naturally focused on U.S. soldiers and their roles, but because the Red Army played such a key role in the war, especially prior to the Normandy Invasion in June 1944, advances by the Soviet fighting forces also drew strong coverage from these news organizations.

The Soviet Union, as reflected in the news and editorial pages of the publications in this study, largely was not an ideological force in 1944, but a fighting force embodied by the Red Army. Fascist conquest was repelled by Soviet men, and sometimes women and children, not Marxist theory. Americans were appreciative of the sacrifices, regardless of the motivation.

Daily war coverage in the publications examined in this study dealt with army advances and lists of casualties with a preference in coverage given to the European Theater. Europe's traditional ties with the United States, the amount of arms and men committed to fighting Germany, and the Europe-first strategy as espoused by U.S. military leaders all provided impetus for priority coverage in Italy and Eastern Europe as opposed to the South Pacific. Coverage, then, was largely tied to military urgency. This did not relate to any particular philosophy the fighting forces might have held, but probably existed in spite of those values. The Soviet Union was a powerful fighting ally, and news stories reflected just that image.

To help illustrate this point and to demonstrate how the thrust of news coverage changed from 1944 to 1947, this study employed a sampling of news and editorial coverage in the four print publications. March and September were selected as sample months from each of the four years. Articles, editorials, editorial columns, and editorial cartoons appearing in the *New York Herald Tribune, San Francisco Chronicle, Chicago Tribune*, and *Time* dealing with the Soviet Union during these months were catalogued as favorable to the Soviet image or unfavorable—"pro" or "con." For the three newspapers the statistics were separated into categories of news or editorial content. *Time*, of course, had no editorials as such, because, though the material was certainly opinionated, the magazine was considered to be entirely news.

The sampling included March and September, because the two periods are six months apart and so reflect opposite ends of the calendar. Also, they include the beginnings of spring and fall when military activities were not hampered by severe winter weather. Most importantly, these months are a measure of news and editorial opinion before and after or around major occurrences. In 1944, for instance, the sampling came before and after Normandy. September 1944 measures news and editorial judgments before the Yalta Conference in the Crimea area and March 1945, just after the conclave. September 1945 was just after V-J Day and March 1945, just before the death of Franklin Roosevelt and before V-E Day. In 1946 Winston Churchill's iron curtain speech in Fulton, Missouri, took place in March, during a sample month. In 1947 the Truman Doctrine speech to Congress occurred in March; George Kennan's article on foreign policy and containment of communism, "Sources of Soviet Conduct," appeared in *Foreign Affairs* in June; and Walter Lippmann's series of articles responding to Kennan were published in September.

Several restrictions and guidelines were established in deriving the sampling. Published letters to the editor were omitted, because those opinions reflected not newspaper judgment, but the random sentiments of interested readers. Letters to the editor and how they appeared in the publications were reviewed in this study but were not considered relevant to the sampling. The charted examples included every article dealing substantially with the Soviet Union during the eight chosen months, such as military coverage, diplomatic reports, human interest stories, columns of personal analysis, editorial cartoons, house editorials, and in-depth analysis by staff and wire service writers. Items mentioning the Soviet Union in passing but that focused mainly on other issues or countries were not included. Each item was identified as essentially anti-Soviet or pro-Soviet in content. This was accomplished by a thorough review of the headline and body-copy content of each.

Among the items categorized, only eight could not be classified as either pro or con because of their neutral content. The remaining 1,402 news and editorial works did merit one or the other label. Often, this was due to the innate thrust of the coverage and not because of any bias or phraseology in the writing. For instance, the military coverage appearing in each publication from day to day or week to week reflected an objective and balanced prose, focusing on casualty reports, geographical positions of the armies, and other objective data. However, the mere reporting of Soviet army casualties and the advances of the Red Army against German battalions left positive Soviet images in the minds of U.S. readers. Constant repetition of such stories reinforced those favorable reactions.

Reporting that Stalin refused to attend a summit meeting in Quebec, on the other hand, left a negative image, though the article might be carefully worded to explain all of the stated reasons for Stalin's absence. Some issues drew articles that were pro one day and con the next. Soviet negotiations with Finland some days drew favorable coverage, when the Soviet Union offered concessions or changed her position to allow movement in the negotiations, and other days the thrusts of the articles were unfavorable because the reports reflected a Soviet ultimatum or general intransigence. If an article contained both pro and con elements, it was categorized one way or the other based on the overall thrust of the article or the main idea in the lead or headline. Nearly all the items examined in the sampling were easily classified, because the general nature of coverage or discussion concerning the Soviet Union in this period usually was heavily weighted one way or the other. Since this sampling technique does not account for amount of bias, importance or placement of the article or editorial, or size of the headline, it does not control for all variables. However, the large sampling and the careful examination of each article or item provides us with a clear feeling of the drift of sentiment from 1944 to 1947. The purpose of the sampling is not to focus on one or two days of coverage or isolated articles, but to demonstrate a general trend in coverage over a four-year period of time.[1]

In 1944, then, the sampling indicates that coverage of the Soviet Union reflected quite a favorable bias in the pages of the four news publications. Yet, by examining the figures in Appendix A, it may also be seen that this bias grew from not only a philosophy sympathetic to Soviet fighting forces, but also from the nature of news appearing in daily newspapers and weekly news magazines. That is, the urgency of the war news pushed aside coverage of diplomatic forays or ideological differences. During March and September 1944, 89 Soviet-related news items appeared in the *Chronicle*, 122 in the *Herald Tribune*, 75 in the *Chicago Tribune*, and 14 in *Time*. Each daily edition of the newspapers and weekly edition of *Time* carried one or more articles on war news concerning the Soviet Union and the Red Army, usually two or three articles in the case of the *Herald Tribune*. That would indicate that at least 60 of the newspaper articles—30 per month—dealt with battlefront news and 8 of the 14 *Time* articles. Between 60 and 80 percent of the news concerning the Soviet Union focused on men in battle. That left little inclination by editors to provide space for discussion of other governmental or diplomatic activities involving the Soviet Union, unless a special conference or meeting provided a daily or weekly newspeg that could compete with war news. In 1944 there were few such meetings.

An examination of the editorials, columns, and editorial cartoons—grouped as editorial content—shows that such opinionated material also often focused on battle or war-related events. Thus, for instance, the *Herald Tribune* in April 1944 eulogized Soviet General Nikolai F. Vatulin, "liberator of Kiev," who was killed in battle. The *Herald Tribune* saw Vatulin's death as a loss to the Allies (not just the Soviet Union) of "a gifted young military leader."[2] An editorial cartoon appearing on the January 15, 1944, editorial page of the *Chronicle* lauded the apparently invincible Soviet fighting forces. In the cartoon a large bear with a sickle and hammer imprinted on its back dwarfs a tiny uniformed German officer who is telling an equally tiny Japanese officer with buck teeth and thick glasses, "Quick! Grab him by the tail!" The Japanese officer responds, "First you grab him by head—prease!"[3]

Ideology played only a minimal part in the editorial philosophy of the newspapers during this period and in the news content in *Time*, during 1944. As the chart in Appendix A indicates, editorial content in the *Chronicle* and *Herald Tribune* did clearly provide a pro-Soviet image. Of the eighteen editorial items in the *Chronicle* during the two sample months in 1944, seventeen were favorable and only one unfavorable. The *Herald Tribune*'s twelve editorial items all reflected a positive sentiment. Only the *Chicago Tribune*'s editorials remained substantially anti-Soviet in nature. Ten of twelve editorial items reflected an anti-Soviet image during the sample sixty editions of the Chicago newspaper. That is because the *Chicago Tribune* neither recognized the Soviet Union as a significant fighting force, nor did the editorial writers ever cease to view the Soviet Union in anything but ideological terms. A *Chicago Tribune* editorial in August 1944 asserted that U.S. soldiers were generally responsible for Allied successes. "The conspirators against America are the social climbers who would return this nation to the status of a colony, to advance their own silly ambitions, and the Communist agents of Russian policy in this country who would disrupt and destroy the industry that has armed the whole world to fight for freedom."[4] However, even with the *Chicago Tribune*, some concession was made to a fighting ally. The two pro-Soviet editorial items from March 1944 were the only two of the entire fifty-two total during the four years of sample editions. The other fifty items were substantially negative. During the early months of 1944, *Time* began to reflect a less favorable inclination toward the Soviet Union. As we shall see later in this chapter and in the next chapter, Henry Luce's innate suspicion of the Soviet Union began to push forward.[5]

II

For the staffs and management of the four news organizations, 1944 brought change and transition. At the three newspapers the changes were generated by the routines of war. The foreign correspondents were fulfilling functions different from those completed during peacetime. Not only were they concerned with reporting on military occurrences instead of diplomatic exchanges, but often they found themselves in far-flung areas as they attempted to document the progress of the war. During peace, these correspondents spent a preponderance of their time in the capitals of Europe. During war, they moved to where news was occurring, and that usually meant military zones.

At the same time many of the jobs on the foreign and domestic staffs had to be filled by substitute reporters and editors, while regular staff members volunteered for active duty or were drafted. For the larger newspapers some newsroom correspondents left their regular duties during the war to become war correspondents stationed around the world. This created headaches for newspaper and magazine publishers just as it did for other businesses. For instance, the *Chicago Tribune* lost "dozens" of reporters and editors to military service in 1942 and 1943, according to John McCutcheon, who had joined the news staff in 1940. McCutcheon was one of those called to the U.S. Navy, where he served as a lieutenant commander until January 1946. War correspondents for the *Chicago Tribune* included Robert Cromie, who had been a columnist and book editor during peacetime; Jack Thompson, former staff reporter; Seymour Korman; Harold Smith; Thomas Morrow; and Arthur Veysey. They all answered directly to the managing editor, J. Loy Maloney, who took over direct responsibility of the foreign news staff from McCormick during the 1940s.[6]

But 1944 produced dramatic changes at *Time* and for reasons only indirectly related to the war. In June Henry Luce relinquished some of his direct management responsibilities over news content. John Shaw Billings became editorial director of all Time, Inc., publications. Billings, a twenty-year staff member, had ably handled his managing editor duties with *Life*, and Luce wanted to spend more time planning a postwar future for *Time-Life-Fortune* in anticipation of the conclusion of the war. Luce still kept a close watch over editorial operations and dictated the philosophical and political scope of the magazine, but Billings became the person responsible for week-to-week decisions. Luce not only wanted to spend more time on long-range planning, but he was dissatisfied with his own performance in handling the weekly operation, and he had an abiding confidence in Billings's abilities.[7] "In short," Luce wrote to his editors, "from Billings you may expect more action and less talk than from the Editor-in-chief."[8]

Billings, however, quickly grew unhappy with his new assignment. He tired of the frantic pace. It was his hope that the change would provide an opportunity to work more closely with Luce, but it did not develop that way. Though he remained with Time, Inc., until 1954, his unhappiness did not abate.[9]

Still, Billings provided strong guidance and a practiced eye on editorial operations, freeing Luce to forge new directions for the magazine, which he began to undertake before the year had ended. It was not so much that the appointment of Billings was a bad idea, but Luce had an opportunity to bring fresh insights and new ideas into a key position at a crucial time and chose instead to fall back on someone who had been an unabashed admirer and who would continue the same philosophy and direction, while viewing his new assignment as a duty and obligation, not a challenge.

The second crucial in-house decision taken by *Time* in 1944 involved the foreign news desk. David Whittaker Chambers became foreign news editor in the summer of 1944, when John Osborne left for France in anticipation of the liberation of Paris. Osborne had been editor of both foreign news and world battlefronts for about a year. The selection of Chambers to such a crucial position at such an important juncture would prove to be a disastrous mistake. He had been one of two senior editors in charge of the book review section and had not really demonstrated a knack for such a demanding assignment.

All his journalistic career, Chambers had envisioned the chance to assume a position involving foreign affairs. In 1924 he had joined the U.S. Communist party but was disenchanted with the party in the 1930s after the bloody Stalinist purges. He had already become a virulent anticommunist when he joined the staff of *Time* in 1939, and he intended to use his position to further his ideology.[10] Not only did Chamber's political leanings begin to affect the foreign news pages, but he also ignored the writing of several respected foreign correspondents, including Osborne and Charles Wertenbaker in Paris, John Hersey in Moscow, and Walter Graebner in London.[11]

Hersey cabled Thomas S. Matthews, *Time* executive editor, in December 1944 that he disagreed strongly with the tone of *Time*'s coverage and the underuse of the information he was sending. He told Matthews:

Without moving one inch to the left of my stated position as a Democrat, I feel that many stories have been grossly unfair to Russia and in some cases, as in the anniversary story in the November 13 issue, actually vicious at this particular moment of history. . . . I have leaned over backwards to be balanced in what I have said and I believe many of *Time*'s writers and editors would agree that wastage is partly the fault of the Foreign News editor since everything that could possibly be construed as friendly to Russia has been killed.[12]

However, Luce backed Chambers, and the controversial editor remained. Luce told Billings in a memorandum in January 1945 that the self-serving positions taken by the Allied nations in the previous several months had confirmed Chambers's good judgment in handling international news. He said he understood the correspondents' complaints, but he could not disagree with Chambers's approach to communist influence.[13] Hersey resigned six months later. Actually, Luce had already developed anti-Soviet sentiments on his own and, for a time, Chambers's ideological approach perfectly suited Luce's outlook. As we shall see in the next chapter, even the Soviet government had taken stock of the *Time* tilt away from Soviet interests as early as March 1944.

Staff changes at the *San Francisco Chronicle*, while apparently not creating the tension that existed at *Time*, did result in makeshift staffing as many employees left for active duty. Editor Paul Smith and Ken McCardle, chief editorial writer, both served as officers in the Navy during the war and were stationed in the Pacific. Royce Breier continued as editorial page director and also wrote a column, while Smith's duties were absorbed by several other editors until he returned from active duty. Also serving on the editorial staff were Benjamin Macumber and Stanley Mitchell, who had been with the newspaper since the World War I era. Thus, the military had claimed key people from the *Chronicle* staff, leaving both news and editorial staffs shorthanded. An aging, overworked editorial staff fought to formulate editorials based on the policies and philosophies of an editor who was several thousand miles away somewhere in the Pacific, according to former *Chronicle* editorial writer Templeton Peck. Smith had not only overseen the news operation of the *Chronicle*, but had also set the tone for editorial policy. Publisher George Cameron concerned himself largely with the business end of the newspaper operation and rarely even attended editorial board meetings.[14]

The smaller newspaper, then, was more crucially affected by the manpower needs of war. The editorial philosophy of the newspaper did not change, but the editorials in 1944 were noticeably less persuasive than after the war. The 1944 editorials were brief—often only a few paragraphs long—and incomplete in their discussions. Though editorials featured a pro-Soviet bent during these years, the expression of those thoughts was not nearly so mechanically sound as after the war. All of the foreign coverage in the *Chronicle* resulted from wire service stories, because such a small-circulation newspaper could not afford foreign bureaus. The *Chronicle* did not have a Washington bureau during the war either. Consequently, war news and foreign coverage were routine and not greatly affected by the manpower shortage, though the handling of the wire stories within the newsroom may have been different and possibly less efficient.

Because of the size of their staffs, the *Chicago Tribune* and the *Herald Tribune* did not face these problems in the same way. Robert R. McCormick, editor and publisher of the *Chicago Tribune*, personally supervised both news and editorial operations. J. Loy Maloney served as managing editor during this period and Leon Stolz as chief editorial writer. Both had McCormick's respect, and he often listened to their arguments, but in all matters McCormick made the final decision. The news and editorial pages reflected McCormick's philosophy and his judgment. "You could argue with the colonel and he would listen, but when he made up his mind, that was it," McCutcheon said. "People often accused the *Tribune* of placing its editorials on the news pages. That was exaggerated but there was definitely a carryover from the editorial to the news pages."[15] Because of McCormick's overwhelming influence, then, as well as the size of the staff of the *Chicago Tribune* and the continuing roles served by key editors, the war did not change the newspaper's daily coverage or emphasis to any great degree.

Similarly, the *Herald Tribune* weathered the wartime claims on its manpower. Editor Ogden Reid took personal interest and pride in the *Herald Tribune* editorial page. Upon his death on January 3, 1947, the newspaper noted that during his thirty-four years as editor he had "felt a personal responsibility for every word on it [editorial page]."[16] Reid, not nearly as dogmatic as McCormick nor as dictatorial in the expression of house opinions, nevertheless had retained a firm hand over the editorial pages for three decades, and the internationalist, conversative tone of the pages did not change during the war years.

Besides, the newspaper's real strength lay in neither its house editorials nor its foreign news coverage. The international stories, while certainly more comprehensive than those in either the *Chicago Tribune* or the *Chronicle*, could not compete with the extensive bureau coverage of *The New York Times*, which boasted about three times as many bureaus and correspondents.[17] The *Herald Tribune*'s edge lay in its columnists, who provided a philosophical balance to its conservative leanings. These writers included Mark Sullivan, George Fielding Eliot, Sumner Welles, William Shirer, and especially Walter Lippmann. Stuart and Joseph Alsop joined the staff in 1946. Shirer provided a particularly insightful perspective during the war years. He had served as a correspondent in Berlin in the late 1930s and had watched Nazi propaganda lull some Americans into a false sense of security. His commentary on the ambitions and motives of Nazi leaders provided a balance to the military-oriented war prose appearing on the news pages.[18] Reading Lippmann's syndicated observations on the national and international scene had been an increasingly prevalent morning ritual for Americans for thirteen years, and in 1944 he not only offered a liberal point of view, but a thoughtful reflection on world affairs that brought a strong newspaper following independent of the appeal of the *Herald Tribune*.[19] The caliber of the columnists on the *Herald Tribune* was a key reason why the University of Missouri in 1936 awarded the medal of honor to the newspaper.[20] Part of the *Herald Tribune*'s strength during 1944 and the early years of the Cold War lay in its variety of editorial expressions provided by its columnists. Unfolding world events received a more thorough airing in the *Herald Tribune* than on the pages of any of the other print organizations in this study.

The news coverage of the Soviet Union during 1944 fell predominantly into the hands of Maurice Hindus, who proved to be as simplistically gullible about Soviet motives and ambitions as Chambers was skeptical. The movements of U.S. journalists in the Soviet Union were greatly restricted on the pretext that wartime counterintelligence operations required a strict limitation on travel by civilians and on the informational flow from war zones. Consequently, as we will see in the next chapter, correspondents were fed a steady diet of propaganda and allowed only carefully orchestrated interviews in the Soviet Union. Hindus often reported these types of stories with earnest enthusiasm and with a much less cynical eye than other correspondents in the Soviet Union. This will become apparent in our discussion on the coverage of issues. In November 1942 *Reader's Digest* editors decided to carry a pro-Soviet article about the Soviet role in the war. They chose Hindus to write the piece.[21] His pro-Soviet bent made him the perfect candidate for the assignment.

It should be noted that Luce and McCormick detested each other, and much of this rancor was aired on the pages of the *Chicago Tribune* and *Time* in 1944. Why did they choose this particular time to take their differences to the pages of their publications? There may have been several catalysts, but the main one appears to have been the presidential election campaign. McCormick backed Thomas Dewey for the Republican nomination, and Luce supported Wendell Willkie, though Luce was far more flexible on the question than McCormick suspected.

An article written by political writer Frank Hughes appeared in the *Chicago Tribune* on February 23, 1944, which amplified the rancor between the two publishers. Hughes compared Luce to Adolph Hitler, calling him the "fuehrer of *Time-Life-Fortune*." He also accused Luce of using "the organized smear, current political weapon of Mr. Roosevelt and his New Dealers" to gain a high position in a Willkie administration. Perhaps the most amazing aspect of the attack was the apparent lack of any provocation, except the political leanings of the Luce empire. The article also appeared on page two, and so was represented as a news story.[22]

The *St. Louis Globe-Democrat* quickly criticized McCormick for the attack. Luce wrote a brief note of thanks to E. Ray Lansing of the *Globe-Democrat*. Luce added:

If I were the proprietor of a daily newspaper with an editorial page I certainly would have done what you did and hope that I would have done it as well. But *Time* has not this same editorial mechanism and a story, whether in our Press or U.S. at War sections, would have to descend to a yes-I-did-no-you-didn't level with the Colonel—which I'm pretty sure you'll agree would be, to say the least, undesirable. So I content myself with the knowledge that I'm in the same boat with you, that means after all that it's a pretty good boat.[23]

Despite Luce's claim, however, the sniping continued for the next several years, and *Time* often did offer sneering comments and snide observations in its press segment about the McCormick–Patterson newspaper empire. McCormick and the *Chicago Tribune* responded in kind and, on occasion, used both the news and editorial pages to attack the Reids and the *Herald Tribune* for their internationalist and pro-British postures. The *Chronicle*, away from the eastern–midwestern clashes and too small to merit notice, escaped the crossfire. War did not change the passions of these publishers.

But for all the news and editorial staffs, war and shifts in personnel provided changes. The urgencies of covering war allowed the impending political and diplomatic decisions to remain recessed in the minds of readers, editors, and reporters alike. As military conquests steadily and ever more readily cornered the Axis powers, opinion leaders in the United States, including editors and reporters, began to worry about how postwar Europe and Asia would align politically and militarily. That led to questions about what these brave Soviets wanted for their sacrifices. Once the questions were asked, the Soviet Union never quite appeared the same to Americans. The military focus began to drift as 1944 ended and the Yalta Conference approached. While the historical and short-term differences between the United States and the Soviet Union did not dominate news and editorial attention quite the way military considerations did in 1944, several incidents did occur that raised questions that later would be magnified far beyond the scope or emphasis that existed during that last full year of war. In the next chapter, we will look at how those issues were treated in the months that preceded Yalta.

NOTES

1. See Appendix A. This approach does not represent a complete content analysis, but because the articles deal with a variety of subjects, word usages, and word contents, it represents the most complete analysis under the circumstances. The sampling technique was verified on two separate occasions. Richard Fruto, a master's candidate at the University of Illinois at Champaign-Urbana, reviewed the sample months in their entirety during April 1986. He counted all the editorial and news items for each edition of all publications during the sample months but did not evaluate the articles as to pro-Soviet or anti-Soviet thrust. The Fruto independent verification resulted in a 94 percent correlation. That is, the sample numbers were found to vary by only 6 percent over the eight sample months for the four news organizations. The individual editorial or news counts actually matched in sixteen

of the fifty-four categories. In November 1986 three master's candidates at the University of Illinois, John Burge, Sharon Raksnis, and Rahul Jacob, systematically sampled the eight months' editions of the four publications. This systematic technique is an accepted methodology for reliability for newspapers as described in Klaus Krippendorff, *Content Analysis: An Introduction to Its Methodology* (Beverly Hills, Calif.: Sage, 1980), 67. See also Krippendorf, *Content Analysis*, 69, 129–54, for additional discussion of reliability and sampling. The verifiers examined every fifth newspaper during the sample months—the first, sixth, eleventh, sixteenth, twenty-first, and twenty-sixth of the month (and thirty-first in March). They tabulated the number of articles and editorial items in each edition and judged them on pro-Soviet or anti-Soviet thrust. The results were tabulated and compared with the complete sampling by the author. The results correlated closely. For instance, in March 1944 the sample in the *Chronicle* had a 20:2 pro–con ratio for news stories and 6:1 for editorial items. The actual count by the author was 52:0 and 12:0. Both sets are overwhelmingly pro, but Ms. Raksnis determined that three items were negative in her sample of thirty. The author did not determine any items to be negative in his count of sixty four. This suggests that judgment differed on only three in twenty items. Results for other publications that month and other months were similar. Sometimes the ratios varied to a larger extent in months in which pro and con discussion was heavily mixed. But the ratios in these situations could be distorted by the low numbers in both the actual counts and the sample counts. For example, the author found two pro and six con editorial items in March 1944 in the *Chicago Tribune*, but Ms. Raksnis found three pro and three con in her sampling. Both sets of numbers are small, and so the ratio is distorted, but it is assumed that a full verification would have resulted in a 5:3 count, which would indicate that the author and the verifier differed in the pro–con analysis of one editorial item. There are institutional reasons that also contributed to the decision to select March and September as sample months. Reporters and editors often take vacations during the summer months and in December and January, and so staffs are filled with substitute employees or have reduced numbers of persons. News makers are normally not as active during those months either for the same reasons. Newspapers often launch subscription drives in September, too, and coverage is at its peak during this month. Reader interest heightens in September, because students return to school and adults are not as distracted by outdoor activities as in the summer months.

2. "Up from the Ranks," *New York Herald Tribune* editorial, April 17, 1944, 14.

3. *San Francisco Chronicle* editorial cartoon, January 15, 1944, 8.

4. "The Victory is American," *Chicago Tribune* editorial, August 2, 1944, 12.

5. Evidence of this trend will be presented later, but for concurring opinions, see Robert T. Elson, *The World of Time, Inc.: The Intimate History of a Publishing Enterprise, 1941–1960*, vol. 2 (New York: Atheneum, 1973), 97; and W. A. Swanberg, *Luce and His Empire* (New York: Charles Scribner's Sons, 1972), 212.

6. John McCutcheon telephone interview, April 30, 1985. See also Lloyd Wendt, *Chicago Tribune: The Rise of a Great American Newspaper* (Chicago: Rand McNally, 1979), 626–27.

7. Henry Luce memo to managing editors, senior editors, and senior executives of Time, Inc., June 7, 1944, 1. John Shaw Billings Papers, Box 1, Caroliniana

Library, Manuscripts Division, Billings Collection, University of South Carolina, Columbia, South Carolina; Elson, *The World of Time Inc.*, vol. 2, 83, 307.

8. Luce memo, June 7, 1944, 2.

9. Carol Bleser, *The Hammonds of Redcliffe* (New York: Oxford University Press, 1981), 391–92.

10. Whittaker Chambers, *Witness* (New York: Random House, 1952), 497; John Kobler, *Luce: His Time, Life and Fortune* (Garden City, N.J.: Doubleday, 1968), 146; Elson, *The World of Time, Inc.*, vol. 2, 101.

11. Elson, *The World of Time, Inc.*, vol. 2, 105.

12. John Hersey to Thomas Matthews, Cable no. 146, December 16, 1944, 1–2; Cable no. 145, December 13, 1944. Billings Papers, Box 1.

13. Luce memo to Billings, January 6, 1945. Billings Papers, Box 1. This reaction to staff complaints typifies the unrelenting hold Luce kept on policy matters. Staffers generally were afraid to challenge Luce. In late 1943 Luce decided that the magazine should draw a written list of guidelines or "Articles of Faith." He was puzzled by a lack of input from the staff. Eric Hodgins, Time, Inc., vice-president, wrote to him on September 22, 1943: "I really don't know anybody in the company who doesn't exhibit a certain amount of moral cowardice in dealing with you. You are the head of the family, papa and the eldest brothers, and, if you choose, you can force any of your children or younger brothers to do as you say. I don't think you have ever taken much cognizance of the possibility that people might exhibit moral cowardice in dealing with you." See Eric Hodgins to Luce memo, September 22, 1943. Billings Papers, Box 1.

14. Templeton Peck telephone interview, March 27, 1985.

15. McCutcheon telephone interview, April 30, 1985. See also Jerome K. Edwards, *The Foreign Policy of Col. McCormick's Tribune, 1929–1941* (Reno: University of Nevada Press, 1971); and Wendt, *Chicago Tribune*, 624–65.

16. "Ogden Reid is Dead at 64; Editor of the Herald Tribune," *New York Herald Tribune*, January 4, 1947, 1, 8.

17. "Old Hand, New Experts," *Time*, January 27, 1947, 49–50. According to the *Time* article, the *Herald Tribune* actually had eight foreign bureaus and the *Times* twenty-seven.

18. For a complete understanding of Shirer and his experiences in Berlin, see William Shirer, *Berlin Diary: The Journal of a Foreign Correspondent, 1934–1941* (New York: Random House, 1941).

19. See Ronald Steel, *Walter Lippmann and the American Century* (Boston: Little, Brown, 1980).

20. See "Ogden Reid Is Dead at 64; Editor of the Herald Tribune," *New York Herald Tribune*, January 4, 1947, 8.

21. Ralph B. Levering, *American Opinion and the Russian Alliance, 1939–1945* (Chapel Hill: University of North Carolina Press, 1976), 104–5.

22. Frank Hughes, "Luce, Magazine Axis Fuehrer, is Ace of Smear," *Chicago Tribune*, February 23, 1944, 2.

23. Luce to E. Ray Lansing memo, February 29, 1944. Billings Papers, Box 1.

Chapter 4
Europe in 1944

As Germany's defeat became increasingly more likely in 1944, policy makers in the United States realized the immediate need for planning a political structure for postwar Europe. Areas liberated by the Red Army would require particular diplomatic finesse. The types of issues and concerns discussed by the four news organizations in relation to the Soviet Union during this time fell into two categories. First, there was the overall U.S. strategy in dealings with the U.S.S.R. and acceptance or rejection of Soviet influence in a postwar world. Second, there were specific boundary or national issues involving smaller European nations as these countries fit into the emerging East–West scenario.

The *San Francisco Chronicle* remained committed to a pro-Soviet stance on nearly all diplomatic issues arising during 1944. "The sacrifices the Russians made during the war were the overwhelming thing," recalled *Chronicle* editorial writer Templeton Peck.[1] This expectation of U.S. reconciliation to Soviet autonomy remained strong at the *Chronicle* even through the first year after World War II, months after many other news organizations had expressed strong opposition to growing Soviet influence in Eastern and Central Europe.

Soviet international interests had identifiable limitations, the *Chronicle* editorial writers believed. An editorial appearing in May 1944 asserted that Soviet expansionism seemed unlikely, and expressions of U.S. distrust appeared misplaced. The editorial added:

Russia's problem seems to be, not to get more, but to use what is already possessed. . . . Moscow's several declarations of intention to change Russian boundaries and to extend a protectorate which in practical effect means an end to unlimited autonomy of buffer states have been interpreted to justify such suspicions. But these declarations have been frank and with such explanations as could hardly be demanded from a military power that did not wish to give them. . . . Stalin beyond dispute has proved himself realistic and the post-war program ahead of him tangible, not emotional.[2]

Stories by James Aldridge, a writer for the North American Newspaper Alliance, received favorable play in the *Chronicle* news columns during this period. In an article on page four, Aldridge observed in March 1944 that he saw no signs of Soviet international designs among the people of Moscow. He wrote:

Russia is a big country with a large army and an enormous future. But the war has taken everything. Most of the stories you have heard about how difficult life now is are probably true.

More than any people alive the Russians need and want peace as soon as possible and for as long as possible.

If you think these people want to be a blind colossus after the war you might as well apply it to yourself. If you have no interest in becoming a colossus you can guess that the Russian hasn't any either.[3]

Pragmatism and ethnocentricity tempered this favorable assessment of Soviet intentions. In a house editorial of January 7, 1944, it was noted that a Roosevelt administration report on war expenditures revealed a major contribution by Americans to the Soviet fighting effort in several important ways. The editorial observed:

The humdrum items of lend-lease to Russia in the President's report seem as significant as the thousands of planes and tanks. There are 5,500,000 pairs of army boots and 16,000,000 yards of woolen cloth for the Red Army. The boots and cloth—enough to shoe and clothe at least half of Stalin's army—may well have made last year's winter offensive possible. Unless they could be kept from freezing, the tanks and planes would not be of much use to them.[4]

The newspaper did not deny the postwar world would bring mutual Soviet–U.S. antagonism. In September 1944 *Chronicle* editorial writers observed that the Soviet Union might offer badly needed support to the United States in the war against Japan, but only to gain Soviet security for Vladivostok and to obtain a warm-water port to the south. "Nobody and nothing has any pull with Stalin except Russian interest," the editorial correctly concluded.[5] If Soviet goals were acceptable to *Chronicle* staffers at that time, these writers also believed that U.S. financial contributions had turned the tide in Eastern Europe and the Soviet self-interest probably would not allow Stalin to recognize easily this fact. While the *Chronicle* acknowledged a Soviet place in the postwar world, the newspaper also saw the inevitability of conflicting future interests. This would lead to the expected divergent interpretations from each side as to the relative importance of U.S. and Soviet contributions to the war effort.

If the *Chronicle* was cautiously understanding of Soviet goals and intentions, the *Chicago Tribune* was completely opposed to any such reflections. The *Chicago Tribune* saw Roosevelt as a dupe for Soviet world ambitions, even during World War II. A cartoon on the front page of the *Chicago Tribune* on February 19, 1944, depicted a cowboy of the "White House Palace Guard" branding a donkey with a sickle and hammer insignia. Three days earlier, Robert R. McCormick, *Chicago Tribune* editor and publisher, told a Republican club in Paducah, Kentucky, that "American troops were not sent to the Pacific in numbers to hold the Philippines and have not been sent in sufficient numbers to recapture the islands and free American prisoners suffering untold tortures in Japanese prison camps because the communists wanted them sent elsewhere." The Democratic party and the government were dominated by communists, though these Marxists composed only 1 percent of the population, McCormick told the group. This was because, of the one million communists in the country, "410,000 of them are in New York State," he added.[6]

The *Chicago Tribune* gave a great deal of coverage to any comments critical of Soviet leadership. For instance, on January 24, 1944, a Chicago-area legislator, Republican Representative Jessie Sumner, criticized a plan for U.S. participation in a joint Allied food program. The article, appearing at the top of page one in the *Chicago Tribune* the next day, quoted Miss Sumner as telling the House that Stalin "helped Hitler start the war." She added, "We owe him nothing except respect for not folding up and for fighting magnificently instead in self preservation."[7] In March a former *New York Times* foreign correspondent, Reg Brook, spoke in Chicago and told a gathering, "Russia's goal in eastern Europe is the occupation and subjugation of the Baltic states." The U.S. people must demand a firm stand against the Soviet Union or "the United States and Britain will be as detested throughout Europe as Germany," he added. The *Chicago Tribune* gave the remarks page-one coverage.[8]

Two months later, Arthur Sears Henning, *Chicago Tribune* Washington bureau chief, wrote that the Soviet Union and "dictator Stalin" were seeking a revision of the Atlantic Charter. "Soviet dissatisfaction with the Atlantic Charter arises from its [charter's] renunciation of territorial aggrandizement and its declaration in favor of self-determination," Henning wrote.[9] Other news organizations used premier or marshall to identify the Soviet leader, but the *Chicago Tribune* called him "dictator Stalin."

This reflection of Stalin as the devil incarnate and as the wily trickster of a gullible Roosevelt was clearly drawn in an editorial in January. The article called on the United States to resist Soviet aims in Poland, but the *Tribune* argued the issue should have been settled in 1943:

Stalin, a male Asiatic, knew the American chief executive was seducible long before he laid eyes on him at Teheran. . . . There are many difficulties in a situation which involves admiration of an associate's fighting ability and distrust of his political good faith.

Nothing in all American history ever produced any one faintly resembling the man Mr. Roosevelt met at Teheran and nowhere, even in medieval English history, could Mr. Churchill find anything like him. Any pretense that Josef Stalin has any social or political consanguinity with the Englishman or American is absurd and dangerous altho Mr. Roosevelt came home with just that affectation. It is possible to use such an illusion in fighting a war. As ingredient in a scheme of post-war collaboration an incongruity of such limitless range may be fatal.[10]

Even during a time when most Americans supported a cordial relationship with the Soviet Union, the *Chicago Tribune* urged the same hard line that formed the basis of U.S. policy toward the U.S.S.R. years later. This attitude reflected an ideological fixation, not a close examination of issues and events of 1944. The *Chicago Tribune* rarely commented editorially on the merits of a given diplomatic exchange by examining the specific pros and cons of the particular occurrence. Anything connected with the Soviet Union involved deceit or attempts to subjugate the midwestern U.S. way of life, the newspaper argued, and all relations with the U.S.S.R. should be approached in such a frame of reference. Communism was the dry rot of civilization, McCormick believed, and specific issues were approached from this general overview.

Consequently, during this wartime alliance, the *Chicago Tribune* sought not only articles that portrayed the Soviet Union in a negative light, but any events that emphasized a struggle against communism. On February 4, 1944, a conservative group in Hollywood created the Motion Picture Alliance for the Preservation of American Ideals. Among those charter members of the organization were studio owner Walt Disney and actor Gary Cooper. The alliance sought to organize those in the movie colony who believed in "the American way of life to combat un-American influences." None of the other news groups provided coverage of the meeting, but the *Chicago Tribune*'s page one article the next day carried the headline: "Group Formed in Hollywood to Fight Reds."[11] A dinner in New York the next month for the National Federation for Constitutional Liberties drew *Chicago Tribune* ire. In an editorial headlined, "The Plot Against America," writers noted that sponsors of the dinner included "Mrs. Ogden Reid, editor of the pro-British *New York Herald Tribune*."

Asserting that the federation was "listed as communist-controlled by no less authority than Atty. Gen. Biddle," the *Chicago Tribune* remarked that "when a blue ribbon aggregation such as this throws a party for a bunch of communists, the ordinary citizen has a right to ask what it is all about and inquire into motives."[12]

The lone exception to anticommunist rhetoric in diplomatic articles came in September when Eric Johnston, president of the U.S. Chamber of Commerce, visited the Soviet Union. The trip was marked by heavy coverage from all of the news organizations, not just the *Chicago Tribune*. *Time*'s Richard Lauterbach followed Johnston throughout the Soviet Union and cabled New York that Johnston had "bewitched, bothered and be-Willkied" the Soviets with his ingratiating personality. But the unusual aspect of the trip was a *Chicago Tribune* front-page article. Johnston found both positive and negative ingredients in Soviet society. He said, among other things, that he admired the Soviet peoples' successful fight against illiteracy, their courage, and their desire to improve, but he found fault with the country's low standard of living and lack of exposure to ideas from outside state-controlled official publications. The tone of this article portraying a balanced look at the Soviet Union was not duplicated in the *Chicago Tribune* during the entire four years of this study.[13] Apparently, Johnston's position as a leader of the business community commanded enough *Chicago Tribune* respect that his balanced remarks still found their way onto the front page of the Chicago newspaper.

The *New York Herald Tribune*'s overall approach to Soviet affairs involved a more complex situation than that of the *Chronicle* or *Chicago Tribune*. Maurice Hindus handled coverage of Soviet battlefronts and civilian industrial areas. He eagerly wrote of the successes of the Red Army and the glowing character of the Soviet peoples and their leaders. A second perspective came from columnist Walter Lippmann, who predicted regional control would be the cornerstone of postwar peace. The house editorial position favoring a limited Soviet role in Europe and a continued strong leadership position for Great Britain provided a third point of view.

Most of Hindus's articles were written in the first person, as if he were writing a letter home to his family, and they were generously peppered with homilies and anecdotes about the fighting spirit and foresightedness of the Soviets. Pointing out that captured Soviet factories had not aided Nazi war efforts because of Soviet anticipation in rendering the machines useless, Hindus observed in January: "So far as I have been able to ascertain not one tractor, not one combine had the Germans manufactured during the occupation. . . . Now the rivers of the Don Kuban, northern Donets, Mais Sozh, and Desna are all in Russian hands again. . . . Despite heavy casualties, the New Year finds the Russian army more powerful than at any time since the start of the Russo–German war."[14]

In October, 1944, Hindus visited the Siberian city of Norilsk. He wrote: "Norilsk is a town which few Americans have heard of, but to Russians it is now a symbol of man's triumph over Nature in the North. This booming industrial community, the largest of its kind in the country for some time has been supplying defense plants with invaluable metallurgical accessories. . . . The story of Norilsk demonstrates the strenuousness with which Russia has been pushing civilization to the Far North."[15]

Both *Herald Tribune* house editorial writers and Lippmann emphasized diplomatic events over insights into the Soviet culture, but Lippmann tended to see Soviet influence as only a natural progression of events. He observed on March 14, 1944: "Our relations with Russia must be considered in relation to the whole war—the war in Europe and in eastern Asia. . . . Russia's real attitude toward collaboration with us will be shaped by the effectiveness of our invasion and the far-sightedness of our political conduct in Europe."[16]

Criticized in *Reader's Digest* in September by roving editor William Hard, Lippmann responded:

Because I have written about the Atlantic community of nations and about the Russian orbit . . . Mr. Hard says that I am a "deviser of spheres of zones," that I am opposed to the unity of mankind. . . . The truth is that these regional groupings were devised by the geography of the earth and the course of history. I did not devise them. . . . I call it a policy of uniting the world by consolidating the natural, the historic and the strategic connections of the nations.[17]

The *Herald Tribune* looked for a more prominent role for the United States after the war. The Soviet Union's place depended on the consignment of U.S. leaders and Soviet willingness to treat its neighbors reasonably. When Soviet ambitions threatened U.S. control, the New York newspaper lashed out at the Soviet Union as in January 1944. *Pravda* had attacked the foreign affairs policies of Republican presidential aspirant Wendell Willkie, and the *Herald Tribune* responded that the U.S. people would never bend to whatever the Soviet Union wanted. The editorial added, however, that Eastern European affairs were primarily the Soviet Union's affair, and "it is in Russia's physical power to organize these central European territories in any way she sees fit. But how she does so will make a very great difference. A policy of reason, moderation and substantial justice will powerfully cement the united nations."[18]

But *Herald Tribune* editorial policy in 1944 always accentuated optimism and a belief that the war had changed Soviet attitudes toward its world neighbors and the handling of its internal affairs. On February 1 Soviet leaders announced that the sixteen republics in the Soviet Union had been granted an increased degree of autonomy with the right to elect their own commisariat of foreign affairs and the right to raise their own armies. Several articles and two editorials in the *Herald Tribune* in the ensuing week heralded a possible new era in the Soviet Union with a less centralized government and a fresh understanding of the needs of a nation of diverse peoples. This move was designed to set the stage for the upcoming organization of the United Nations, when the Soviet Union would claim representation in the general assembly for three of its sixteen republics. The subtlety of the move in early 1944 was lost on the *Herald Tribune*, displaying the newspaper's inclination for greeting Soviet moves with a degree of optimistic hope.[19]

Two months later, the newspaper reviewed the guidelines for a postwar world as set forth in the Atlantic charter nearly three years earlier. The charter was outdated, the *Herald Tribune* concluded, and a new diplomatic agreement for postwar relations had to be forged. Would 1939 or 1941 boundaries be recognized? Would the Soviet Union annex the Baltic states? Intentions needed clarification from all sides. In essence, the newspaper called for a conference to reshape Europe, and that conclave eventually was held at Yalta ten months later. But in so doing, the editorial writers recognized that the Atlantic Charter did not bear any Soviet input, since only Churchill and Roosevelt had met near the coast of Newfoundland two years before. Now it was time for an Atlantic peace with a Soviet stamp of approval.[20]

As with the *Chronicle*, *Herald Tribune* willingness to accept Soviet influence in 1944 stemmed from sympathy for a war-torn nation. In March the newspaper observed:

It is not exactly pretty: the [Russian] passion which here speaks is not exactly predictable. But this is the deep passion of a people who have not simply waged war beyond distant seas, but have met it in a peculiarly brutal and hideous form, in their own homes and farms and cities. It is a people to whom war has taught a bitter realism, a simple grimness that goes beyond all fine-spun international theories, elaborate political calculations, ulterior intrigue.[21]

This, then, was the legacy of the postwar world: a mediated peace with the United States accepting a certain inevitable Soviet influence. However, the newspaper reasoned, it would be the United States that would ultimately decide the general political structure with Soviet input considered—this along with the comments and pressures from the other nations of Europe and the world. The year 1944 was marked on the editorial pages of the *Herald Tribune* with a wait-and-see attitude.

The rigors of the Eastern front did not generate a like sympathy from either *Time* or Henry Luce. Luce and his editors were wary of Soviet intentions and had openly expressed apprehension in the pages of *Time* even before Whittaker Chambers had assumed the duties of foreign editor. Chambers's retention in that position despite heavy staff opposition did, of course, provide one indication of Luce's anticommunist philosophy, but there were others, and Luce genuinely felt the Soviet Union was not worthy of a great deal of postwar influence.

One indication of this attitude was a memo Luce wrote to his policy committee in late 1943. He described what he thought the alignment of the postwar world would be by dividing the earth into six federations. The first was the United States of Europe, supported financially in large part by the United States "to the extent of $100 per year per U.S. family."[22] The Soviet Union comprised another federation, and its function was to "demonstrate in her vast domain, her ability to develop a prosperous and noble society," while the United States develops to a "stronger industrial (and hence military) power than any other two nations combined." Were Luce's outline to come to fruition, he felt that "throughout the world man's eyes would open as upon a glorious morning inviting men to work and to happiness."[23]

A year later, Luce observed that he was not certain if the United States ought to export democracy, but he was sure that world cooperation would create problems. "What the dopey good-willed internationalists must be made to understand is that internationalism means trouble," Luce wrote. "And therefore the pragmatic question: how much trouble for what?"[24]

Time's increasingly hostile tone toward the Soviet Union did not escape the attention of Soviet Ambassador Andrei Gromyko, who in March 1944 questioned a *Time* Washington bureau correspondent as to who created *Time* editorial policy. The staffer replied that there was no single source of *Time* policy making. This infuriated Luce, who directed Eric Hodgins, Time, Inc., senior vice-president, to circulate a memo to Time, Inc., editors. The March 6 memo said: "The chief editorial policymaker for TIME Inc. is Henry R. Luce—and that is no secret which we attempt to conceal from the outside world. But the difference between policymaking at TIME Inc. and some other places that could be named is that policy is not handed down as a one-man ukase."[25] In the furor over the Washington staffer's response to Gromyko, *Time* and Luce lost sight of the real significance of the exchange. That is, Gromyko had sensed such negativism at *Time* over the previous few months that he had been compelled to make the inquiry in the first place.

Information sent from the Soviet Union to the United States was heavily censored during the war, and as Richard Lauterbach noted a few days after the Gromyko inquiry, *Time* and *Life* had particular difficulty with the censors. Lauterbach cabled John Shaw Billings, *Life* managing editor, that Soviet officials had for four months ignored requests for pictures of military officers and spot news events. He said a request to visit the Ural area in the Soviet interior "had not been benignly received." Lauterbach speculated that one reason for the lack of cooperation was the "resentment and suspicion induced mainly by a series of articles which Walter Graebner, a *Time* correspondent, wrote after leaving the Soviet Union." Lauterbach said the articles were printed in the *London Daily Mail*. "I'm sorry as can be that this hasn't been more productive for LIFE, but I know you didn't expect much when I left," Lauterbach added.[26]

Also in March *Time* carried two articles that emphasized increasing uneasiness between the Americans and Soviets. Entitled "Cause for Alarm," a foreign relations section piece described mounting apprehension among writers and diplomats in the United States concerning Soviet motives. Accompanying the article was a letter written by several judicial, political, business, and labor leaders in the United States to the Kremlin. The letter called on Soviet policy makers to demonstrate an appropriate mood of cooperation and said Americans were shocked by Soviet intentions to resolve the Polish political situation unilaterally.[27] Not only was the timing of the articles critical—coming soon after the Gromyko incident—but also notable was the expressed urgency of the situation and the amount of attention given the issue. An entire page was devoted to the letter and several columns to the lead article.

If *Time*'s tone did not express the virulence of the *Chicago Tribune*, the belligerency toward the Soviet Union was there. Certainly, Soviet war losses were diminishing in importance in the estimation of *Time* editors and, as the Yalta Conference approached, *Time* openly questioned the Soviet Union's right to guide decisions about postwar Europe.

The most potentially explosive national issue in Europe in the overall United States–Soviet Union backdrop in 1944 concerned the postwar political situation in Poland. The Pact of Nonaggression remained one of the greatest single sources of U.S. antagonism toward the Soviet Union, especially among Polish Americans. The Polish London government-in-exile had restored relations with the Soviet Union after Hitler turned on the Soviets in June 1941.

However, those relations were severed again in April 1943, when the Germans had announced the discovery of the mass graves of 11,000 Polish officers in the Katyn Forest near Smolensk. These officers had been taken prisoner by the Soviets in 1939. The Germans called for an investigation by the International Red Cross, and the London Poles reluctantly decided to associate themselves with this request. The Soviets responded by claiming that the men had actually been executed by the Nazis after the German Army had overrun the area in July 1941, and the Soviet Union once again severed relations with the London Poles.[28]

In January 1944 the Soviets invited Western journalists to visit the site of the massacre. Kathy Harriman, the twenty-five-year-old daughter of U.S. Ambassador W. Averell Harriman, attended the briefing. Considering the impact of the issue, none of the four news organizations dwelled much on the conference or the Soviet revelations.

For instance, the *Chronicle* carried a news story on page two that emphasized Soviet claims that a special Soviet commission had performed autopsies and investigated before concluding that the men had been killed by the Germans in August and September 1941. The commission produced evidence that it claimed was indisputable, the *Chronicle* story noted. The article carried no byline and no wire-service identification but was datelined from Smolensk, which is ten miles from the murder site. A *Chronicle* editorial two weeks later concluded that the London Poles had made a mistake by associating themselves with the charges, and that was a mistake "that may well prove fatal" to the Poles.[29]

Time carried a picture of the murder site and an eleven-paragraph article. The story said that the Soviets had issued a weak response to a question about why the dead officers were wearing fur-lined coats, if they were murdered in August and September. The Soviets said Smolensk was cold at night, even during the summer. However, the story concluded, "Cabled TIME Correspondent Richard Lauterbach: 'As far as most of us were concerned, the Germans had slaughtered the Poles.' "[30] The *Herald Tribune* and the *Chicago Tribune* carried wire-service articles but did not comment editorially.

The Katyn massacre embodied only one facet of the strained relations between the Poles and the Soviets. The United States the same month offered to mediate the differences, but the Soviets declined the offer, causing the *Chronicle* to reflect that Eastern European boundary issues ought not be the business of the United States, but the Soviet Union would decide these questions fairly.[31]

The other news organizations did not subscribe to this pro-Soviet stance on the Polish question. The *Herald Tribune*, while critical of the London Poles, constantly aired the complaints of the exiled leaders. In March, after a communist-sponsored government arose to challenge the exiles, the *Herald Tribune* carried an article datelined in London in which the exiles claimed a communist government was being forced on the people of Poland. Two months earlier, the same group predicted in a news story that despite the fact that the Polish underground was fighting Nazis, Soviet policy makers would make the Polish leaders prisoners of war, if they were taken by the Red Army.[32]

In October Lippmann expressed despair over the Polish situation, not because of Soviet aggression but because of indecisiveness by Roosevelt. The columnist argued that a Polish government-in-exile acceptable to the Soviet Union should have been constructed in 1942 to replace the recognition of the London Poles, who were dominated by the reactionary Polish aristocracy. He added: "But the President was badly advised, and instead of urging General Sikorski to dominate the irreconcilable Poles and work out a settlement, General Sikorski was told that these questions could be postponed until after the war. . . . Mr. Churchill with Mr. Roosevelt supporting him, has tried to settle the problem on the lines which Mr. Roosevelt would not approve in 1942. But now their terms are offered too little too late."[33] Lippmann neither favored nor opposed Soviet moves but merely sought a reconciliation of the situation that would allow Poland to coexist with the Soviet Union and retain some degree of independence.

Time did not devote a great deal of space to the Polish question until Chambers became foreign news editor in July. Then the issue became a touchstone for the ominous Soviet threat. As Stanislaw Mikolajezyk, premier of the government-in-exile, prepared to travel to Moscow to meet with Stalin in mid-August, *Time* predicted that he was heading into an atmosphere of "accomplished facts." A pattern had already been set in Czechoslovakia, and a communist-backed government would likely be forced on Poland. Two months later, *Time* emphasized that the London Poles had been deprived of their right to govern, and their land and other possessions had been confiscated by the communists, known as the Lublin Poles.[34]

The stories revealed a one-sided emphasis. The London Poles lacked popular appeal, and the polarization between London and Lublin left the middle-road Poles in a quandary. Also, the Red Army had evicted the Nazis from Poland at great cost. The issue was more complex than could be discerned from the pages of a magazine in which foreign affairs reporting was edited by a fanatical anticommunist.

The *Chicago Tribune* found two reasons to attack Soviet policy on Poland. McCormick's anti-Soviet philosophy led the editorial writers to decry any Soviet influence in Poland. Secondly, the heavy Polish–U.S. population in Chicago was naturally concerned about their home country and what would befall that nation if it were left to the mercy of a country that had invaded Poland just five years before. Yet, in 1944 the *Chicago Tribune* did not carry a great deal of foreign news away from the battlefields, and the Polish issue received airing in the *Chicago Tribune* only when a local angle came into play or when McCormick needed another excuse to attack Roosevelt.

For instance, in January 1944 and later in September the newspaper carried stories about people who had made observations in Chicago about the Polish situation. One story, on page two, concerned the comments of a Harvard professor of Slavic affairs, Waclaw Lednicki, who had delivered a speech in Chicago. Lednicki said the chief question before Poles was whether the Red Army entered Poland as conquerors or liberators.[35] Similarly, eight months later, a Chicago Polish American told a reporter about a colony in Mexico where about 1,400 Poles had made a home because other Poles "still are suffering from slavery in Russia."[36]

When Mikolajczyk visited Stalin, the *Chicago Tribune* described his journey as a "Canossan pilgrimage to Moscow." The editorial added that Roosevelt should have resolved the issue in 1943, but "as an ally Mr. Roosevelt has proved himself the greatest Good Time Charley in history."[37]

Other lesser European countries affected by Soviet policy drew generally sporadic attention from the four news organizations in 1944. As the war came to a close, decisions about the face of Europe had to be hammered out by the Soviet Union, Great Britain, and the United States. In some cases, especially where small countries had fought on the side of the Axis powers, these questions could generate ambivalence.

Finland, as an example, had been invaded by the Soviet Union in 1939 and had spent much of the war fighting with Germany. In early 1944 the Soviet Union began offering Finland peace terms, which were turned aside until September. This gained the attention of the news organizations, which would in one instance laud the Soviets for their patience and diplomacy and criticize them in another instance for their power politics.

Only the *Chicago Tribune* remained aloof from the issue, perhaps because the editors cared little for events not directly related to the United States or because Finland's posture on the side of Germany made it awkward for the *Chicago Tribune* editors to criticize the Soviet Union as they were wont to do. The newspaper did carry several front-page wire stories throughout the year, which objectively reported the Finnish situation.[38]

Not surprisingly, the *Chronicle* saw the Soviet Union as generous with the Finns. On March 2 the *Chronicle* observed that "the peace terms Moscow offers Finland seem no harsher than, perhaps not so harsh, as the conditions put to any loser in modern war." The key issue was whether a Soviet–Finnish border drawn in 1940 and favoring the Soviet Union would be recognized. "What warranty could we give stronger than the realistic recognition that the world's future, and ours as part of it, depends in large degree upon the integrity of Russia's proclaimed spirit for peace?" the editorial asked.[39]

Time found more cause for flip-flopping on the issue. In Finland *Time* correspondent John Scott wrote in July that the Soviet Union sought only a friendly neighbor. "Neither now nor later do they want to annex Finland. . . . What they want to do in Finland is liquidate the war on this front. . . . But they believe the present Finnish government must go."[40] This feeling changed later in the year when Chambers became foreign editor. An article in October, not bylined and apparently edited by Chambers, found the Soviet armistice terms signed by Finland in September to be harsh. The $300 million reparations would make Finland "an economic colony of Russia" but "Finland still had her nominal independence," *Time* noted.[41] The change in authors certainly affected the sentiments, but the issue itself caused dual feelings among Americans.

This divergence was most apparent in the *Herald Tribune*. In late February the newspaper featured a page-one United Press article in which the Soviet Union outlined reasonable terms for armistice, not asking unconditional surrender. Two weeks later, Soviet leaders were seen as "sternly demanding" an answer from the Finns, according to a page-one Associated Press story "heavily censored by the Russians." Two months later, the newspaper's editorial writers observed that the Allies, particularly the Soviet Union, had been too magnanimous with the small nations of Europe still supporting the Axis forces.[42]

These swings in temperament not only reflected ambivalence about the Finnish issue but indicate a lack of understanding of the Soviet resolve to ensure that the Soviet Union would henceforth be surrounded by friendly, if not docile, neighbors. These deep-rooted Soviet suspicions had been greatly enhanced in the years from 1939 to 1944, and the U.S. news organizations did not fathom the strength of the Soviet determination. Neither

Finland nor any other border nation would field an army to threaten the Soviets again. This was an unshakable tenet of the postwar world, as far as Soviet leaders were concerned, but it was not something that many editors firmly grasped in 1944.

Bulgaria faced a similar Soviet resolve as the war came to a close. The Bulgars had sought to remain neutral, but in September 1944 the Soviets demanded that they declare war on Germany. When the Bulgars resisted, the Soviets declared war on them. The smaller country then acceded, but the Soviet Union did not grant an armistice immediately, and for a few days Bulgaria was at war with both sides. Once the situation had been stabilized, the *Chicago Tribune* expressed fear that Bulgaria would "come under the Russian yoke," while *Time* observed that "once more tough minded Russian diplomacy had paid off." The *Herald Tribune* merely noted the occurrence in passing, while the *Chronicle* carried an editorial cartoon of four men (Balkans) singing and trying to woo a friendly United States. Earlier in the year the *Chronicle* had asserted that all of the Balkan countries had nothing to lose by assuming the role of bystanders and, consequently, aiding the Soviet advance.[43]

Finally, in 1944 the Allied countries met in the United States for two world conferences. The first was in Bretton Woods, New Hampshire, in July, when forty-four countries attempted to create a coherent postwar monetary system. As the only communist country in the world, the Soviet Union declined to attend but managed to grab some headlines by announcing from Moscow during the conclave that they might accept some of the tenets established at the conference. Except for the *Herald Tribune* the news organizations largely ignored the parley. The *Chicago Tribune* did not even carry wire stories.

The second conference at the Dumbarton Oaks estate in Washington was designed to draft an outline for the United Nations Organization. The delegates from the Soviet Union, the United States, Great Britain, and China worked in secrecy, which angered both the *Chicago Tribune* and the *Herald Tribune*. The New York newspaper carried an indignant editorial, and the Chicago newspaper a page-one article focusing mainly on the conference's secrecy. Lippmann held that whatever the results, the United States would have to remain an influential power in Europe, unlike the days after Versailles in 1919. Both the newspaper and the columnist indicated that the Dumbarton Oaks Conference was the time for the United States to take its place as the leading nation in the world.[44]

The *Chicago Tribune* and *Chronicle* focused their attention on a meeting between John Foster Dulles and Cordell Hull prior to the forty-four-nation parley. The two met in Washington—Dulles being Thomas Dewey's foreign affairs adviser and Hull being the secretary of state—to discuss the U.S. position. That way no matter how the 1944 election in November ended, U.S. policy would be uniform. In an article written by Marquis

Child the *Chronicle* reflected how the two were studies in contrast but that the nonpartisan discussion boded well for the United States. The *Chicago Tribune*, on the other hand, found nothing to cheer about in the meeting, noting that Hull "represents the views of the British foreign office" and Dulles "is the impersonation of the big dough of Wall Street."[45]

The Big Three leaders did not meet in 1944 and, as the year ended, it was obvious that the tentative agreements at Teheran the year before would not suffice for much longer. A visit to Stalin by Churchill in July 1944 brought polite perfunctory remarks from the news groups. A Churchill–Roosevelt parley in Quebec two months later resulted in similar comments, though *Chicago Tribune* reporter William Moore saw a sinister connection between Stalin's absence in Quebec and Soviet terms for European nations in Red-Army-occupied areas.[46]

As 1945 began, the four news organizations carried more words of optimism than they had at any time since Pearl Harbor, but the diplomatic coverage was buried beneath the overwhelming attention given the war news. In the second month of the new year the Allied leaders gathered in an obscure city on the Baltic Sea, and Yalta thereafter would symbolize postwar Europe. The war news would linger, but increasingly diplomacy would begin to supplant the fighting, and this shift would signal a change in both news coverage and in the image of the Soviet Union in the pages of U.S. publications. The time for Red Army diplomacy and attendant U.S. sympathies had nearly ended. Americans would read of another Soviet Union as they spread their newspapers over their breakfast tables each morning and as they took their news magazines from their mailboxes each week.

NOTES

1. Templeton Peck telephone interview, March 27, 1985.

2. "Stalin Policy," *San Francisco Chronicle* editorial, May 11, 1944, 14.

3. James Aldridge, "The Soviet Colossus, Or Nightmares in the West/That 'Power Mad' Russia Wants Only Peace—And Plenty of It," *Chronicle*, March 5, 1944, 4.

4. "Boots and Clothes," *Chronicle* editorial, January 7, 1944, 10.

5. "Russia and Japan," *Chronicle* editorial, September 8, 1944, 14.

6. *Chicago Tribune* editorial cartoon, February 19, 1944, 1; "Col. McCormick Says Reds Balk Arms to Pacific," *Chicago Tribune*, February 16, 1944, 3.

7. "Stalin Called Hitler Helper in War Plots," *Chicago Tribune*, January 25, 1944, 1.

8. "U.S. Correspondent Charges Reds Aim at Huge Conquest," *Chicago Tribune*, March 13, 1944, 1.

9. Arthur Sears Henning, "Stalin Scheme for Land Grab Stirs Tempest," *Chicago Tribune*, May 9, 1944, 1.

10. "Russian Political Morality," *Chicago Tribune* editorial, January 18, 1944, 14.

11. "Group Formed in Hollywood to Fight Reds," *Chicago Tribune*, February 6, 1944, 1.

12. "The Plot Against America," *Chicago Tribune* editorial, March 31, 1944, 16.

13. Richard Lauterbach to John Shaw Billings, Cable no. 236, September 4, 1944, 4, Box 1. John Shaw Billings Papers, Caroliniana Library, Manuscripts Division, Billings Collection, University of South Carolina, Columbia, South Carolina; "Johnston Finds Both Good and Bad in Russia," *Chicago Tribune*, September 17, 1944, 1.

14. Maurice Hindus, "The Russian Army Strong as Ever as Year Starts," *New York Herald Tribune*, January 3, 1944, 2.

15. Maurice Hindus, "Russians Build Nickel Empire in North Siberia," *Herald Tribune*, March 14, 1944, 21.

16. Walter Lippmann column, "Today and Tomorrow," *Herald Tribune*, March 14, 1944, 21.

17. Lippmann column; "Today and Tomorrow," September 5, 1944, 17.

18. "Futile Polemics," *Herald Tribune* editorial, January 6, 1944, 18.

19. See especially "Reds Accord War Power to 16 Republics," *Herald Tribune*, February 2, 1944, 1.

20. "The Atlantic Charter," *Herald Tribune* editorial, April 12, 1944, 22.

21. "What Russia Wants," *Herald Tribune* editorial, March 19, 1944, 22.

22. Henry Luce to Policy Committee memo, November 3, 1943, 1. Billings Papers, Box 1.

23. Luce to Policy Committee memo, November 3, 1943, 2, 4.

24. Luce to Billings memo, December 9, 1944. Billings Papers, Box 1.

25. Eric Hodgins to editors memo, March 9, 1944. Billings Papers, Box 1; Hodgins to staff memo, March 6, 1944. Billings Papers, Box 1; also see Robert T. Elson, *The World of Time, Inc.: The Intimate History of a Publishing Enterprise, 1941–1960*, vol. 2 (New York: Atheneum, 1973), 78–79; and W. A. Swanberg, *Luce and His Empire* (New York: Charles Scribner's Sons, 1972), 215.

26. Richard Lauterbach to Billings memo, March 21, 1944, 1–2. Billings Papers, Box 1.

27. "Cause for Alarm," *Time*, March 20, 1944, 17; "Russia Must Choose," *Time*, March 20, 1944, 20.

28. See George F. Kennan, *Russia and the West Under Lenin and Stalin* (Boston: Little, Brown, 1960), 359–60.

29. "Russ Reveal Final Proof to Show Nazis Slaughtered Poles," *Chronicle*, January 27, 1944, 2; "Russia-Poland," *Chronicle* editorial, February 12, 1944, 10.

30. "Day in the Forest," *Time*, February 7, 1944, 27–28.

31. "Poland," *Chronicle* editorial, January 27, 1944.

32. "Poles Contend Underground Opposes Reds," *Herald Tribune*, March 1, 1944, 4.

33. Lippmann column, "Today and Tomorrow," *Herald Tribune*, October 3, 1944, 21.

34. "Poland—Mission to Moscow," *Time*, August 7, 1944, 32; "Poland—Fruits of Appeasement," *Time*, October 9, 1944, 36.

35. "Poles Doubtful of Reds' Intent, Says Fugitive," *Chicago Tribune*, January 4, 1944, 2.

36. "1,419 Enslaved in Russia Find Mexico Haven," *Chicago Tribune*, September 16, 1944, 1.

37. "Paying the Fiddler for Stalin's Tune," *Chicago Tribune* editorial, August 1, 1944, 8.

38. See "Peace Parley with Finland Planned: Reds," *Chicago Tribune*, March 1, 1944, 1; "Finnish Cabinet Debates Reds' Peace Offer," *Chicago Tribune*, March 3, 1944, 1; "Report Finns Refuse Peace," *Chicago Tribune*, March 4, 1944, 1; "Finland's Reply to Russia!" *Chicago Tribune*, March 9, 1944, 1; "Finns Break with Germany," *Chicago Tribune*, September 3, 1944, 1; "Finn-Russian Armistice Ends All Hostilities," *Chicago Tribune*, September 4, 1944, 1.

39. "Finland," *Chronicle* editorial, March 2, 1944, 12.

40. "Finland—Fateful Hour," *Time*, July 3, 1944, 36.

41. "Finland—Hard Terms," *Time*, October 2, 1944, 40.

42. "Reds Tell Finns to Intern Nazi Troops and Ships and Offer to Help Do It," *Herald Tribune*, March 1, 1944, 1; "Russian Reply Tells Finns to Decide at Once," *Herald Tribune*, March 15, 1944, 1; "Statement of Fact," *Herald Tribune* editorial, May 14, 1944, 6.

43. "Russia in the Balkans," *Chicago Tribune* editorial, September 8, 1944, 14; "Bulgaria—One Strike and Out," *Time*, September 18, 1944, 45; "Soviets Herald Shaping of New Balkan Front," *Herald Tribune*, September 6, 1944, 10; "Russian Moderation," *Chronicle* editorial, April 4, 1944, 12.

44. "Secret Diplomacy," *Herald Tribune*, October 2, 1944, 16; "Allies Begin Talks on Peace Outline Today," *Chicago Tribune*, August 21, 1944, 1; Walter Lippmann column, "Today and Tomorrow," *Herald Tribune*, September 2, 1944, 13.

45. "The Washington Conference," *Chicago Tribune* editorial, August 21, 1944, 10; Marquis Childs, "Hull, Dulles Contrast in Characters," *Chronicle*, August 23, 1944, 4.

46. William Moore, "Busy Fighting Stalin Shuns Quebec Parley," *Chicago Tribune*, September 12, 1944, 1.

Chapter 5
Yalta to San Francisco

I

On December 16, 1944, the German Army launched a last-gasp offensive in the Ardennes Forest against a poorly reinforced section of the U.S. front. Hoping Allied ground troops were overextended, the Nazis tried to split the lines and forge a retreat. The strategy failed at a cost of nearly 100,000 German casualties, and the unsuccessful Battle of the Bulge ensured that the defeat of Germany would come in a matter of months. By the end of January the rapidly approaching Red Army stood on the banks of the Oder River only forty miles from Berlin.[1]

Consequently, Allied leaders knew that the February 1945 three-power meeting of heads of states and their foreign ministers in the Crimea area of the Soviet Union would be momentous. Despite this, reporters were kept away from the conference and, in fact, the public was not even informed that the meeting was in progress until after it began. Consequently, early stories after Yalta reflected information from official communiqués, and complaints about the agreements reached came weeks later. This left problems for the future.

At Yalta military matters still dotted the agenda, of course. For instance, the question remained as to how to finally subdue Germany and with what troops. Soviet participation in the Pacific also was a priority in the eyes of the Americans. But in general, it was apparent that the Yalta Conference would address diplomatic questions on postwar Germany and Europe, as a whole. The geopolitical character and influences of nearly an entire continent, historically the world's most powerful area politically, came under Big Three scrutiny at this eight-day gathering.

The top leaders at Yalta were the same men who had presided over the previous wartime Big Three conferences. They were Great Britain's Winston Churchill, the Soviet Union's Josef Stalin, and the United States' Franklin D. Roosevelt, who had just begun his fourth term as president. Twelve years of the rigors of office through depression and war had taken their toll. Roosevelt appeared haggard and exhausted in the weeks prior to the conference. Assistant Press Secretary Eben Ayers observed in his diary on January 17, 1945, that Roosevelt had suffered through a bout of influenza and had lost ten pounds, making him appear weak and emaciated.[2]

Great Britain was financially and militarily drained by six years of war, and Churchill, too, approached the meeting in a poor frame of mind. He was depressed by the increasingly aggressive moves of the Soviet Union in Poland and Eastern Europe, and his attention to his work had deteriorated over the first few weeks of 1945. But as historian Diane Shaver Clemens observed, regardless of the moods or health of Churchill and Roosevelt, the large numbers of supporting diplomats made certain those interests would be protected.[3]

More than three years later, disgruntled U.S. conservatives would assert that the United States and Great Britain had not bargained forcefully at Yalta, partly because of both Roosevelt's and Churchill's health. These accusations were fostered by charges from Whittaker Chambers against Alger Hiss. Chambers, who was *Time*'s foreign news editor during the Yalta meeting, accused Hiss in 1948 of conveying U.S. secrets to the Soviet Union. Hiss had been a key aide at Dumbarton Oaks and at Yalta and was later the coordinator of the San Francisco Conference. It was felt in the late 1940s and early 1950s that revelations about Hiss and others meant that these men had taken advantage of Roosevelt's declining health to influence him into making decisions adverse to U.S. interests.[4]

It is difficult to determine what effect Roosevelt's health and Churchill's depression may have had, though as Clemens indicates and as a thorough examination of the discussions at the conference reveals, the two leaders handled themselves well.[5] What is germane to this study is the structure of the conference that gave rise to these speculations.

Reporters in the United States were excluded from Yalta entirely. A. Merriman Smith, United Press White House reporter, recalled in 1946 that he and his press association colleagues at the White House had learned of the impending conference in December 1944, and he knew the location in January 1945, but voluntary press guidelines from the Office of Censorship had prevented Smith from making public his knowledge. Press Secretary Stephen Early told Smith that Roosevelt and Churchill had agreed with Stalin that no reporters of any nationality would be allowed at the conference.[6] According to *Time*, Smith and the two other wire-service reporters had been given medical shots and told to be ready to travel but had been left at home when Roosevelt departed without warning.[7] Given Stalin's penchant for secrecy and his unpopularity among disaffected Eastern Europeans, Roosevelt and Churchill could not gain support for direct press coverage.

But when the charges of complicity came later, a lack of free and open discussion contributed to the expressions of suspicions that were generated by a vociferous group opposed to the Yalta settlements. The attempt at secrecy met only partial success anyway. Churchill's aides managed to leak sketchy information to the British press during the conference as they had during all of the wartime meetings.[8] It was probably a mistake on Roosevelt's part not to have worked harder to provide more and better information to U.S. newsmen during the eight days of meetings. The secrecy combined with the health issue ensured that Yalta would always be subject to second guessing.

Attempts to suppress the existence of the conference failed almost immediately. The day the conference began, February 4, 1945, a *Herald Tribune* editorial speculated that talks were underway and that they were probably taking place in the Soviet Union. Three days later, Ned Russell, *Herald Tribune* London correspondent, wrote that an announcement of the conference had confused British censors. The following day, an official acknowledgment of the meeting's existence was released simultaneously in Washington, Moscow, and London, but the whereabouts of the conclave and the issues discussed were still left to speculation.[9]

During the eight days, the three delegations attempted to hammer out a basic approach to postwar Europe, but the differences among the representatives left the Yalta agreement with vague references to vital issues. Poland remained the most divisive question. At Yalta the Curzon Line once again became Poland's eastern border, the boundary that existed just after World War I. The Poles got some new territory in the west of Germany. The conferees directed that free elections under Allied supervision be held in Poland involving all of that nation's democratic forces. This unclear wording proved meaningless, especially because the Red Army already occupied Poland and the Soviet Union had recognized the Lublin government on January 5.

The rest of Eastern Europe found little solace in vague promises for self-determination. For Yugoslavia, already controlled by communist Josip Broz Tito, the three leaders decided on a supervised political settlement similar to Poland's, while the Axis satellites in Europe received vague promises of free elections.

Disposition of Germany and postwar world relations dominated much of the discussion during the eight days of meetings. The accord included plans for a three-nation occupation in Germany with the country divided into zones. At the last minute the three leaders recognized France as a ruling power and decided that Germany would have a fourth zone. The Soviet Union agreed to enter the war against Japan ninety days after Germany's surrender in exchange for concessions in China. For obvious reasons this part of the document remained secret until August 1945. The agreement also provided that a world conference would be held in San Francisco in April to establish the final shape of the United Nations Organization with the provision that the United States, the Soviet Union, Great Britain, and two other countries comprise the security council.[10] At the conclusion of the conference a joint communiqué outlined the basic points of the meeting. The famous official photographs of Stalin, Churchill, and Roosevelt seated together and smiling broadly were released to the world.

Eager anticipation gave way to hearty approval among the four print organizations as they first waited for the announcement of the results of the conference and then pored over the points in the accord. The editors and reporters, like their reading public, anxiously wanted a new air of peaceful coexistence to pervade the postwar world, and they felt Yalta would certainly be the beginning of this trend.

In a series of editorials following the historic meeting, the *Chronicle* continuously expressed hope and optimism. "The leaders appear to have agreed remarkably. The thorniest issues, those of Poland and the Balkans, turned out to have been handled on lines that speak of mutual respect and reason," the *Chronicle* declared. A second editorial, concerning the United Nations, concluded, "That the Big Three were able to set a date [for the U.N. conference] must be taken to mean that no important disagreements remain between them." A front-page Associated Press article on February 14 observed that stiff opposition concerning Poland had developed among congressional leaders, but generally the world received the accords with great enthusiasm. An editorial noted that the London Poles were rightfully unhappy with the vague language at Yalta and that assertions about concessions by Stalin on Poland were probably "only a mirage." The editorial added, "Nevertheless it is difficult to see how they [Poles] could have expected anything much different." In early March the newspaper said that Roosevelt's assertion at Yalta that German exsoldiers should be sent to the Soviet Union to repair destruction there was "implicit in the Stalin program to restore what the Germans have so wantonly wrecked."[11]

Similarly, the *Herald Tribune* gushed with praise for the three delegations and rejoiced at the decisions reached. The newspaper editorialized, "Those all over the world who have been looking to the conference beside the Black Sea for mutual understanding, for clarity of purpose and for concrete decision amid the tempestuous issues of the war's great climax have not been disappointed."[12] The next day, editorial writers found satisfaction over the Nazis' unhappiness with the Yalta declaration. The Allies were truly unified and Yalta certainly did not represent a final triumph of the Soviet Union over the rest of the Allied world, as the Nazis had predicted, the newspaper concluded.[13]

A week after Yalta Moscow correspondent Maurice Hindus in a lengthy article praised Soviet strength and potential. The *Herald Tribune* responded with an editorial philosophically reflecting on the Soviet people and the future. The editorial said in part:

The creation of such an army in the very jaws of the appalling initial defeats will always remain one of the amazing achievements of history. . . . Totalitarian communism was not, of course, solely responsible. The stubborn, self-sacrificing and deeply patriotic spirits of the Russian peoples [were]. . . . Does it mean that the Communist system is "better" than our own for the world which now lies ahead? It probably is better for waging war. . . . One can sincerely wish them well. But one can feel that the whole case is very far from being proved.[14]

Even the *Chicago Tribune*, caught up in the euphoria of an apparently successful summit conference, noted that "no American in his right mind can fail to hope that the decisions at Yalta produce a stable and peaceful Europe." The United States should not be part of a United Nations until it could be determined that "the spirit of Yalta is followed in reconstituting Europe," the newspaper added. This reaction came the day after the Yalta statement had been released. The same day, the Chicago newspaper devoted an entire front page to the announcement with several other stories inside. In a less positive vein one of the additional stories by staff writer E. R. Noderer asserted that Yalta meant the finish of the London Poles.[15]

It did not take long for even minimal *Chicago Tribune* support for Yalta to evaporate. Upon Roosevelt's return to the United States the newspaper fired a fusilade of angry charges, beginning with a March 1 story by Arthur Sears Henning, Washington bureau chief. Under a page-one headline, "FDR Admits Making Secret Deal at Yalta," Henning wrote ironically that Roosevelt's physicians had found the president to be in excellent health. The story added, "There is much speculation on Mr. Roosevelt's secret commitments. They are supposed to include indefinite American occupation of Germany [and] colossal American credits for European postwar rehabilitation."[16]

Two days later, *Chicago Tribune* editorial writers complained that Roosevelt had told Congress nothing of what was decided at Yalta and warned darkly that a United Nations would mean the same Holy Alliance as existed after the Napoleonic Wars. "This time the men and wealth of the United States will be thrown into the balance. This will assure that when the next war comes we shall be in it on the side of oppression," the newspaper concluded.[17]

As weeks passed, *Chicago Tribune* discomfiture over Yalta led to even more shrill attacks. In April, with the Soviet Union insisting on three votes in the United Nations general assembly, Henning wrote in a classical overstatement that because of Yalta, Roosevelt was facing the "greatest diplomatic crisis of his career." Henning claimed that Stalin "made no bones of his contempt" for Roosevelt and Churchill, as well as plans for peaceful relations. The next day, a page-one editorial cartoon depicted caricatures of a crafty Stalin and a scheming Churchill playing cards with Roosevelt by candlelight. A ditty accompanying the cartoon suggested that Roosevelt had been duped at Yalta and had gambled away U.S. interests.[18] Following the initial editorial after Yalta, the *Chicago Tribune* was obsessed with the decisions reached there and became the earliest proponent of the theme that Roosevelt had sold out U.S. interests.

At *Time* Chambers's influence over foreign affairs reporting became markedly evident during the weeks before and after the Crimean Conference. An article in the January 22 edition referred to probable "Soviet blackmail of its western allies" at the anticipated Big Three meeting. In the same edition a story concerning Bulgaria argued that communists, through Soviet influence, were setting up a government "as unbearable and distasteful to the vast majority of Bulgars as was the former Nazi-inspired fascist government." Such a force may have been unpalatable to many Bulgars, but January 1945 was an early date for decrying the inevitability of a communist government. The Bulgarian leadership was split among four factions, including the communists. Chambers, however, sought to emphasize what he saw as spreading Soviet influence and treachery.[19]

On February 5, as the Yalta Conference opened, *Time* carried a cover picture and story on Stalin. Unlike the cover story in January 1943, however, *Time* found Stalin's "ambiguous political purposes were giving the creeps to practically everybody except professional Communists and those men of goodwill for whose professional unrealism (when it turns up among Russians) Stalin had always saved his most scathing barbs." The foreign news item also said that the Soviet Union had already begun a domination of Europe and that only Stalin could decide if the next Big Three Conference would push the world in the proper direction.[20]

After the announcement of the Big Three agreement, *Time*, like the *Chicago Tribune*, greeted the results with muted optimism. The lead article on Yalta in *Time*'s February 19 edition merely reported the details of the joint declaration from Yalta and concluded that "if words mean anything, the Big Three did more for their nations and their world at Yalta than they did at Teheran." A separate story dealing with the ramifications for Poland and Germany, however, argued that Poland had become subservient to the Soviet Union and that the industrialized part of Germany to be controlled by the Soviet Union would soon follow. A week later, *Time* retrenched further. Though the overall tone of the article was still positive, it was riddled with misgivings. In part, it said, "In the first glow, some optimists had read more into the Big Three declaration on liberated Europe than the Big Three actually said. Even among the Big Three, contests for power and spheres of influence were not finally abolished at Yalta."[21]

Two weeks later, Chambers thrust his personal philosophy into the pages of *Time* in an extraordinary way, as he wrote a long diatribe against Yalta that covered two full pages of the magazine. The article was entitled,

"Ghosts on the Roof," and sprang from a statement by author George Bernard Shaw that the Yalta Conference was an "impudently incredible fairy tale."[22] Chambers created a story in fairy-tale form about how the bolsheviks had murdered the family of the czars and their ghosts were dancing on the roof of the Yalta palace where the principals met. The meandering article saw Yalta as a naïve mistake on the part of the West. In a conversation between the czarina's ghost and the Muse of History, the Muse says, "I never expect human folly to learn much from history."[23]

At *Time* staff hostility toward both Luce and Chambers was running high at this time, both because of the way Luce had backed Chambers against the bureau correspondents and because the virulent anti-Roosevelt and anti-Soviet tone of foreign coverage offended their sensibilities. Aware of this, Luce in early March decided not to accept or reject the article personally. He wanted it published but did not want to be blamed for it. Instead, he gave the article to the more liberal Thomas S. Matthews, editor of *Time*, and told Matthews it was his decision.[24] Matthews reluctantly allowed publication of the unsigned piece. The incident indicated both how Luce had abandoned control over Chambers and how drastically anti-Soviet Chambers had pushed the expressed philosophy of *Time*.

About the same time Time, Inc., editors received a confidential memo from Washington Bureau Chief Robert T. Elson, who had discussed Yalta with James Byrnes, a member of the delegation at the conference and soon to be secretary of state under Harry S Truman. Stalin had expressed a great deal of emotion about Poland, and the United States probably gained as much from Stalin on Poland as was possible, Byrnes told Elson. He also confided that reparations for Germany was the key issue left unresolved and that another conference would have to be held to "ratify and confirm" the Yalta accord. Finally, Byrnes told Elson, Stalin had frequently spoken bluntly at Yalta. He had continuously told Churchill and Roosevelt that he could be trusted, adding, "My word is my bond." Byrnes told Elson, "I would rather trust a man who said his word was his bond than the man who didn't say so. . . . After all, if a man says his word is his bond often enough he is likely to believe it."[25]

The *Time* treatment of Yalta indicated that the Elson memo had largely been ignored and certainly an off-the-record conversation between Luce and Secretary of State Edward Stettinius completely negated Byrnes's input. Stettinius told Luce a few weeks later that Roosevelt was a "too much devious boss." Luce filed a self-serving memo to his editors telling them of how he had milked information from Stettinius. The tone of the memo and some of the language construction suggests that Luce may have embellished a bit on what Stettinius actually said. It is clear, though, that the secretary of state disagreed with Roosevelt and expressed his disappointment with Yalta to Luce in no uncertain terms. Stettinius told Luce he feared all of Europe would be dominated by communism. He also said that both he

and Roosevelt were placing a great deal of hope in the potential power and
influence of the soon-to-be-formed United Nations. The emphasis Luce
placed on the memo and the wording suggests that the conversation with
Stettinius had a profound effect on the Time, Inc., publisher. Any hope of
toning down the anticommunist rhetoric in the magazine had ended for the
time being. This was an instance in which a government official directly
influenced the policy of a publication, but only because the publisher heard
what he had been hoping to hear.[26]

The decisions at Yalta set the framework for postwar Europe and established a basis for bitter anticommunist feelings in the United States in the
late 1940s and early 1950s, and even later. However, immediately after the
conference, criticism was muted and, in fact, two of the print news organizations in this study found much to celebrate. The initial positive reaction
of all four news groups represented overall U.S. press reaction to Yalta.
Historian Ralph Levering pointed out that after the Yalta announcement 75
percent of U.S. news institutions sampled approved of the agreement, and
only 11 percent disapproved.[27]

There appear to be three reasons for this initial positive reaction and
negative comment later. First, the three leaders tightly controlled information emanating from Yalta, and the final communiqué, worded in the
most optimistic terms, provided the basis for most early news reports.
Secondly, February 1945 found Americans and Soviets still struggling with
a stubborn German Army, and sympathy for the Soviet Union remained.
Finally, the closed format at the conference allowed Soviet diplomats to
argue their points of view in their usual self-interested and intransigent
manner without engendering the ill will of the U.S. public.

After Yalta U.S. leaders increasingly sensed a drifting mutual interest
between the two countries, but the public failed to gain this impression
through published news reports. This dichotomy would soon end, but the
secrecy at Yalta damaged postwar world relations. It would be several years
before this would become apparent. Understanding Soviet interests and
Stalin's method of dealing with the West would be an educational process
for Americans and that learning experience did not grow through the Yalta
Conference. The short-term goal of an apparent mutual public admiration
between the two countries was achieved, but later that goal would seem
appallingly shortsighted.

II

Through the Crimean Conference, the three Allies attempted to establish
a format for coexistence after the war, but though these nations were the
most powerful of the Allies, they were only three countries. Since the
Atlantic Charter had been established in 1941, it was clear that some form
of world organization with most nations participating would be the only

long-range answer to potential world disunity. The League of Nations had failed because of internal dissension about the League in the United States and because of recalcitrant attitudes by the victorious European leaders. Roosevelt and most of the world's leaders hoped to avoid a repetition of 1919.

By early 1945 the format and approach to the new world organization had been established, and at Yalta the three Allied leaders agreed to convene a general meeting of most of the world's nations to arrange the final details of the postwar United Nations. The San Francisco Conference, set for late April, would provide a forum for both powerful and weak nations to voice their individual hopes and aspirations for a restructured geopolitical order. At the same time the meeting also would allow many Americans and U.S. newspersons their first close-up glimpses of European, and particularly Soviet, diplomacy in a U.S. setting, away from the demands of war. Published articles during the months of March and April reflected a great deal of anticipation.

However, just prior to the conference two key events occurred. First, Franklin D. Roosevelt died after barely beginning his fourth term in office, the longest presidential tenure in the history of the nation. Americans plunged into a special kind of mourning reserved for the death of a leader, especially one whose policies and programs touched each citizen personally through the Great Depression and World War II. Even the *Chicago Tribune*, which had vilified Roosevelt for years, observed: "History will appraise his work. For the moment we can only express the deep sorrow which all Americans feel at the passing of their chosen leader." The Republican *New York Herald Tribune* noted, "There was no one, of whatever party or persuasion, who did not feel in the first instant that a gallant figure had been snatched suddenly from our common life."[28]

Roosevelt's death left an apparent leadership vacuum in the United States. Vice-President Harry S Truman had been poorly informed about foreign policy matters, and Soviet leaders were left to deal with an unknown and relatively unprepared president at a crucial time.

The Allies, meanwhile, agreed that U.S. troops would remain outside Berlin across the Elbe River where the two armies had met, and the final assault on Berlin would be left to the Red Army. This saved U.S. lives but also ensured that postwar political dominance of East Germany would fall into Soviet hands.

These two events tended to draw interest away from the momentous world conference. The final decisions on the shape of the world forum were made while most Americans and most of the peoples of the planet, for that matter, watched with divided interest. The newspapers and *Time* in late April emphasized that the delegates should commit themselves to ensuring that forty million lives were not lost during World War II so that new tyrants could take Hitler's place.

For coverage of the San Francisco Conference the *Chicago Tribune* and *Herald Tribune* both sent their Washington correspondents, the writers who were most familiar with diplomats and members of the U.S. delegation. The *Herald Tribune* also assigned London correspondent Ned Russell to San Francisco to monitor feelings among Europeans. Walter Lippmann attended and offered his insights through his column. *Time* used summaries that sounded a great deal like rewrites of Associated Press copy but apparently sent one or two correspondents to California.

The conference posed a unique and interesting challenge for the *Chronicle*. A small newspaper in a highly competitive market faced the task of covering one of the key diplomatic events of the decade in its own hometown. None of the *Chronicle*'s writers had any appreciable experience covering major diplomatic events. The newspaper did not have a Washington bureau at the time. Its editor and other key staff members were still serving overseas in the military.

The editors decided to cover the world meeting as they would a political convention. Veteran staff writer Charles Raudebaugh provided daily lead coverage, and backup writers were assigned to write secondary news stories or features about delegates or plenary sessions. The first day coverage dominated the front page and additional pages inside, including a picture page. Through the six weeks of the conference, the *Chronicle* carried two to three articles a day, far more than either of the other two newspapers, especially in the latter weeks when the conclave had dragged, draining the interest of readers and editors alike. However, this saturation coverage did not evince the *Chronicle*'s obvious lack of sources. All of the newspaper's coverage consisted of reports on open sessions and comments made by delegates at various press conferences. Insights that writers would normally gain from key sources with whom they had personal relationships were noticeably lacking, as would be expected from a staff unaccustomed to the procedures and persons at such a meeting. Still, the amount of coverage for the first time focused attention on what San Franciscans could expect from postwar diplomacy and especially what kind of attitudes the Soviets displayed in such settings.

Aside from establishing a myriad of rules and procedures that naturally accompany the formation of such an organization, the delegates at the meeting faced three controversial issues that dominated press attention. First came discussion of the acceptance or rejection of a request by the Soviet Union that Byelorussia—or White Russia—and Ukrainia each have separate votes in the general assembly. The Soviet Union claimed these two areas were autonomous states and, through this ploy, sought to increase Soviet influence in the world body. Secondly, the delegates faced the issue of admitting Argentina, a neutral with Axis sympathies until late in the war. The Soviet Union unalterably opposed admitting Argentina. Thirdly, the limitations, if any, on member vetoes in the Security Council, needed final agreement. The Soviet Union, against the wishes of the United States, Great Britain, France, and China, sought unlimited veto power.

Eventually, the two Soviet states were granted seats, Argentina gained admittance, and a compromise limiting veto power was accepted. The veto could be used in cases of suggested formal investigations of a complaint by a U.N. member, to block decisions on peaceful settlements of disputes, and against the deployment of U.N. member troops to forcefully end international border violations.

To the Soviets, this combination reflected a great deal of compromise. They had suffered greatly during the war, and their fears of Western betrayal ran deep. The United States was closely aligned with South American leaders at the time, and the Soviet Union felt that the United States controlled at least twenty-five votes because of this relationship. The three votes seemed only fair, in the eyes of the Soviets. Many of the Eastern European countries west of the Soviet Union had fought on the side of the Nazis, and the Soviets felt these countries could not be trusted. In fact, as the only longstanding communist government in the world, the Soviet Union felt completely isolated. Any compromise at this time was seen as a potential risk to Soviet security. But none of the print media in this study could completely grasp these Soviet anxieties.

For *Time* and the *Chicago Tribune* Soviet insistence on their own terms for the United Nations offered proof of the futility of dealing with communist leaders. A sarcastic *Time* article argued that even the representative for the Byelorussians and Ukrainians considered themselves as citizens of the Soviet Union. "In one respect the Byelorussians were truly autonomous," the article concluded. "They set up their own bar."[29]

Arthur Sears Henning wrote in a page-one *Chicago Tribune* article that "as a consequence . . . Russia will have three votes in the general assembly . . . the British empire will have six votes, and the United States one."[30] For Henning and the *Chicago Tribune* both Great Britain and the Soviet Union were not to be trusted. As the meeting opened and Soviet delegates blocked a move to make Stettinius permanent conference chairman, the *Chicago Tribune*, in an editorial delicately headlined, "Once a Commy, Always a Commy," noted that it was customary for a host country to have one of its delegates serve as chair. The Soviet Union's resistance in this case showed its unwillingness to compromise even on the smallest issues, the editorial said, and the *Chicago Tribune* concluded that these were the kind of tactics communists had used to push their way into U.S. labor unions. As always, the *Chicago Tribune* saw communism as a universal logic, which mechanically dictated a certain approach, whether in a domestic labor situation or in a world diplomatic forum. Surprisingly, the editorial gave a pat on the back to the new president, a Democrat. The *Chicago Tribune* observed, "Perhaps, also, Mr. Molotov has become so voluble in San Francisco because he found out in Washington that President Truman is a fellow who can push back."[31]

Time viewed the West's triumph on the Argentine issue as actually a defeat and an example of Soviet scheming to garner world opinion. The magazine concluded:

Some of the wisest diplomats in San Francisco felt that his [Stettinius's] seeming victory in getting the shabby Argentine Government admitted to the conference had in fact been a triumph for Molotov. Stettinius' forthright support of Argentina, said they, unnecessarily pointed up the disproportionate voting strength of the U.S.'s noisy Latin American bloc, gave Molotov a brilliantly used opportunity to pose as the conference's moral spokesman in opposing the Argentine jingoes, and generally cost the U.S. more than it gained.[32]

As the conference dragged on and the initial words of optimism faded, the tone of the articles became more belligerent. The *Chicago Tribune* summarized:

The disagreements at San Francisco over the acquisition of territory and the government of colonies prove that those of us who have always said the Atlantic Charter was sucker-bait were right all the time. . . . As might be expected, our delegation, most of whose members are either Wall streeters or do-gooders hasn't been of much use in solving the problem. The do-gooders are in a panic lest the Russians withhold their assent and thus defeat the purposes of the meeting.[33]

Because these two news organizations expressed philosophies that were so anticommunist, perhaps these reactions could be expected. The real damage to Soviet goodwill came not from foes, but friends. The *San Francisco Chronicle* and the *New York Herald Tribune* had expressed a great deal of sympathy for the Soviet people in the months before the San Francisco meeting and had dutifully and fully reported all of the occurrences at the conference. Raudebaugh described the three votes for the Soviet Union as a compromise, not a victory for the Soviet Union. But Bert Andrews of the *Herald Tribune* added a more contentious note when he described the Argentina vote as the "first out-in-the-open battle of the United Nations Conference."[34] The constant Soviet delays frustrated the *Herald Tribune* editors. "Why . . . have the Russians kept the conference in a stew for over a week with these minor procedural issues?" the newspaper asked.[35] A week later, Molotov left the meeting, and the two newspapers expressed disappointment and puzzlement, fearing Molotov had left in a huff. The *Herald Tribune* concluded, "About the only firm fact that has made its way to the fore amid the headlines has been that once again our Russian allies have proved difficult to understand."[36]

On the same page Joseph Barnes, foreign editor and former Moscow correspondent, offered some additional explanation. He said the Soviet delegation was shorthanded at the conference because most of their leaders had devoted their energies to the Battle of Berlin. Barnes offered four possible explanations for Soviet behavior but admitted he was puzzled. He speculated that the Soviets were cautious because of traditional Soviet suspicions of the West, were improvising because of a lack of diplomatic experience, did not understand the Americans, or refused compromise because traditionally they insisted on dealing with future issues from a position of strength.[37]

At the same time the *Chronicle* observed, "Something like a wave of uneasiness, both among the American public and, to some extent, among delegates to the San Francisco Conference, attended the report that Mr. Molotov was leaving San Francisco for Moscow." The editorial concluded that the conference would end properly and the uneasiness should not "give way to the first vagrant wind of defeatism," but for the first time in several years the *Chronicle* reflected negatively on Soviet actions.[38]

These seeds of doubt perhaps reflected an unrealistic appraisal of Soviet willingness to compromise. As Lippmann wrote when the conference opened: "It is true the future depends upon the relations between the Soviet Union and the other countries. But these relations will become hopeless if we yield at all to those who, to say it flatly, are thinking of the international organization as a means of policing the Soviet Union."[39] Nevertheless, the mood prior to San Francisco on all sides seemed to reflect a hope for a successful world forum possessing the universal acceptance that eluded the League of Nations. The Soviets approached the conference, however, with the same stubbornness that marked such meetings in the past. The conference lasted far longer than anyone had anticipated.

If the newspapers and magazine were puzzled, so were U.S. diplomats. Historian John L. Gaddis observed: "It exposed prominent Republicans like Dulles and Vandenberg to the frustrations of dealing with the Russians. Both men came away from the experience convinced that the only way to negotiate with Moscow was to take a firm position and avoid compromise. It also made clear to the American people the depth and extent of the divisions which separated the Soviet Union and the United States."[40] Harrison E. Salisbury, *New York Times* Moscow correspondent, attended the conference. He recalled thirty-eight years later: "I was not enthused by the San Francisco proceedings. . . . I thought there had been a dangerous deterioration in relations between the Russians and the West. 'Most of the fault, I feel, and I think I can judge it pretty accurately,' I wrote, 'lies with the Russians. Some with us but much more with them.' "[41]

This was not the one, easily separated, single occurrence that soured Soviet–U.S. relations. The two nations were still allies, and what appeared to be a monumental military task—subduing Japan—remained. As the analysis of the stories from March 1945 indicates, the newspapers and magazine content remained largely pro-Soviet. Only *Time* had moved to a more antagonistic posture as reflected in its stories, and that probably resulted from Chambers's influence.[42] The editors at the *Herald Tribune* and *Chronicle* still saw the Soviet performance at San Francisco as a minor diplomatic foray.

Yet, the meeting raised questions for the first time. Yalta had brought optimism, because the press and the public had not been allowed to see the extent to which U.S. diplomats had been frustrated by Soviet intransigence. San Francisco provided no such shield. It was San Francisco, not Yalta, that alerted many of these news people to a potential postwar clash. The goodwill planted on the battlefields remained, but when the fighting ended, both sides looked for a new way to cement the Alliance. After San Francisco the two newspapers with pro-Soviet sympathies began asking whether there existed such a cement. *Time* and the *Chicago Tribune* found reason to believe their previous anti-Soviet feelings had been correct.

NOTES

1. See especially John Toland, *Battle: The Story of the Bulge* (New York: New American Library, 1960); Stephen W. Sears, *Battle of the Bulge* (New York: American Heritage, 1969); William K. Godrick, *Battle of the Bulge* (Alexandria, Va.: Time-Life Books, 1979); John Pimlott, *Battle of the Bulge* (New York: Galahad Books, 1981); Charles Brown MacDonald, *A Time for Trumpets* (New York: Morrow, 1985).

2. Eben Ayers Diary, January 17, 1945, entry, Box 16. Harry S. Truman Library, Manuscripts Division, Ayers Collection, Independence, Missouri.

3. Diane Shaver Clemens, *Yalta* (New York: Oxford University Press, 1970), 102, 104.

4. See John L. Snell, ed., *The Meaning of Yalta: Big Three Diplomacy and the New Balance of Power* (Baton Rouge: Louisiana State University Press, 1956).

5. See *Foreign Relations of the United States: The Conference at Malta and Yalta 1945* (Washington, D.C.: United States Government Printing Office, 1955), 562–948.

6. A. Merriman Smith, *Thank You, Mr. President: A White House Notebook* (New York: Harper and Brothers, 1946), 162–63.

7. "Old Hand at Work," *Time*, February 26, 1945, 66.

8. See especially Ned Russell, "Big Three Meeting Is Underway, Citrine Reveals," *Herald Tribune*, February 8, 1945, 1.

9. "The Big Three Conference," *Herald Tribune* editorial, February 4, 1945, Section 2, 3; "Secrets," *Time*, February 12, 1945, 57; Ned Russell, "London Elated by Evidence of Big Three Unity," *Herald Tribune*, February 8, 1945, 2; "The Conference Has Begun," *Herald Tribune* editorial, February 8, 1945, 16; "Big Three Accord," *San Francisco Chronicle*, February 8, 1945, 1; Arthur Sears Henning, "Report Stalin Will Join War on Japs After Nazis' Defeat," *Chicago Tribune*, February 12, 1945, 1.

10. Clemens, *Yalta*, 280–300; Cabell Phillips, *The Truman Presidency: The History*

of a Triumphant Succession (New York: The Macmillan Company, 1966), 86–87; *Foreign Relations of the United States*, 966–87; Edward R. Stettinius, Jr., *Roosevelt and the Russians: The Yalta Conference* (Garden City, N.J.: Doubleday, 1949), pp. 295–307; Snell, ed., *The Meaning of Yalta*, 209–17.

11. "Big Three," *San Francisco Chronicle* editorial, February 13, 1945, 10; "Miracle," *Chronicle* editorial, February 13, 1945; "Reaction to Big 3 Plans," *Chronicle* editorial, February 14, 1945, 1; "London Poles," *Chronicle* editorial, February 15, 1945, 12; "War Damage," *Chronicle* editorial, March 3, 1945, 10.

12. "Unity and Decision," *Herald Tribune* editorial, February 13, 1945, 22.

13. "The Blunt Facts," *Herald Tribune* editorial, February 21, 1945, 16.

14. "Russia's Great Achievement," *Herald Tribune* editorial, February 21, 1945, 16.

15. Walter Lippmann column, "Today and Tomorrow," *Herald Tribune*, February 15, 1945, 21.

16. Arthur Sears Henning, "F.D.R. Admits Making Secret Deal at Yalta," *Chicago Tribune*, March 1, 1945, 1.

17. "Congress Hears About Yalta," *Chicago Tribune* editorial, March 3, 1945, 10.

18. Arthur Sears Henning, "Ghosts at Yalta Rise to Peril League Plans—F.D.R. Faces His Greatest Crisis in Diplomacy," *Chicago Tribune*, April 12, 1945, 1; *Chicago Tribune* editorial cartoon, April 13, 1945.

19. "Russia," *Time*, January 22, 1945, 33–34; "Bulgaria—Enemies of the People," *Time*, January 22, 1945, 38–39.

20. "Russia—Historic Force," *Time*, February 5, 1945, 32–38; *Time* cover, February 5, 1945.

21. "Conferences—In the Shadow of Ai-Dagh," *Time*, February 19, 1945, 22–23; "Poland—From Failure to Victory," *Time*, February 19, 1945, 34–35.

22. "Ghosts on the Roof," *Time*, March 5, 1945, 36.

23. "Ghosts on the Roof," *Time*, 37.

24. W. A. Swanberg, *Luce and His Empire* (New York: Charles Scribner's Sons, 1972), 229–30; Robert T. Elson, *The World of Time, Inc.: The Intimate History of a Publishing Enterprise, 1941–1960*, vol. 2 (New York: Atheneum, 1973), 114.

25. Robert T. Elson "restricted" memo to editors, March 1, 1945, 1–5. John Shaw Billings Papers, Box 1, Caroliniana Library, Manuscripts Division, University of South Carolina, Columbia, South Carolina.

26. Luce to editors "strictly confidential" memo, March 19, 1945, 1–4. Billings Papers, Box 1; addendum to Luce to editors "strictly confidential" memo, April 17, 1945. Billings Papers, Box 1; also see Swanberg, *The World of Time, Inc.*, vol. 2, 233.

27. Ralph Levering, *American Opinion and the Russian Alliance, 1939–45* (Chapel Hill: University of North Carolina Press, 1976), 186.

28. "A Nation Mourns," *Chicago Tribune* editorial, April 13, 1945, 12; "The President," *Herald Tribune* editorial, April 13, 1945, 10.

29. "The Conference—The Other Russians," *Time*, June 4, 1945, 29.

30. Arthur Sears Henning, "Rotation Plan for Chairmen Vetoed," *Chicago Tribune*, April 28, 1945, 1.

31. "Once a Commy, Always a Commy," *Chicago Tribune* editorial, April 28, 1945, 10.

32. "Ed and His Friends," *Time*, May 14, 1945, 10.

33. "The Real Conflict at San Francisco," *Chicago Tribune* editorial, May 14, 1945, 16.

34. Charles Raudebaugh, "Charting Security," *Chronicle*, May 2, 1945, 1; Bert Andrews, "Russia Loses First Test—Parley Seats Argentina," *Herald Tribune*, May 1, 1945, 1.

35. "Two San Franciscos," *Herald Tribune* editorial, May 2, 1945, 22.

36. "A Guide to the Russians," *Herald Tribune* editorial, May 11, 1945, 18.

37. Joseph Barnes column, "Wanted: A Guide to the Russians," *Herald Tribune*, May 11, 1945, 18.

38. "Conference Leaders," *Chronicle* editorial, May 4, 1945, 12.

39. Walter Lippmann column, "Today and Tomorrow," *Herald Tribune*, April 24, 1945, 22.

40. John L. Gaddis, *The U.S. and the Origins of the Cold War, 1941–47* (New York: Columbia University Press, 1972), 230.

41. Harrison E. Salisbury, *A Journey for Our Times* (New York: Harper and Row, 1983), 289.

42. See Appendix A.

Chapter 6
War's End and Potsdam

Few U.S. presidents faced the type of challenge Harry S Truman met when he took office in the spring of 1945. Massive reconstruction in Europe and a stubborn Japanese military in Asia posed immediate problems, but growing Soviet influence increasingly required the new president's most delicate diplomatic skills, a talent he sorely lacked. As a senator from Missouri, Truman had developed a reputation as an honest but tough-talking legislator, who had roundly criticized the Soviet Union on several occasions. He did not shrink from that position in the spring of 1945. Upon taking office, he quickly and bluntly indicated that he would not allow Soviet expansionism to go unchallenged. These were views actually similar to those held by Roosevelt just prior to his death, but Truman's lack of tact and his previous record of anti-Soviet rhetoric caused alarm in the Soviet Union. As John L. Gaddis noted, "Truman's abrasive personality may well have led the Russians to conclude, prematurely, that Roosevelt's goals had been abandoned."[1]

Truman, however, was an intelligent, incisive man who blustered publicly but privately waited for a Soviet accord during the first months after the war. This chapter will trace the unfolding events in the United States and Europe from the time Truman took office to the end of the Potsdam Conference on August 2, 1945. The summer of 1945 was a crucial time in world history. As the war in Asia neared an end, it became apparent that the United States and the Soviet Union would dominate the postwar era. Truman's portrayal of the Soviet Union, his success or failure at Potsdam, and his influence over the U.S. press would all be factors in the origins of the Cold War. At the same time the Soviet image hung in the balance, and Stalin's efforts to cultivate a positive image in the United States might also have had lasting ramifications. As will be seen, press relations before and during the Potsdam conclave received scant attention from both Truman and Stalin, and even the modest gains of the conference suffered from a lack of press exposure. Potsdam engendered a spirit of suspicion and mistrust, not mutual understanding, and the poor attitude toward press relations only fanned that hostility.

This chapter will examine the early part of the Truman administration and reveal how the reporters from the four news organizations perceived the developing foreign policies of the new president. Much of the discussion will focus on the Potsdam Conference, where the three world leaders refused to provide adequate details to reporters. This created a confused public perception of Soviet–U.S. relations and established a poor precedent between the president and the press.

Truman's succession to office came just when the last vestiges of mutual Soviet–U.S. admiration were disappearing. With the end of the war in Europe, Americans and Soviets shared a mutual outpouring of goodwill for the last time. In Germany and elsewhere Soviet and U.S. troops observed a common celebration, and Truman, Stalin, and Churchill exchanged words of admiration and good hope.

The good wishes only papered over an increasing distrust of the Soviet Union, especially on Churchill's part. The British prime minister first coined a famous expression in a telegram to Truman on May 12, 1945. He warned that while the United States hastily began to shift nearly all its manpower to the Pacific, Eastern Europe moved toward Soviet domination, and Greece, Austria, and the Balkans would soon follow. "An iron curtain is drawn down upon their front. We do not know what is going on behind," Churchill wrote.[2] The famous "iron curtain" observation would be repeated by Churchill nearly a year later in a speech at Fulton, Missouri, and would become a rallying cry for anticommunist conservatives for decades.

Sensing a need to repair the drifting relationship with the Soviet Union, Truman sent Harry Hopkins, lend-lease administrator and former secretary of commerce, to visit Stalin in Moscow in mid-May. James F. Byrnes, director of the office of war mobilization, who would become secretary of state six weeks later, recalled in his memoirs that Hopkins reported a frank exchange of views at the meeting. Stalin, however, clearly indicated that he feared a cooling friendship with the United States and a harder line from the Americans, because the war in Europe had ended.[3] The meeting salved both Truman's and Stalin's anxieties momentarily, but it was clear that another Big Three meeting was needed. The three leaders began preparation for a conference inside the Soviet zone of Germany thirty miles from Berlin near a former movie colony in Potsdam.

At the same time Truman's sudden elevation to the presidency drew a great deal of sympathy and support from editors and writers around the country. The four news organizations wholeheartedly backed Truman in his first few months in office, despite his being a Democrat and having served as Roosevelt's vice-president. The new president took care to provide adequate information to the Washington press corps and, though he did not hold as many press conferences as Roosevelt, he met with reporters enough to keep them happy. After a June 1 press conference Eben Ayers, assistant press secretary, noted in his diary, "He is making a hit with the correspondents [and] replies decisively."

Ayers remained assistant press secretary, while Stephen Early transferred from press secretary to aide to the president. Charles G. Ross, former *St. Louis Post-Dispatch* Washington bureau chief and editorial editor, became the new press chief. Ross, Truman, and Truman's wife, Bess, all had attended high school together in Independence, Missouri, and Ross had long been Truman's trusted friend. Upon Ross's appointment, Truman and Ross telephoned their old high school English teacher, Tillie Brown, who told the pair she was extremely proud.[4]

Truman had watched on the sidelines while animosity grew between Roosevelt and many of the nation's publishers. He shared Roosevelt's suspicion of these men and their Republican leanings. Two exchanges occurred shortly after Truman took office that illustrated his lack of concern for influencing the editorial policies of the print organizations.

The first involved a request from Arthur Hays Sulzberger, publisher of *The New York Times,* who was about to leave for Moscow. Sulzberger thought it would help for Truman to let Sulzberger carry a special letter to Stalin about the postwar situation in Europe. In a staff meeting at the White House on May 24, Ross, Ayers, and Early all urged Truman to accede to Sulzberger's request, not because it would have much influence with Stalin, but because it would allow the president to establish a positive relationship with Sulzberger. Truman, however, responded, "I want no more special envoys." He added that the nation had ambassadors capable of acting as couriers and, if not, he would "get some who are." Four days later, Truman decided to send a note with Sulzberger to Averell Harriman, U.S. ambassador to the Soviet Union, but clearly this did not fulfill the vision Sulzberger had for enhancing Sulzberger's image in the eyes of the men involved, particularly Stalin.[5]

The second exchange took place a week later when Ross and Ayers met with Truman concerning a request from publisher William Randolph Hearst. The West Coast publisher had acquired newspapers all over the country, and his extreme conservative views had been legendary for decades. The Hearst flagship newspaper, the *Examiner,* had the highest circulation of any San Francisco daily. Ross reminded Truman that a Hearst aide had requested that Truman extend an invitation to the publisher so that the two might meet at the White House. The two press advisers urged Truman to act on the request. The president declined. Clearly, Truman would not cater to Sulzberger, Hearst, nor any other publisher. Administration policy, including diplomatic relations with the Soviet Union, would be accepted or rejected on its merits, as far as Truman was concerned, with no special favors to influence the opinion makers of the nation, especially those who had bitterly opposed the previous administration.[6]

But the president continued to deal amicably with White House reporters and those newsmen whom he had known as a senator and later as vice-president. On June 11 Truman invited several aides and five newsmen for a weekend of fishing and poker playing aboard the presidential yacht, *Potomac*. One of the reporters, Robert Elson, *Time* Washington bureau chief, told his editors about the trip but cautioned them to keep confidential what he had heard. They complied.[7]

Truman confided to Elson that he and Churchill both disliked Charles De Gaulle and would help push him from office as president of France "when the time was right." Frequently, he surprised Elson with his earthy language and referred to De Gaulle as a "bastard" and a "stuckup asshole." He also said Britain's value as a world force had dropped drastically, and the British served as a weak partner. "We don't have to worry about old Churchill," the president said. He quickly expanded the conversation to include the Soviet Union, which he speculated would become the most powerful nation in the world in as few as twelve years, if left unchecked. But Truman would not allow that to happen, he told Elson. The president reviewed Hopkins's conference with Stalin and explained that Hopkins had saved the San Francisco Conference from failing, while convincing Stalin of the need to cooperate. Truman also told Elson he disliked the Poles, who, he felt, had brought most of their troubles on themselves.

Truman then turned his attention to the Soviet leaders. He did not trust Molotov and bragged of having told off the Soviet foreign minister during a meeting in April. He also explained his attitude toward the Soviets. He saw a dark future for Josef Stalin. The Soviet leader likely would be assassinated someday, Truman predicted. "Let me tell you: that god damned old son of a bitch Molotov is cutting Stalin's throat every time he gets a chance. Stalin knows it, but he can't do anything about it," Truman said. The president added that the United States would have to maintain a large military force long after the war had ended. "There's going to be an end to this lip service to the thesis that the U.S. must lead the world in military know-how and weapons. We're going to stop talking about it, and do it," Truman added.[8]

Clearly, Truman intended to take a firm line with the Soviets, and following Elson's memo, the editors of Time, Inc., knew it. The path toward open contentiousness with the Soviet Union had been established, and no one could have been happier than Henry Luce.

Also aboard the ship that day were Ernest Vaccaro, Associated Press; Ray Lahr, United Press; Joe Short, *Baltimore Sun;* and Sam Bell, *New York*

Herald Tribune. Presumably, Truman in a talkative mood confided in Bell, who informed his editors in New York as well.[9]

Meanwhile, during the spring and summer of 1945, U.S. armed forces moved toward the outer islands of Japan, capturing first Iwo Jima and then Okinawa at great cost in both men and materials. Truman anxiously wanted Soviet participation in the war against the Japanese, and he, Churchill, and Stalin all needed a resolution to questions on Europe left unanswered at Yalta. The San Francisco Conference ended in June, and the Senate quickly approved U.S. participation in the United Nations. Truman appointed Byrnes to replace Stettinius as secretary of state just as final preparations for Potsdam got underway.

The question of press coverage at Potsdam again posed problems for conferees and reporters as it had at earlier Big Three meetings. Realizing Stalin would never accept open coverage or even the presence of newspeople at the conference, Churchill proposed that the press be excluded and suggested a public announcement of the decision to "avoid disappointment and sending to Berlin of high-powered press representatives." Both Truman and Stalin quickly agreed, and for the first time a wartime summit meeting was announced beforehand, though still the press could not attend or receive daily reports of any substance.[10]

This brought about a series of botched decisions by the White House in its dealings with reporters. Shortly before Truman embarked for Europe, Ross called the White House press corps into his office and explained the decision to exclude reporters from the conference meeting area. He proposed that three wire-service correspondents, a representative from the radio news corps, and a Paramount Pictures newsreel team accompany Truman to the conference aboard the U.S.S. *Augusta.* The remaining twenty newsmen were to follow by ship or plane later. For security reasons Ross asked and the newsmen agreed that Truman's departure and whereabouts would not be disclosed until he reached Europe. Columnist Drew Pearson did not attend the White House meeting with Ross and reported Truman's whereabouts just hours after he departed. Ross then lifted the blackout.[11]

Soviet–U.S. relations needed a boost from press coverage in July 1945, but Potsdam failed in this area. The aborted news embargo was one of many failed attempts to coordinate press activities prior to the Big Three meeting. Clearly, Ross and Ayers did not work well together. Ross saw the Potsdam Conference as an opportunity to show his good faith with reporters and editors. Indeed, many newspersons had pressured him to allow open coverage of the meeting. Paul Miller, assistant general manager of Associated Press, wrote to Ross in June to say publishers and editors were all urging that reporters be allowed to attend. "It would be another home run for Harry Truman, in the eyes of newspapermen everywhere, if it can be arranged."[12]

But Ayers knew of the impossibility of such a task, having been involved with other conferences during Roosevelt's tenure, and he did not care for the way Ross made statements to reporters without coordinating with him. When Ross told reporters on June 27 in Salt Lake City that the president would have an important announcement about the coming conference, Ayers back in Washington was inundated with inquiries. He did not know what Ross meant, and his helplessness angered him.[13] While the *Augusta* steamed toward Europe, Ayers had to soothe the feelings of indignant reporters, who had been told no dispatches could be filed during the voyage. Ayers cabled to the *Augusta* for help. Ross, sympathetic but unable to control the situation, could only express anger toward the reporters. "I should like to give you my thoughts on some of these reporters but it would have to be written on asbestos paper," he cabled back.[14]

On July 15 the U.S. delegation arrived in Germany and prepared for the first sessions the next day. For security reasons Stalin chose to delay his trip across Europe by train, and so plenary sessions did not get under way until July 17, and reporters wrote inconsequential stories. For instance, they wrote that the president had fish for lunch. As the conference opened, photographers entered the meeting area in the Potsdam Palace of former German Kaiser Wilhelm for quick pictures before the entire press contingent moved to headquarters three miles from the palace, against their wishes. Throughout the conference no reporters were allowed in the vicinity of the meetings. During the second day of talks, Churchill suggested that a statement be issued explaining what had been discussed, but Stalin said he saw no need for any conciliatory gestures, and Truman agreed that brief, nondescript press releases were sufficient.[15]

Complaints from reporters grew louder as the conference progressed, bringing reactions back in the United States. One Republican Senator, Alexander Wiley, of Wisconsin, complained in a speech to the Senate on July 19: "It is high time that [press] delegates to the Potsdam Conference were stopped being treated like indiscreet maidens who talk too much. This is censorship and a ghastly example of dictatorial behavior. Correspondents are being spoonfed a dish of trivial mush."[16] Editorials and articles discussing the news blackout emphasized that the newspersons attending did not seek to cover the discussions firsthand, but sought only to receive adequate news briefings to better analyze the meeting's progress. It was all to no avail.

For the moment Truman ignored the press furor and concentrated on Poland, the most divisive issue. As a gesture of conciliation, the United States and Great Britain had recognized the Lublin government just before the conference started. At the bargaining table both Western nations sought free elections in Poland and a reasonable compromise on the future political situation there. Stalin refused to budge, and Truman realized he would have to settle for vague promises.

The rest of Europe remained an open question, and aides in the State

Department warned that a pattern had formed in areas liberated by the Red Army. The disintegration of much of Europe had left an open invitation to the Soviet Union, George Kennan, chargé d'affaires in the Soviet Union, wrote to Stettinius before the conference. Raymond E. Murphy, special assistant on European affairs, observed in a briefing paper that communist governments were replacing popular fronts. Another aide wrote in an unsigned briefing paper that communist activities in Greece could be crucial to the security of Europe and the United States should take "an active and benevolent interest in Greece at this time."[17]

The conference turned out to be a reaffirmation of most of the agreements reached at Yalta with most controversial questions left unresolved or addressed with vague, ineffective language. The conferees promised Austria and Eastern bloc countries free elections and access to the Western press but did not say how this could be achieved. Germany, it was decided, would remain divided until final peace terms were reached. Although the Soviet Union had urged a figure of $20 billion for reparations, the three nations established no exact amount. They agreed that each country would exact from its zone in goods and materials what it deemed fair. The Soviet Union had already begun to ship materials, food, and machinery from her zone back to the Soviet Union and continued the process for the next several months. Poland and the Soviet Union absorbed much of East Prussia. The Soviet Union moved to eradicate what was left of fascism. Spain, ruled by fascist Francisco Franco, was not allowed to enter the United Nations, and provisions were established for prosecution of Nazi war criminals.

News coverage throughout the summit conference remained sketchy. The *Chicago Tribune* and *Chronicle* relied on wire-service reports written mostly by Daniel De Luce, of Associated Press, and A. Merriman Smith, of United Press. Smith, who had covered the White House for five years, was sympathetic to Truman. His articles praised Truman's efforts and painted pictures of the president bargaining forcefully with Stalin while suggesting that the entire conference pivoted around the Soviet Union's willingness to declare war on Japan, something that had been secretly resolved at Yalta. De Luce and the staff correspondents for the *Herald Tribune* and *Time* wrote more objectively, but their reports provided no more insight than Smith's stories.

The conference recessed after the July 24 meeting so the British delegation could return home and await the results of a nationwide election. Voting took place on July 5, but because British military remained scattered all over the world, electoral officials needed three weeks to round up and count the ballots. Churchill's Conservative party lost, and Clement Attlee, who had attended the Potsdam Conference at Churchill's invitation, returned after the recess as the new British prime minister. Churchill remained in England. This created a stir and drew heavy interest in U.S. newspapers and magazines. Americans admired Churchill, and his defeat caught most by surprise. However, the remaining unresolved details at Potsdam were not affected by the election results. Attlee concurred with Churchill on the British position. Their differences were largely centered on domestic issues. Besides, British influence at Potsdam remained relatively inconsequential compared to that of the two emerging military and economic giants, the Soviet Union and the United States.

During the recess, the United States, Great Britain, and China issued the Potsdam Proclamation calling for Japanese surrender. This declaration demanded immediate Japanese capitulation in exchange for which Japan would be guaranteed sovereignty for her four main home islands of Honshu, Hokkaido, Kyushu, and Skikoku. The three powers promised utter destruction should the surrender be rejected. Historians, such as Charles Mee and Gabriel Kolko, maintain this represented a veiled threat to use the atomic bomb, but the Japanese apparently did not understand the proclamation in these terms. The request for surrender did not succeed.

After Attlee replaced Churchill, the conference resumed but achieved only a few additional minor agreements before adjourning on August 2. Truman then quickly flew to Plymouth, England, and boarded the *Augusta* for the trip home. The wire-service correspondents had to rush away from Germany with the Truman coterie in order to leave on the *Augusta* with the president. Consequently, they did not have time to file stories in response to the Potsdam Declaration, issued immediately after the conference and summarizing the details of the agreements reached. After weeks of waiting for substantial information about the inner workings of the conference, travel logistics prevented the correspondents from writing timely, meaningful stories. The long days of waiting and hoping for a break on an important series of stories did not pay off for those reporters accompanying Truman to the ship. Finally, the conferees released all details of the agreements, but the breaking postconference stories had to be written in Washington from copies of the official communiqués.[18]

As *Time* noted, "In 17 days at Potsdam, the Big Three made surprisingly little news (much of what they did and said had already been decided and predicted)." In part, this lack of news and background caused a muted response to the announced results of the meeting. In fact, the *San Francisco Chronicle* carried an editor's note on its editorial page on August 3, 1945, the day after the issuance of the Potsdam Proclamation. The note explained to readers that the editors would analyze the proclamation an extra day before issuing editorial comment. The editorial writers used this delayed approach only a few times during the four years of this study. It represented a conscious effort to resist hasty reaction to news events. But in this instance it also seemed to indicate that the newspaper writers expected some additional developments the next day. They guessed wrong.[19]

When the *Chronicle* did issue editorial comment on August 4, the results were predictable. The newspaper found the decisions that were announced "appear to make common sense" though it singled out "two or three places where a cynical eyebrow could be lifted if it were worthwhile." Germany should be converted to a peaceful, industrial nation, not reduced to an agrarian state with no chance for economic advancement, the editorial urged, and the writers noted that the conference appeared to institute just such an approach. The Soviet Union should be allowed to remove equipment and machinery from her zone in Germany, and German-speaking nationals should be forced to move from Poland, Czechoslovakia, and Hungary, as provided in the conference agreement, the editorial continued. The writers also praised the conferees' decision to continue postwar discussions by scheduling a foreign ministers conference in London in the fall.

But the editorial waxed cynical about language in the agreement advocating free elections and a free press in Poland and Eastern Europe. "We are mindful that the English-speaking countries and possibly France are the only ones in the world that know what freedom of information is," the editorial observed. "Only a process of evolution, and only if they want it, will bring this freedom into bloom in the countries that lack it."[20]

Much of the discussion in the *Chronicle* after the Potsdam Proclamation centered around the future of Europe, in general, with surprisingly little reference to how the Soviet Union fit into the overall scenario. The lone exception was an editorial on August 5. The *Chronicle* expressed surprise at the disappointment voiced by several newspapers that the announced agreement contained no Soviet commitment to enter the war in the Pacific. The writers asked: "What did they expect? That Josef Stalin, assuming that he intends a blow at Japan, would telegraph his punch to the enemy? It is our belief that if and when Russia joins . . . it will be strictly because the Kremlin judges this called for [sic] by Russian interest."[21]

In the first days after the conference ended, the *Herald Tribune* spoke infrequently of the Soviet Union. Russell Hill had remained in Germany after the conference ended and filed a story summarizing results of the meeting and emphasizing treatment of Germany and former Nazi leaders. The article, based almost exclusively on the details of the official press release, merely summarized the provisions of the overall agreement and emphasized that there had been no mention of the Soviet Union's entry into the war against Japan. The Soviet Union's role in Europe was not mentioned at all.[22] Hill's straightforward, nonanalytical approach did not capitalize on whatever information he had obtained through sources during the conference. Consequently, his presence in Germany did not enhance the newspaper's coverage. The postconference story could have been written in New York.

The newspaper editorial writers similarly did not spend a great deal of time discussing the Soviet role in Europe or at Potsdam, but concerned themselves with what they considered unusual steps taken there. The conferees essentially declared the German nation bankrupt and indefinitely divided, and an August 3 editorial emphasized that much remained to be accomplished at the London foreign ministers' meeting.[23]

The *Chicago Tribune,* which for months had ranted about perceived trickery and secret deals at Yalta, used Potsdam as an outlet for its frustrations with U.S. diplomacy. The page-one banner headline on August 3, 1945, declared, "Here's Big 3 Treaty Plan! Make Reich a Farm Nation." The secondary headline added, "War Against Japan Almost Ignored; Truman Sees King, Sails for Home." The story referred to the Soviet leader as Dictator Stalin.[24]

In anticipation of the Potsdam communiqué, but before they had read the document, *Chicago Tribune* editorial writers harkened back to Yalta. The *Chicago Tribune* noted: "A great many people all over the world thought from a first reading of the Crimean document that it promised a decent and honorable settlement of the Polish question. . . . In fact, as we now know and as a careful reading of the communique made clear at the time, Mr. Roosevelt and Mr. Churchill gave Mr. Stalin everything he wanted. . . . What Europe needs is a relaxation of hate and a revival of hope. If the Potsdam conference didn't provide both, it failed."[25]

The next day the newspaper carried three editorials dealing with Potsdam, and all three indicated that the *Chicago Tribune*'s worst fears had come to pass. "As on previous occasions, Mr. Stalin got what he wanted, for the most part because what he wants is potentially under the guns of the Red Army," one editorial concluded. A second editorial added, "Nobody won but Russia at Potsdam. Russian hegemony is confirmed over half of Europe . . . it is only a question of time until Moscow becomes the center of gravity for the entire continent." The third article of opinion warned that the agreement would dismantle European industry and, by implication, leave an open economic field for the Soviet Union.[26] The conference in Germany only served to reinforce the newspaper's isolationist instincts and shatter whatever temporary admiration the *Chicago Tribune* had for the new president.

Time's coverage of Potsdam did not contain the same virulent rhetoric as after Yalta. Articles appearing during the conference concentrated on the meeting's superficial aspects, such as protocol observed and how the conferees spent their leisure time. Postconference summaries dealt almost strictly with the details of the overall agreement with little editorial comment. The articles were buried among other international stories. The magazine published four days after the conference ended, and the lack of timeliness probably had as much to do with the lack of play as anything.

Time did carry six articles about Potsdam in its August 13 edition (actually delivered about August 7), but each merely explored one area of agreement. Much of the magazine's discussion centered around the disposition of Germany and Nazi war criminals. The only negative reference to the Soviet Union came in the lead article. *Time* noted that "subterfuge no longer

obscured Russia's intention to dominate Eastern Europe" and that the communiqué "tacitly recognized the new Poland's status as a satellite of Russia."
Probably the article overstated the actual situation slightly, but the writer
noted that Stalin had been stubborn about conceding anything on the Polish
question. The disposition of Poland at that time could have taken several
twists and turns, but the knowledge of Stalin's attitude made the assessment
fairly accurate. Besides, the article was balanced with the observation that
the West had wedged its democratic philosophy into the document.[27]

Overall, Potsdam did not damage the Soviet image in the U.S. periodicals
nearly as much as the Crimean conference or the San Francisco meeting.
For one thing, there was less to damage. By August the war in Europe had
been over for nearly three months, and the image of the Soviet Union's
role as an Allied war partner began to fade in favor of an image as a potential
world competitor. But also, Potsdam did not represent the same category
of achievements as Yalta. It reaffirmed much that had been decided. Only
a serious change in the Yalta agreements would have made Potsdam a
momentous meeting.

The news blackout made press assessment difficult. Reporters felt much
more frustration. This time they knew of the conference in advance but
reported little more information than had originated from Yalta. *Time* observed: "They heaved & hauled to make something of nothing. By & large,
the reporting from Potsdam's fringe last week was no credit to the world's
press."[28]

Truman's failure to insist on a freer flow of information did not distort
public perception as at Yalta, however. Yalta had set a precedent for Europe.
Potsdam did not. The impact of the conference did not create the same
furor, especially in later years. Also, the use of the atom bomb and the
subsequent end to the war in Asia just days later caused Americans to forget
about Potsdam. Truman's radio address about the conference, delivered on
his return to the United States, barely drew any public attention. People
wanted to hear about the new weapon and whether it would end the war.
Potsdam faded quickly and was largely forgotten until historians began to
analyze its impact years later.

In human terms Truman and his aides learned much more from the
conference than did the reporters or the public. Ayers realized that his
relationship with the new press secretary and the new president had gotten
off to a poor start. The attempts to soothe reporters had failed miserably.
The structure of the conference had dictated the inevitability of problems,
but the lack of coordination between Ross and Ayers had exacerbated the
situation. Eddie Lockett of *Time* met with Ayers for several hours two days
after the Potsdam Conference. He told Ayers there was a general feeling
of disappointment among Washington reporters with both Ayers and Ross.
He said Ayers needed to be more aggressive in getting information to
newspersons. Tom Reynolds, of the *Chicago Sun,* also met with Ayers and

expressed similar feelings.[29] Truman spent a great deal of time talking with the wire-service reporters aboard the *Augusta* during the trip back to the United States, and that removed some of the hostility, but the other reporters continued to harbor resentment.

Truman learned of Stalin's personality and of what he would face in his personal dealings with the Soviets in the future. The president had not wanted to go to Potsdam in the first place. As he traveled to Europe aboard the *Augusta*, he wrote to his sister and mother: "I wish this trip was over. I hate it. But it has to be done."[30] He wanted to stay in the United States and reckon with domestic, postwar problems. He was also anxious to settle the issue of Soviet participation in the war against Japan, and so he felt he had no choice but to go. As he watched Stalin in action, the new president realized that the Soviet leader had a very different idea of what the Soviet Union's role would be in a postwar world and that Stalin always wanted to talk about what would benefit the Soviet Union, not the United States.[31]

The Soviet diplomats also displayed the same kind of inferiority complexes that Churchill and Roosevelt had seen in the past. For example, Byrnes recounted that the conferees had agreed not to have more than ten members of their delegations in the room at one time. At one point a female assistant brought Byrnes some papers during a meeting and waited a few minutes for him to review them. Byrnes remembered that "she had scarcely seated herself when two women from the Russian staff promptly came in and took chairs by the side of their male associates."[32] The Soviets would never concede an edge to the Americans even in the smallest of matters.

The bombing of Hiroshima and Nagasaki in the next week and the fall of Japan a few days later changed the entire perspective of the world for U.S. and Soviet leaders and for editors and reporters of the four news organizations.

Potsdam represented a chance for mutual understanding and in-depth reporting of the differences and points of common interest between the United States and the Soviet Union. The reporting turned out to be inconsequential and the results of the conference unremarkable. As fall approached and war ended, the relationship between the two countries would deteriorate rapidly and all four news organizations would harden their attitudes toward Soviet–U.S. rapprochement.

NOTES

1. John L. Gaddis, *The U.S. and the Origins of the Cold War, 1941–1947* (New York: Columbia University Press, 1972), p. 200.

2. Winston Churchill, *Triumph and Tragedy* (Boston: Houghton Mifflin, 1953), 573.

3. James F. Byrnes, *Speaking Frankly* (New York: Harper and Brothers, 1946);

also see especially Herbert Feis, *Between War and Peace: The Potsdam Conference* (Princeton: Princeton University Press, 1957), 97–98.

4. "News for Miss Tillie," *Time*, May 7, 1945, 19; see also Ronald T. Farrar, *Reluctant Servant: The Story of Charles G. Ross* (Columbia: University of Missouri Press, 1969); Biographical folder, Charles G. Ross Papers, Box 1. Harry S Truman Library, Manuscripts Division, Ross Collection, Independence, Missouri; Letter from Ross to Marion Horowitz, Brooklyn, N.Y., July 26, 1945, Ross Papers, Box 1.

5. Eben A. Ayers Diary, May 24, 1945, and May 28, 1945, entries, Box 16. Harry S. Truman Library, Manuscripts Division, Ayers Collection, Independence, Missouri.

6. Ayers Diary, June 4, 1945, entry, Box 16.

7. Robert Elson to Edward Lockett memorandum, June 11, 1945, cover letter, John Shaw Billings Papers, Box 1. Caroliniana Library, Manuscripts Division, Billings Collection, University of South Carolina, Columbia, South Carolina.

8. Elson to Lockett memorandum, June 11, 1945, 1–9, Billings Papers, Box 1.

9. Elson to Lockett memorandum, June 11, 1945, 16, Billings Papers, Box 1.

10. Commission for the Publication of Diplomatic Documents under the Ministry of Foreign Affairs of the U.S.S.R., Document nos. 500, 498, and 495, *Stalin's Correspondence with Churchill, Attlee, Roosevelt, and Truman 1941–45* (New York: E. P. Dutton and Company, 1958), 371, 371, and 370. Also see U.S. Department of State, *Foreign Relations of the United States: Conference of Berlin (Potsdam)*, vol. 1, 122 (Washington, D.C.: U.S. Government Printing Office, 1960), 139.

11. A. Merriman Smith, *Thank You, Mr. President: A White House Notebook* (New York: Harper and Brothers, 1946), 228. For original manuscript of the book, see also A. Merriman Smith Papers, U.S. Mss 72AF. State Historical Society of Wisconsin, Manuscripts Division, Madison, Wisconsin. Aboard the *Augusta* were Robert Nixon, International News Service; Morgan Beatty, National Broadcasting Company; Earnest Vaccaro, Associated Press; Smith, United Press; and Hugo Johnson, Al O'Eth, and Thomas Thompson, newsreel syndicates and Paramount Pictures. See Smith, *Thank You, Mr. President*, 229. Other correspondents at Potsdam from print organizations in this study included Charles Christian Wertenbaker, *Time;* and Carl Lewis and Russell Hill, *New York Herald Tribune*. The *San Francisco Chronicle* and *Chicago Tribune* did not send correspondents to the conference, but instead relied on wire-service stories. Other reporters at Potsdam were Pierre J. Huss, I.N.S.; Price Day, *Baltimore Morning Sun;* W. B. Ragsdale, *U.S. News;* J. Emlyn Williams, *Christian Science Monitor;* Raymond Daniell, *The New York Times;* Daniel De Luce and Kenneth Dixon, A.P.; and Charles Arnot, U.P.; as determined through the author's review of fourteen newspapers.

12. Paul Miller to Ross letter, June 10, 1945. Charles G. Ross Papers, Box 1.

13. Ayers Diary, June 27, 1945, entry, Box 16.

14. Farrar, *Reluctant Servant*, 167.

15. Churchill, *Triumph and Tragedy*, 650; U.S. Department of State, Raymond E. Murphy briefing paper no. 226 and Document no. 442, unsigned briefing paper of June 29, 1945, *Foreign Relations of the United States, Conference of Berlin (Potsdam)* vol. 1, 267 and 651.

16. "Potsdam Censorship Hit," *New York Times*, July 20, 1945, p. 5.

17. U.S. Department of State, *Foreign Relations of the United States: Europe 1945*,

vol. 5, George F. Kennan to Edward Stettinius, undated dispatch, early summer 1945, p. 853; *Foreign Relations of the United States: Conference of Berlin (Potsdam)*, vol. 1, Raymond E. Murphy, briefing paper, no. 226, p. 267; *Foreign Relations of the United States: Conference of Berlin (Potsdam)*, Document No. 442, unsigned briefing paper of June 29, 1945, p. 651.

18. Smith, *Thank You, Mr. President*, 255.
19. *San Francisco Chronicle* editor's note, August 3, 1945, 8.
20. "Control of Germany," *Chronicle* editorial, August 4, 1945, 8.
21. "Russia and Japan," *Chronicle* editorial, August 5, 1945, 8.
22. Russell Hill, "Big Three Agree on War Trials, Reparations," *New York Herald Tribune*, August 3, 1945, 1.
23. "Charter for the Transition," *Herald Tribune* editorial, August 3, 1945, 14.
24. "Here's Big 3 Treaty Plan! Make Reich a Farm Nation," *Chicago Tribune*, August 3, 1945, 1.
25. "What Should Have Come From Potsdam," *Chicago Tribune* editorial, August 3, 1945, 10.
26. "Planned Chaos for Europe," "The Red Star Rises," "The Potsdam Folly," *Chicago Tribune* editorials, August 4, 1945, 6.
27. "Conferences—Seventeen Days," *Time*, August 13, 1945, 27.
28. "Conference—Minuct in Potsdam," *Time*, July 30, 1945, 32.
29. Ayers Diary, August 4, 1945, entry, Box 16.
30. Harry S. Truman, *Year of Decisions* (New York: Doubleday, 1955), 338.
31. Truman, *Year of Decisions*, 360, 411.
32. James F. Byrnes, *All in One Lifetime* (New York: Harper and Brothers, 1958), 292.

Chapter 7
The Bomb

Throughout World War II U.S. scientists worked to develop a secret weapon that would devastate the enemy and quickly end the war. The successful development of atomic weaponry came in the summer of 1945 after Germany had surrendered. On July 16 military officers and civilian scientists witnessed the first atomic explosion, an underground blast in the desert near Alamogordo, New Mexico.

Truman arrived in Germany for the Potsdam Conference just hours before the detonation. George Harrison, an aide assigned to act as liaison between Alamogordo and Potsdam, cabled to Secretary of War Henry Stimson in Germany that preliminary indications suggested results that "already exceed expectations."[1]

Five days later, a special courier delivered to the U.S. delegation in Germany a full report on the explosion, and the Americans realized that the Soviet Union's main bargaining chip, the commitment to enter the war against Japan, had disappeared. If the test at Alamogordo proved to be a clear indication of the destructive force of the atomic bomb, the key reason Truman had come to Germany no longer seemed important. Truman, however, decided immediately not to alter the course of the conference, although clearly the mood and attitudes of the Americans did change.[2]

While the military created two new bombs for shipment to the Pacific Theater, the president wrestled with the problem of how to inform Allied leaders of the weapon's existence. The British had worked with the Americans on developing the bomb during the early part of the United States' involvement in the war, but by 1945 the project had become entirely a U.S. venture. Because the British had known of the research and because it appeared Churchill posed no immediate threat as an adversary, Truman quickly informed the prime minister of the new discovery.

Telling Stalin and the Soviets presented a different situation. Officially, Soviet leaders had not known of the U.S. research, and Truman by this time had grown uncertain about sharing anything with Stalin. Still, the Soviets would obviously know about the bomb soon enough, and it would likely damage Soviet–U.S. relations, if the weapon were used against Japan before Stalin even officially knew of its existence.

Stimson expressed those fears at a July 4 meeting in the Pentagon of the Combined Policy Committee of the Department of War. Anticipating that the atomic bomb probably would be available in a few weeks, Stimson told the committee that he had advised the president to test the mood at Potsdam. If an amicable atmosphere existed, Truman would probably tell Stalin of the imminent development of the bomb but not be specific about when the United States might use the weapon, Stimson told the group.[3]

Truman decided to mention the bomb at the end of a plenary session just before the conference recessed for the British elections. When informed, Stalin seemed hardly surprised and quickly brushed over the topic. Byrnes recalled years later that he did not feel Stalin grasped totally what Truman had told him, and he had expected an additional inquiry the next day, though one never came.[4] But historian Charles Mee, who reviewed Soviet documents years later, quoted a Soviet general, Marshal Zhukov, as remembering the situation differently. Zhukov claimed that after Stalin left that meeting, the Soviet premier immediately ordered his researchers to speed up work on atomic fission.[5] Either way, Truman had taken the Soviets into his confidence before the bombing, but the United States did not allow the Soviet Union to share in the secrets of atomic fission.

On the night of August 2 Truman boarded the *Augusta* near Plymouth, England, and the president told the newsmen aboard that he would meet with them the next morning to tell them something special. Probably to make up for the hurt feelings caused by the news blackout at Potsdam, Truman spent a great deal of time chatting with reporters aboard the *Augusta*, but this meeting provided the reporters with the scoop of the century. They entered the cabin that morning with great anticipation. "He laid out a big loose-leaf notebook and began to tell us the fascinating story of the atomic bomb," Smith recalled. But Truman swore them to secrecy and Smith noted: "Here was the greatest news story since the invention of gun powder. And what could we do with it? Nothing. Just sit and wait. . . . The secret was so big and terrifying that we would not discuss it with each other. I locked my notebook on the first atomic bomb briefing in a safe."[6]

The United States transported two atomic bombs to the Pacific in early August. At 0915.5 hours on August 6, 1945, local time, which corresponded to 1915.5 hours Eastern War Time on August 5, an atomic bomb was released from the aircraft, *Enola Gay,* over the industrial city of Hiroshima in Japan's home islands. More than 200,000 civilians died immediately and an untold number sustained radiation-related injuries. Nearly the entire city was destroyed.

Truman, in an unfeeling display of joy, celebrated with crewmen aboard the *Augusta* when told of the bombing. In a prepared statement released at the White House at 8:00 A.M. Eastern War Time on August 6, Truman warned of further bombings and reminded the world that the Japanese had brought the devastation upon themselves by rejecting the Potsdam Declaration. He added, "If they do not now accept our terms they may expect a rain of ruin from the air, the like of which has never been seen on this earth."[7]

The awesome force of the bomb stunned the world as nothing had before. Ayers delivered the president's statement at the White House and told the newsmen of the new weapon. He recalled, "For a moment the reporters seemed unable to grasp what it was about. They did not break for the door on a run or run to their phones. Some of them had difficulty in getting their news desk to grasp the import of it. But it was not long in developing."[8]

John Hightower, State Department correspondent for the Associated Press, worked the wire-service news desk in Washington the afternoon of August 6, just hours after the bombing. Hightower wrote the second-day story on Hiroshima, and he recalled nearly forty years later that that day was one of the busiest of his life. Newsmen scrambled to get whatever bits of information they could find on the nature of the bomb.[9] William Laurence, science writer for *The New York Times,* had met in Oak Ridge, Tennessee, with General Leslie R. Groves, director of the bomb project, in the spring of 1945. Laurence at that time consented to write a history of the project, and after the bombing he briefed newsmen on the intricacies of the research.[10]

The Soviet Union declared war on Japan as agreed at Yalta and Potsdam, and the Soviets invaded Manchuria. The Americans dropped a second atomic bomb on the city of Nagasaki on August 9, and five days later the Empire of Japan announced it had accepted the Potsdam terms of surrender.

Historians have debated for decades the propriety of Truman's decision to use the atomic bombs. Some maintain that the United States unleashed these weapons against Japan not to end the war, but to impress the Soviet Union and force the Japanese to surrender before the Soviet Union could become a force in Asia.[11] Although the question of the necessity of the bombings is beyond this study, it is worth noting that the second-guessing came years later when the political climate in the United States had changed.

In August 1945 the news organizations in this study questioned neither the propriety of bombing Hiroshima and Nagasaki nor the motives behind the destruction. Throughout the nation newspapers carried words of praise and support for Truman. The *New York Herald Tribune* editorialized, "No sane man can take any satisfaction in the swift and terrible annihilation of Hiroshima and most of Nagasaki, but no sane man has taken any satisfaction from any part of this frightful war. . . . If these two bombs have sufficed to end the war, they are justified." The *Chicago Tribune* carried a front-page editorial cartoon with a globe depicted. On one side of the globe was a sign that said "Pearl Harbor." An arrow extended from that point around the globe to a sign that said "Hiroshima."[12]

Americans feared the fanaticism of the Japanese. In the summer of 1945 no one questioned whether the Japanese would eventually lose the war. U.S. warplanes bombed the home islands at will. The Imperial Air Force barely had any aircraft left to resist. But strategic bombing could not force a Japanese surrender. Japan had to be conquered by invading ground troops, and the Japanese appeared to be unbending in their defense of the home islands. Hightower noted that he and a colleague at Associated Press, Elton Faye, wrote a series of articles during the summer of 1945 outlining the plans for transfer of U.S. troops from Europe to the Pacific. Military leaders at that time estimated the war would last another fourteen months at a cost of about 1 million U.S. casualties, Hightower recalled.[13]

Truman, himself, always insisted he authorized the bombings solely because of military necessity. Herbert Feis, a historian largely sympathetic to the U.S. position, wrote to Truman in 1962 asking him to explain how the atom bomb order was carried out. In a response found in Truman's papers, but never sent to Feis, Truman said that he had consulted with Churchill and all of his military advisers and decided the bomb had to be used. But though Feis leaned toward Truman's point of view, the question nettled the president, and he added, "Now if you can think of any other, 'if, as, and when' egghead contemplations, bring them out." Truman never could understand the second-guessing.[14]

News of the Hiroshima bombing naturally brought banner headlines in newspapers across the country. The newspapers in this study carried the first stories of Hiroshima the morning of August 7 and used Hightower's story from Associated Press. Because Laurence provided detailed information to reporters, most of the first stories carried fairly complete explanations of the history of the atom bomb project and the nature of nuclear fission, but of course, such an intricate and awesome story required a myriad of follow-up details. As Ayers pointed out, the newspeople may have been stunned when they first heard the news, but that condition was only temporary. One of the most insightful articles was by Robert S. Bird, of the *Herald Tribune*. "It would be incorrect to say these [Hiroshima] victims were burned to death, because death-dealing rays generated at that incredible heat explode atoms," he wrote. "What happened to the people of Hiroshima never happened to human beings before." Similarly, radio newscaster Raymond Gram Swing, of the American Broadcasting Company, was shaken by the bombings and, as a result, devoted much air time after early August to the cause of world government.[15]

After the shock of the new weapon wore off, the print organizations turned philosophical and speculated on the meaning of the atomic age—again ignoring the tough question of the new adversarial role of a Soviet Union, without nuclear weapons. The *San Francisco Chronicle* mused that the bomb would be a deterrent to war, and the editorial writers noted that they had no fear that scientists had unleashed a weapon that might destroy the world. The *Herald Tribune* echoed, "Perhaps war has, indeed, been rendered at last too costly in life and civilization for peoples to face it any longer."[16] James Agee wrote the first story on the atomic bomb for *Time* magazine under the close scrutiny of Managing Editor Thomas S. Matthews, who returned early from a vacation to oversee reporting on the rapidly breaking series of events that week. In one of the most prosaic articles to appear in *Time* during the entire war, Agee wrote in part:

The greatest and most terrible of wars was ending, this week, in the echoes of an enormous event—an event so much more enormous that, relative to it, the war itself shrank to minor significance. . . . The bomb rendered all decisions made so far, at Yalta and at Potsdam, mere trivial dams across tributary rivulets. When the bomb split open the universe and revealed the prospect of the infinitely extraordinary, it also revealed the oldest, simplest, commonest, most neglected and most important of facts: that each man is eternally and above all else responsible for his own soul, and, in the terrible words of the Psalmist, that no man may deliver his brother, nor make agreement unto God for him.[17]

The *Chicago Tribune* was the only one of the four news organizations that expressed overwhelming pessimism. The editorial writers doubted the bomb meant the end of war, adding, "The secret of atomic energy has not changed the hearts of men." A few days later, in a characteristic *Chicago Tribune* fixation with fiscal matters, the newspaper calculated that research on the atomic bomb cost about $2 billion but that even shortening the war by nine days would net a return on investment because the war cost $239 million a day. The *Chicago Tribune* then called on the government to cease immediately production of conventional weapons and rely on the bomb to defeat the Japanese. Apparently, in the opinion of the writers, Japanese lives certainly were not worth the cost of an unbalanced budget![18]

In the months after the summer of 1945 three areas of public debate developed around nuclear arms and international relations. First, should the United States share its atomic secrets with the world community, including the Soviet Union? Second, should the United States develop additional atomic weaponry during peacetime, even though the United States possessed both military and economic superiority, or should national security continue to depend on conventional weapons? Third, who should retain control over atomic development—military leaders or civilian scientists? The former would indicate a greater emphasis toward military preparedness, which the Soviet Union likely would translate as hostility.

The discussion of these issues in the three newspapers and in *Time* increasingly assumed political overtones in the two years after the bomb's use. This weapon, after all, was not just another destructive piece of equipment, such as a tank or a rocket, which could be neutralized. There was no defense against the atom bomb in 1945. Soon after Japan surrendered, the editors and writers from the print organizations began to contemplate what this new world would be like. Most peoples had just suffered through the most devastating war in history. Yet, if the secret of nuclear weaponry spread with no regard to who had the secret and how it might be used, the next war could bring more destruction and loss of life in fifteen minutes than had been wrought in the entire six years of World War II. How the United States parlayed its nuclear monopoly affected more than just a discussion of weaponry. It also took into account the places the United States and other countries assumed in the world.

To this end, the *Chicago Tribune* combined the natural fear of atomic energy with an ethnocentric paranoia about the world in general. The day after the bombing of Hiroshima *Chicago Tribune* editorial writers voiced the theme that would dominate *Chicago Tribune* policy on atomic armaments for the entire period of the origins of the Cold War. "The secret belongs to all the American people," the *Chicago Tribune* observed. "It must be guarded and withheld jealously until they have the proof that those who obviously will want to share it cannot use it to the detriment of this nation."[19]

As relations between the United States and the Soviet Union deteriorated throughout 1946, the *Chicago Tribune* attacks became more shrill. Three sets of occurrences in the spring and summer of that year convinced the newspaper's editorial writers that only a U.S. monopoly over nuclear arms could protect the world. In March minor government officials were arrested in Canada for passing atomic secrets to the Soviet Union. The Soviet Union acknowledged that documents had been obtained but labeled them insignificant. During the trial of a Canadian official, evidence presented suggested that the Soviet Union had obtained secret documents describing the test at Alamogordo within days of the underground blast.[20]

In July 1946 the United States tested the feasibility of using atomic weapons to destroy battleships by bombing U.S. surplus warships docked at Bikini Atoll in the South Pacific. The test reaffirmed the awesome power of the nuclear arms but also underscored their weaknesses. As weapons for physical destruction of enemy hardware, nuclear armaments proved ineffective. After the bombing most of the ships remained afloat in the harbor. Historian Paul Boyer argued that the test needlessly raised U.S. fears and uncertainty about nuclear energy and "was nearly swamped in publicity, ballyhoo, and sensationalism."[21]

Finally, in September 1946 Bernard Baruch, U.S. representative to the United Nations Atomic Energy Commission, presented a plan for U.N. responsibility over atomic energy. The "Baruch Plan" essentially called for world control with no veto power by individual members. The plan did not include a provision for the United States to destroy its existing nuclear weaponry, a point on which the Soviets insisted. Objections by the Soviet Union eventually dashed the resolution. In response the *Chicago Tribune* editorialized, "National security demands that this nation be in instant readiness to defend itself from atomic weapon attack and that it hold to this policy until it is certain that there never can be an atomic war . . . our defense consists of assembling as large a stock of weapons as we can and . . . of being ready to launch greater destruction at him than he can at us."[22]

The *Chicago Tribune* reactions to related nuclear issues and policies dealing with the Soviet Union were a welter of contradictions. In April 1946 the *Chicago Tribune* observed that U.S. leaders had not listened closely enough to scientists, and a test of the atom bomb was needed to remind the world of its terrible destructive force. Two months later, the newspaper carried a front-page editorial cartoon showing a mad scientist sitting in a chair with beakers on a table in front of him. The beakers are labeled "atomic poison" and "disease germs." The scientist says, "If all the people are killed off we won't have any more war!" The newspaper, in other editorials, also favored the tests at Bikini and then groused about the unnecessary cost.[23]

Chicago Tribune writers quickly turned against Truman after his first few months in office. They bemoaned the fact that a "New Deal Democrat" was in office when crucial decisions over nuclear policy had to be made. The *Chicago Tribune* favored keeping a nuclear monopoly and lashed out at Truman for suggesting the secret be shared with the Soviet Union under supervised conditions. Another front-page cartoon appeared the day after the mad-scientist drawing. This one depicted a mountain-climbing Truman placing a flag entitled, "Surrender of Atom Bomb," on top of a peak. The peak is labeled, "Height of New Deal Imbecility." Lower peaks in the backgound are described by similarly insulting signs that refer to Roosevelt administration policies. The caption suggests that Truman wanted to gain mutual trust with Stalin by giving him the atom bomb.

This continued the trend of contradictory arguments. The newspaper editorial writers realized the secret could not be kept for long, and their attacks seemed misguided. In an editorial just three months later, the newspaper acknowledged that the creation of nuclear weapons would not remain a U.S. monopoly forever. The *Chicago Tribune* called for a massive nuclear buildup to stay ahead of everyone else, but also in later editorials called for reductions in spending on defense and all manner of weaponry including nuclear arms.[24] The newspaper feared nuclear war, but the changing international posture of the United States and its involvement in policing world problems seemed to be the antithesis of *Chicago Tribune* philosophy. Confused, the newspaper lashed out at all persons and groups associated with the problem, concluding only that the United States had to guard its own interests, no matter what the cost. If a nuclear war was necessary, the United States had to make certain it "won" the war.

The *Chronicle* approach did not require such convoluted logic. Throughout the eighteen months after Hiroshima, the *Chronicle* expressed confidence in the Soviet Union and the willingness of both sides to come to agreements about nuclear arms. The newspaper's editorial writers called for destruction of all nuclear weapons, international supervision by civilians, and cooperation with the Soviet Union in avoiding any nuclear arms buildups. But Soviet intransigence seemed to be the key roadblock, the newspaper editorialized. When Soviet Foreign Commissar V. M. Molotov issued a statement in November 1945 decrying U.S. secrecy concerning atomic research, the *Chronicle* quickly pointed out that this was a matter for foreign ministers of the leading nations to resolve and, as a member of that club, Molotov had not acquitted himself well. A year later, the *Chronicle* pointed out that Stalin continually had changed the Soviet Union's position on nuclear controls and it was time for the Soviet Union to get down to business. The *Chronicle* concluded by observing that if Stalin wished to play politics with the issue, that was fine as long as the goal of destruction of atomic weapons was met.[25]

Walter Lippmann argued that atomic energy must come under U.N. control. Just two months after the bombing of Hiroshima and Nagasaki, Lippmann described in his column what he considered to be the best hope for the world. "The object of our policy cannot be to keep the secret," Lippmann wrote. "Our object must be to prevent the secret use of the knowledge as a military surprise. To those who contend that we should guard this secret, we must, I believe, reply that on the contrary, the safest course is to guard against its being a secret anymore."[26]

In April 1946 the *Herald Tribune* carried a series by Lippmann that explained the nature of the atomic bomb and the political and military implications of its existence. "It follows, therefore, that treaties must be designed directly to nullify the sovereign right and to destroy the actual power of any governement [sic] to make a state secret of the development of atomic energy," Lippmann wrote. The United Nations must have complete control of atomic energy and any nation that failed to sign a treaty agreeing not to produce atomic weapons should be considered an outlaw, Lippmann urged.[27]

At first the *Herald Tribune* also advocated a policy of international control, but as events unfolded in 1946, the newspaper changed its policy along with its attitude toward the Soviet Union. After the Canadian spy incident the

Herald Tribune noted that enough suspicion existed on both sides that spying would probably be necessary in the coming years, as long as the secret of the atomic bomb remained a secret. The newspaper also rejected General Leslie R. Grove's request that the bomb be left to military control and supported congressional efforts to legislate control, obviously not trusting the Democratic president. The newspaper also supported the testing at Bikini, calling it a necessary reminder of the bomb's awesome force.

The Soviet Union's rejection of the Baruch proposal for international supervision of atomic energy brought a vociferous response from the *Herald Tribune*. The Soviet Union called for the United States to surrender its atomic weaponry. The newspaper noted that such a suggestion was so impractical that "if they are trying to fight a concealed atomic war with us, of course, there is no hope." When Molotov gave a speech at the United Nations in November 1946 attacking the U.S. position on arms control and once again calling for destruction of the United States' atomic weapons, the *Herald Tribune* concluded that the United States had pursued a practical and fair position, which the Soviets, unfortunately, could not accept.[28]

Time pursued a cautious path in its approach to the political and military realities of atomic energy. Ralph Delahaye, *Fortune* managing editor, asked to publish an article in November 1945 detailing the atomic process. Luce rejected the idea, fearing the author, physicist Louis N. Ridenour, might reveal secrets. The article ran anyway, but the incident demonstrates Luce's caution on the topic.[29] *Time*, of course, did not have editorials, but the type of information used on its pages suggested that editors realized the futility of both an arms race and U.S. attempts to keep secret the source of atomic weaponry. An article in November 1945 listed twelve points that *Time* considered relevant to atomic energy. Among those points *Time* noted that "no big secret" protected the U.S. monopoly, all major powers have access to the necessary raw materials for atomic weapons, and out-producing the enemy is not much of an advantage with atomic armaments.[30]

Yet, *Time*, like the *Herald Tribune*, eventually concluded that international cooperation on control of atomic energy was thwarted by the Soviet Union. However, the rhetoric in *Time* dealing with the topic generally was restrained. The magazine, for instance, treated the Canadian spy incident lightly, making plays on words about "red faces" and pointing out that spying is a natural course of events. Much of the discussion in *Time* concerning Bikini Atoll dealt with the natives living on the island who were forced to leave their homes forever. When the Soviet Union refused to agree to a provision in the Baruch Plan that allowed aerial inspections of nations agreeing to the control of atomic energy, *Time* plainly indicated the Soviet Union was responsible for failure to reach a basic agreement.[31]

Time explored atomic energy with a more thorough and well researched logic than the newspapers, particularly the *Chicago Tribune* and *Chronicle*. This was an instance in which the news magazine had an advantage over the newspapers. The topic was complex, both from a scientific and political viewpoint. The newspapers too often became caught up in daily coverage of congressional hearings, U.N. speeches, and presidential pronouncements. Each week *Time* successfullly placed the volatile issue in its proper perspective and demonstrated how a weekly magazine could provide needed information not available in a newspaper, something the magazine had missed with its continual harangues during the Chambers tenure.[32]

The presence of atomic armaments put increased pressure on the two major powers of the world, the United States and the Soviet Union, to resolve their political differences. It also pressured the news organizations to use their power as vehicles of information and government watchdogs to insist that some accord be reached on atomic weaponry. In late 1945 and early 1946 all but the *Chicago Tribune* attempted to follow such a route. The *Chicago Tribune*'s urgings for a massive nuclear buildup bordered on the reckless and irresponsible, illustrating that publisher Robert R. McCormick's logic no longer followed an acceptable conservative line, but an ethnocentric paranoia that hardly reflected the realities of an emerging, intertwined world order.

But for the other news organizations, the revelations of spying, Soviet intransigence, and lack of agreement in the United Nations all too soon brought a halt to optimism and support for nuclear accord. Such a reaction is only human, and chastising the writers and editors for such moves is all too simple in retrospect. Yet, the truth is, these news organizations did give up too soon. Soviet attitudes had always been confusing and balking. Patience with such tactics would have served the country and the public well. The nuclear threat to humankind was overwhelming and, as government watchdogs, the editors and writers had obligations to push mightily to control that threat.

There was obviously a clear understanding of the potential of nuclear weapons immediately. Nuclear proliferation was unthinkable to all but the *Chicago Tribune* in this study. It is unclear whether the world ever had the opportunity to prevent the massive atomic weapons buildup that ensued in the decades that followed the Hiroshima and Nagasaki attacks, because though U.S. efforts seemed sincere, Soviet motivations remain a mystery. But the period after World War II was not a time for tentative words on the subject, and the editorials and stories that appeared at this time needed a firm commitment to the elimination of nuclear escalation. It was a time for the newspeople to lead the public and demand of the U.S. government that no effort be spared. Political ideology and misunderstanding of Soviet motives prevented news managers from taking those stands. As the Soviet Union and the United States went separate paths, the world was left to live with the possibility of a nightmarish nuclear holocaust.

NOTES

1. Charles L. Mee, Jr., *Meeting at Potsdam* (New York: M. Evans, 1975), 79, 86.

2. Cabell Phillips, *The Truman Presidency: The History of a Triumphant Succession* (New York: Macmillan, 1966), 98; Bert Cochran, *Harry Truman and the Crisis Presidency* (New York: Funk and Wagnalls, 1973), 172.

3. U.S. Department of State, Document no. 619, "Minutes of a Meeting of the Combined Policy Committee," *Foreign Relations of the United States: Conference of Berlin (Potsdam),* vol. 1 (Washington, D.C.: U.S. Government Printing Office, 1960); 941.

4. James F. Byrnes, *All in One Lifetime* (New York: Harper and Brothers, 1958), 300–1.

5. Mee, *Meeting at Potsdam,* 222, 287.

6. A. Merriman Smith, *Thank You, Mr. President: A White House Notebook* (New York: Harper and Brothers, 1946), 254–56.

7. Harry S. Truman statement after bombing of Hiroshima, 2, Charles G. Ross Papers, Box 7. Harry S. Truman Library, Manuscripts Division, Ross Collection, Independence, Missouri.

8. Eben A. Ayers Diary, August 6, 1945, entry, Box 16. Harry S. Truman Library, Manuscripts Division, Ayers Collection, Independence, Missouri.

9. John M. Hightower letter to author, February 20, 1983.

10. Meyer Berger, *The Story of the New York Times, 1851–1951* (New York: Simon and Schuster, 1970), 512.

11. See especially Mee, *Meeting at Potsdam,* 223; Cochran, *Harry Truman and the Crisis Presidency,* 173.

12. "It Had to Be Used," *New York Herald Tribune* editorial, August 13, 1945, 16; *Chicago Tribune* editorial cartoon, August 9, 1945, 1; author review of fourteen newspapers nationwide.

13. Hightower letter to author, February 20, 1983.

14. Monte Poen, ed., *Strictly Personal and Confidential: The Letters Harry Truman Never Mailed* (Boston: Little, Brown, 1982), 35. A Gallup poll taken on August 10, 1945, just a day after the bombing of Nagasaki asked Americans, "Do you approve or disapprove of using the new atomic bomb on Japanese cities?" Eighty-five percent approved and only 10 percent disapproved with 5 percent having no opinion. George H. Gallup, *The Gallup Poll: Public Opinion 1935–1971,* vol. 1, 1935–1948 (New York: Random House, 1972), 521–22. See also "Fortune Survey: Use of Atomic Bomb," *Fortune* 32 (December 1945): 305; "Fortune Poll, Nov. 30, 1945," *Public Opinion Quarterly* 9 (Fall 1945): 530; American Institute of Public Opinion poll, August 26, 1945, *Public Opinion Quarterly* 9 (Fall 1945): 385. In Paul Boyer, *By the Bomb's Early Light* (New York: Pantheon, 1985), 14–15, Boyer argued that Americans were gripped by fear and depression after the bombings. The overwhelming support for Truman's decision was muted by the realization that under different circumstances it could have been a U.S. city that was destroyed. For additional studies, see Gregg Herken, *The Winning Weapon* (New York: Knopf, 1980), 9–22; and Michael J. Yavenditti, "American Reactions to the Use of Atomic Bombs on Japan, 1945–1947," dissertation, University of California, Berkeley, 1970.

15. Robert S. Bird, "A Death No One Ever Died Before: Scientists' Picture of Hiroshima," *Herald Tribune*, August 9, 1945, 1; Boyer, *By The Bomb's Early Light*, 33.

16. "Are Armies Obsolete?" *Herald Tribune* editorial, August 11, 1945, 14; "Atomic Bomb," *San Francisco Chronicle* editorial, August 7, 1945, 10.

17. "The Nation—The Bomb," *Time*, August 20, 1945, 18. See also Robert T. Elson, *The World of Time, Inc.: The Intimate History of a Publishing Enterprise, 1941–1960*, vol. 2 (New York: Atheneum, 1973), 135.

18. "The Atom in War," *Chicago Tribune* editorial, August 9, 1945, 16.

19. "Atomic Energy," *Chicago Tribune* editorial, August 7, 1945, 8.

20. In Herken, *The Winning Weapon*, 136, he argues that the atomic spy case along with the Iranian insurgency provided a base for tougher Truman administration policy toward the Soviet Union.

21. Boyer, *By the Bomb's Early Light*, 82–83.

22. "Atomic Strategy," *Chicago Tribune* editorial, September 13, 1945, 18.

23. "Is Only Hirohito Wise?" *Chicago Tribune* editorial, April 7, 1946, 18; "Peacemaker," *Chicago Tribune* editorial cartoon, June 16, 1946, 18.

24. "He Has Reached the Pinnacle," *Chicago Tribune* editorial cartoon, June 17, 1946, 1; "Old Adam, New Atom," *Chicago Tribune* editorial, September 20, 1946, 16.

25. See especially "Atomic Bomb," *Chronicle* editorial, August 7, 1945, 10; "Russia and the A-Bomb," *Chronicle*, November 7, 1945, 1; "The Molotov Speech," *Chronicle* editorial, November 8, 1945, 12; "In One Month's Time," *Chronicle* editorial, December 2, 1945, 12; "Disarmament Debate," *Chronicle*, January 1, 1947, 2; "There is Only One Way to Harness A-Bomb," *Chronicle* editorial, August 4, 1947, 16.

26. Walter Lippmann column, "Today and Tomorrow," *Herald Tribune*, October 2, 1945, 21.

27. Lippmann column, "Today and Tomorrow," April 2, 1946, 25.

28. See especially "Protocol and Espionage," *Herald Tribune* editorial, February 22, 1945, 22; "Control of the Atom Bomb," *Herald Tribune* editorial, March 5, 1946, 26; "Atomic Policy," *Herald Tribune* editorial, April 5, 1946, 26; "In Control of the Atom," *Herald Tribune* editorial, June 4, 1946, 26; "Bikini Is Needed," *Herald Tribune* editorial, June 11, 1946, 26; "The Last Best Hope," *Heralld Tribune* editorial, June 15, 1946, 12; "On the Edge of Annihilation," *Herald Tribune* editorial, July 1, 1946, 18; "First Reactions to Bikini," *Herald Tribune* editorial, July 3, 1945, 18; "The Atomic Argument," *Herald Tribune* editorial, August 2, 1946, 18; "American Atomic Policy," *Herald Tribune* editorial, November 1, 1946, 18.

29. Elson, *The World of Time, Inc.*, vol. 2, 138.

30. "Twelve Points," *Time*, November 12, 1945, 28.

31. See especially "The Atomic Age—Russian Cosmos," *Time*, November 26, 1945, 28–29; "Espionage—Red Faces," *Time*, March 4, 1946, 25; "The Atomic Age—The Goodness of Man," *Time*, April 1, 1946, 28; "Crossroads," *Time*, July 1, 1946, 52–55; "Army & Navy—Test for Mankind," *Time*, July 8, 1946, 20–21; "Atomic Age—Either—Or," *Time*, January 6, 1947, 23; "The Administration—Atomic Diplomacy," *Time*, January 13, 1946, 21–22; "The United Nations—Where We Stand," *Time*, March 17, 1947, 27.

32. Chambers relinquished his position as foreign editor in late 1945. See Chapter 8.

Chapter 8
China: The Open Door Closes

I

The tension between the United States and the Soviet Union in the years after World War II sprang, in part, from growing Soviet dominance in Eastern Europe and an increasing U.S. presence in Western Europe. But the fear of spreading interests elsewhere and possible worldwide encirclement by one side or the other eventually became the underpinnings of mutual discontent. After 1945 Europe no longer remained the only key ideological battleground.

One of the first and most critical battlegrounds in this ideological war was in China, a country split between a corrupt, dictatorial Nationalist government and revolutionary Marxist forces seeking to assume power. The ruling Kuomintang party, headed by Chiang Kai-shek, was formed in 1927, three years after the death of liberal reformist, Sun Yat-sen, who had overthrown the Manchu dynasty in 1911. The Manchus were the last of the emperors to rule China, for centuries under increasing foreign interference and domination.

Years of warfare between the communists, led by Mao Tse-tung, and the Nationalists halted in 1936 with an unspoken truce as both sides sought to oust the invading Japanese. By 1943 the ceasefire began to disintegrate, and U.S. concern over postwar China heightened. A special Foreign Service report written by State Department officers who traveled to China in 1943 concluded that civil war appeared imminent and the communists would win. The United States should prevent this by changing the country's ruling structure and replacing regional feudal lords who controlled most of the nation's wealth, the report concluded.[1]

Ironically, though Americans came to see the Chinese civil war as one of the first postwar struggles between Western capitalism and Soviet communism, Stalin gave Mao little help in his efforts. As historian Kenneth E. Shewmaker observed, "Chinese Communists may have derived inspiration from Leninist doctrine and have been impressed by the Soviet model, but they made their own way." William Appleman Williams also pointed out that Americans who assumed that Chinese communists were dupes of the Soviet Union found a convenient explanation for failure of U.S. policy in China.[2] The Soviet Union, badly damaged by World War II, involved itself in areas where immediate security was concerned. That did not include China, but this did not convince many Americans who feared Soviet intervention. Historian Steven I. Levine wrote, "American apprehension about Soviet intentions in China was linked to U.S. perceptions of the Chinese Communist Party (CCP)." He added that Marshall saw the CCP as a stalking horse for the Soviet Union.[3]

Actually, the Soviet Union had already ensured the security of its Chinese borders. At Yalta the three parties agreed that the port of Dairen in Shangtung would be internationalized, that the Chinese–Eastern railroad in Manchuria would be jointly run by China and the Soviet Union, and that the Soviet Union would gain control of the Kurile Islands. China agreed to the provisions of the Yalta accord, and the Nationalist government and the Soviet Union pledged not to interfere in each other's internal affairs.[4] The Soviets seemed content to allow the Americans to mediate between the two long-time and bitter rivals in the emerging civil war.[5]

One key question had to be answered in China: Could U.S. diplomatic influence restrain communist insurgency in a large, undeveloped nation such as China and stem possible Soviet encroachment before it began? Americans needed reassurance that a worldwide communist domination was not in the making.

By fall 1945 Truman faced a great deal of domestic pressure to bring about a popular Chinese government friendly to the United States. Patrick J. Hurley had been appointed by Franklin D. Roosevelt as special representative to China in August 1944, and four months later he assumed a second role as U.S. ambassador to China, replacing Clarence E. Gauss. As special representative, Hurley was to use U.S. influence to settle the Chinese strife, but his abrasive style alienated both sides.[6]

Truman cast about for a more prestigious and diplomatic emissary whose stature would convince the Chinese of the president's sincerity. On November 27, 1945, he chose George Catlett Marshall, who had been chief of staff of the army during the war with overall responsibility for U.S. military planning. He commanded a great deal of respect worldwide. Truman told Marshall to speak to both sides with the "utmost frankness."[7]

Hurley resigned his diplomatic post in a huff when he learned of Marshall's appointment as special representative, and Hurley charged he had been doublecrossed. He said that the United States had a weak and unreliable foreign service, that he had been unable to make progress because of "secret U.S. diplomacy," and that a third world war "was in the making."[8] Alarmed by Hurley's statements, reporters pressed the Truman administration for answers, largely ignoring Marshall. Hurley testified before a Senate Foreign Affairs Committee and repeated his claims. Byrnes testified a few days later and told the committee Hurley's charges were reckless and without foundation and the United States fully supported the Nationalist government. The committee decided to ignore the accusations, and the furor died.

Marshall quietly left for China, but lost in the flurry was a crucial point of foreign policy. How could Marshall negotiate a truce between warring factions in China when the U.S. secretary of state had already told Congress the nation stood fully behind the Kuomintang? Indeed, Truman released a statement on December 15, 1945, saying that "the U.S. and other United Nations have recognized the present Nationalist Government in China. . . . It is the proper instrument to achieve the objective of a unified China."[9] Historian Tsang Tsou noted, "The *overriding* objective of the United States was to support the Nationalist government and to establish its authority as far as possible."[10] At a press conference on March 11, 1948, after the Marshall mission had ended, Truman told reporters he had sent Marshall to assist Chiang Kai-shek and he had wanted liberals from other parties to help rule China, but never the communists.[11]

Marshall faced other difficulties as well. As he tried to convince both sides of U.S. sincerity in stabilizing the Far East, the United States throughout 1946 reduced its military presence in China from 112,000 servicemen to fewer than 12,000.[12] The dwindling U.S. military presence belied Marshall's reassurances of support for China.

Part of this decreasing military presence reflected the inclinations of the U.S. public and U.S. leaders to favor Europe over Asia. Historian William Stueck noted that the United States risked war with Japan only after British and Dutch empires were threatened in Southeast Asia. The European Theater always received priority material and manpower during the war. After World War II Chiang Kai-shek overestimated U.S. commitments to China and his government. "It [China] was important but not sufficiently to risk American objectives in Europe," Stueck concluded. As will be seen, this tendency spilled over to the print organizations, and often China news received secondary consideration to news in Europe.[13]

Yet, Marshall had one advantage that he used to bring the two sides together. Sun Yat-sen's program for revitalizing China envisioned a period in which one party, the Kuomintang, would rule only until conditions had settled. His program then called for establishing a multiparty system through a constitution and a national assembly. A constitution had been drafted on May 5, 1936. Marshall then hoped to use Sun Yat-sen's vision of a national assembly to unify the country. Surprisingly, both the communists and Nationalists immediately agreed to accept Marshall's offer, and on January 10, 1946, delegates from both sides met for the Political Consultative Conference in Chungking. Representatives from two minor parties, the Democratic League and the Youth party, joined the conclave.

Just before the assembly opened, Marshall met separately with communist representative Chou En-lai and Kuomintang official Chang Chung. On the day the national conference convened, Marshall announced that the communists and Nationalists had agreed to a ceasefire. The four-point plan essentially called for a cessation of troop movements and no interference with communication lines.[14] In a few weeks Marshall had brought together two opponents who had been fighting for nearly twenty years.

<h1 style="text-align:center">II</h1>

Coverage of the Marshall mission to China posed a challenge for the four news organizations. China had not occupied center stage in foreign coverage in most U.S. periodicals since the Japanese invasion and occupation of Manchuria in the 1930s. The tendency for editors to think of Europe first and Asia second in their views of the world reduced reader interest in China, especially compared to articles about the Soviet Union.

China had a certain fascination for Americans but certainly did not pose an imminent threat as a world power. The interest in Chinese internal affairs was only superficial. As Nancy Tucker pointed out, "Peking and Canton datelines often succumbed to more compelling events in Europe or downtown Buffalo." A survey of U.S. citizens in 1948 found little interest in foreign affairs, in general, and newspapers did not tend to dissuade Americans from the inclination to ignore the world's trouble spots. Historian Robert A. Pollard also pointed out that the U.S. government was much more interested in resurrecting Japan as an economic force.[15] Yet, Hurley's accusations, the growing fear of world communism, and the unique nature of the assignment given to a major war hero drew some common interest among all four news groups.

Additionally, a number of internal factors affected coverage of the mission. Aggravated by Yalta and Potsdam, the *Chicago Tribune* sought to produce evidence of a spreading communist menace in the world. Articles and editorials in the Chicago newspaper, then, were framed to prove that a soft Truman administration had opened the door to humiliation of Americans and domination of China by communists. Articles about corruption and poverty in China were withheld from the *Chicago Tribune* in favor of politically oriented articles that portrayed Soviet expansionism in China or communist insurgency. Most did not deal with Marshall's activities at all. For example, an article by Joseph Hearst in March 1946 asserted that the Soviet Union remained in Manchuria to loot the country and Mukden had been stripped of all its industry. An Associated Press article the next month emphasized that the communists were predicting a return to civil war. In July 1946 an Associated Press story told of the kidnapping of seven U.S. marines by the communists. An article by *Chicago Tribune* correspondent Donald Starr in December 1946 dealt with a statement from the communists assailing Truman and U.S. policy in China. As with nearly all *Chicago Tribune* coverage of China, the articles cited here appeared on inside pages with small headlines.[16] Hearst and Starr covered China for the *Chicago Tribune* but on a sporadic and selective basis.

The *Herald Tribune* despised the corrupt Chiang Kai-shek regime and saw China as an independent country with its own problems, but the newspaper also feared a communist takeover and spreading Soviet influence. For instance, the newspaper editorial writers pointed out in May 1946 that the United States was supporting the conservatives in Japan and should follow a similar course in China. Communists had to be opposed. Yet, the newspaper observed, supporting feudal barons was not the proper route, either. Similarly, a skirmish between U.S. marines and Chinese communists prompted the newspaper to condemn the Chinese communists and to observe that a policy that sent U.S. marines to support a corrupt government had to be altered. The newspaper also observed in April 1946 that the answer in China was self-rule, but only if communism could be repelled. Columnists Joseph and Stewart Alsop also emphasized the communist threat in China. Two of the three columns they wrote on China in 1946 dealt with the question of Soviet influence there.[17] A. T. Steele and Christopher Rand, veteran correspondents, covered the Marshall mission for the New York newspaper.

Despite San Francisco's large Chinese-American population and the business community's links to East Asia, the *Chronicle*'s reporting of the Marshall mission usually landed on page four or five and consisted of wire-service articles or syndicated reports from the *Chicago Sun* news service. For instance, a *Chicago Sun* article by John G. Dowling on September 12, 1946, focused on the drastic reduction in perceived U.S. sympathy for the CCP. The article, significant in its implications, appeared in an innocuous place on page four. An Associated Press article two months earlier explained that fighting had broken out in China again, and all-out civil war appeared imminent. That article also appeared on page four. On the last day of 1946, just a week before Marshall was recalled, the *Chronicle* relegated to page ten an Associated Press article by James D. White about student demonstrations in China and the resulting political impact.[18]

Chronicle editorials on China appeared infrequently, about twice a month, when some dramatic event dictated an editorial response or when U.S. interests were directly affected. In February 1946 the newspaper commended the Chinese for their "reasonable spirit" and rejoiced at the negotiation of a ceasefire. An editorial in May 1946 urged Congress to authorize a half billion dollar loan to China. The *Chronicle* argued about U.S. financial capabilities and U.S. activities in China, saying the Truman administration had not been open enough about what U.S. marines were doing in China. Two months later, the newspaper's editorial writers lamented that a U.S.-sponsored food program was being subverted by the Kuomintang's (KMT) refusal to allow shipments to CCP-controlled areas.[19] These sporadic and ethnocentric editorials reflected the editors' feelings that China coverage had to be closely tied to U.S. interests. Templeton Peck recalled nearly four decades later that the *Chronicle* management in 1946 saw no need for special coverage in China. The editorial board did consider China important but reviewed events there with respect to U.S. interests with no special concern about Chinese-American readers. Many local Chinese Americans read foreign-language newspapers anyway, Peck said.[20]

The internal staff developments that had the greatest effect on stories about China occurred at *Time* magazine. Publisher Henry Luce, born and raised in China by missionary parents, took an intense interest in China. Although aware of the inadequacies of the KMT and hopeful that a Western-style democratic government would emerge in China, Luce bitterly spurned any talk of accord with the CCP. Luce visited China for a month in October 1945 to view for himself how the country had changed through years of war. He even attended a dinner honoring Mao.[21]

Luce's diary of his trip recorded pleasant meetings with Chiang Kai-shek and the generalissimo's wife, who both impressed Luce with their ideas about Chinese democracy. To round out his knowledge of Chinese politics, Luce had a "back-alley" meeting with Chou En-lai, Mao's second in command. Time, Inc., had not been treating the Chinese communists well, Chou argued, and Luce replied that left-wing activities in the world left things "just as nasty as a skunk." Apparently receiving little satisfaction from the talk, Chou did promise to put Luce in touch with other communists later.[22]

Upon his return to New York and just two weeks before Marshall's appointment, Luce wrote a "Super-confidential" memorandum to his senior editors. "For nearly twenty years we have been backing Chiang and his government. Now that he's on the 10-yard line of victory is a hell of time for us to be thinking about abandoning the long 'investment' we have in him," Luce summarized. He added that China appeared to be a test of Byrnes's "grasp of policy" and whether the secretary of state had "any guts." The opportunity for clear, forthright foreign policy and effective leadership at home would be reflected in China, Luce wrote.[23]

To Luce's way of thinking, the United States could follow only one logical path: support of Chiang. Luce was a member of the informal China lobby of publishers and industrialists, those influential Americans who emphasized the importance of China and its anticommunist elements. Nancy Tucker observed, "Luce devoted the resources of his publishing empire to preserve the dwindling prestige of the Kuomintang, believing he might effect a significant change in United States policy." This swayed Time, Inc.'s coverage drastically, though not always in favor of Marshall. John Chamberlain, *Life* editorial writer, recalled that Luce requested an editorial in 1946. Luce wanted it to state that Marshall had to commit himself to supporting Chiang Kai-shek against the communists and that Marshall had been blind to this fact. Luce eventually opted to water down the editorial, fearing it might push Marshall into a corner, but Chamberlain acknowledged that the *Life* editorial page belonged to Luce, and his commitment to China often graced those pages.[24]

Meanwhile, two writers on Luce's staff found his smothering influence on China coverage more than they could bear. In July 1946 Theodore White, a well known China correspondent and a Luce favorite, left the staff. White had argued that the CCP was a viable force and had to be included in any government coalition. Luce refused to listen, and the two did not speak to each other for ten years.[25] John Hersey also left the staff when Luce ordered him to return from China to cover other topics.[26] Throughout Marshall's mission Luce gave personal attention to *Time*'s coverage, and *Time* remained firmly committed to the Kuomintang. With the departure of White and Hersey, *Time* relied mostly on Dick Lauterbach and Fred Gruin for coverage.

Newspersons in China not only had to contend with influences from within, but also with external problems. Chiang Kai-shek heavily censored news reports. Just before Marshall left for China, the government ejected noted correspondent Edgar Snow of the *Saturday Evening Post*. Snow, author of *Red Star Over China* in the 1930s and a communist sympathizer, continued to write about the communist cause, and this led to his expulsion. The U.S. government's protest fell on deaf ears.[27] Marshall's chief aide, John Robinson Beal, noted this systematic effort to censor the news. Beal pointed out in his memoirs that Chou En-Lai was not even allowed a radio in Chungking until Marshall provided him with one. Earlier, Beal had spoken with Nationalist officials about the handling of news information, but Chiang Kai-shek insisted that communist views were "vicious and slanderous" and had to be suppressed.[28] This censorship had existed in China for several years. Historian Kenneth Shewmaker noted that the Chinese government had heavily censored news written by Western correspondents from 1939 to 1944 and denied the writers' travel requests.[29]

While conducting regular press conferences and providing background, Marshall did not discuss the progress of talks very often. Even Beal periodically had to call correspondents and question them as to what was occurring. Marshall did not even confide in his chief aide, and sometimes the reporters knew more about diplomatic exchanges than did Beal. Despite having been a correspondent for *Time* at one point before 1945, Beal refused to leak information to reporters.[30]

Transportation problems continued to plague newspersons in China after the war. During late fall of 1945, the United States tried to ship home military personnel as quickly as possible. After nearly four years of war and overseas duty, nearly everyone wanted to go home. Overseas personnel seeking transportation received orders on a priority basis. Usually, civilians rated low priority, and such was the case with newspeople trying to travel to and around China.

In October Hugh Baillie, president of United Press Associations (UP), wrote to his home office from Shanghai that newspeople in China were not being accredited and were losing access to many amenities including transportation. Lyle C. Wilson, general Washington manager of UP, wrote to President Truman the same day asking that the situation be corrected. Ross apparently got the accreditation process resumed, but still newspersons halfway around the world were at the mercy of unsympathetic military officers in the field.[31]

Finally, newspeople had to deal with primitive transmission facilities. Teletypes frequently broke down, and radio transmissions were nearly impossible. Telephone connections were out of the question. Stringers often sent their stories by mail, sacrificing timeliness. Radio newscasters actually suffered more of a disadvantage, because they relied heavily on mechanical voice transmissions, something that did not burden print reporters. The Columbia Broadcasting System moved its Far East headquarters from Chungking to Tokyo because of the lack of facilities in China.[32] Americans received sketchy reports because of censorship and tight-lipped diplomats, but also because China was not geared to dissemination of news to other parts of the world.

III

Despite the many extraneous problems affecting coverage of the Marshall mission in China, editors controlled coverage, and their decisions made the most impact. This was a classic example of how the gate keeping function of the editor affected reader perceptions.

Among the four print organizations, the coverage varied dramatically. Luce's interest, of course, blew *Time*'s coverage far out of proportion to that of the other news organizations. During mid–1946 when interest in China waned, *Time* kept up a torrent of articles and even a cover story on Marshall explaining how Marshall's and Chiang's leadership had helped China.[33]

At the other extreme the *Chicago Tribune* never editorialized on the mission and confined its coverage to a few paragraphs daily from the wire services on the back pages. Publisher Robert R. McCormick's extreme ethnocentricity, combined with China's distance and third-world status, relegated the coverage to inside pages. Though McCormick backed Chiang

Kai-shek in the battle against the CCP, the publisher's support was only rhetorical. China certainly was not a major priority, in McCormick's estimation, and he opposed any financial support to Chiang.[34] Coverage of the Marshall mission illustrates the bias of the *Chicago Tribune* at this time. The poor coverage in China, an offshoot of the newspaper's philosophy, prevented its readers from even gaining a minimal insight into Far East problems. Lack of coverage may have been McCormick's way of making a statement about U.S. internationalism, but its practical effect was to spread ignorance about China at a time when knowledge was desperately needed.

Coverage in both the *Herald Tribune* and *Chronicle* was steady in early 1946, dropped off for several months, and commanded daily coverage again in late 1946. Walter Lippmann devoted little or no attention to China, however. Unlike the Soviet Union, the United States' chief rival, China had to compete with other nations for space on the pages of U.S. periodicals and often did not get any attention.

But Marshall's initial success did bring response, mostly optimistic and misleading. The *Herald Tribune* mistakenly credited a change in U.S. policy for the immediate success, claiming that previous support of the KMT had only provided comfort for Chinese reactionaries. The newspaper assumed that the agreement to bargain meant an abandonment of reactionaries. "There is now reason to believe that China may be unified and that a democratic constitutional government may be created," the newspaper editorialized. The *Chronicle* added, "The agreement is a triumph for the eminently reasonable spirit of the Chinese and for the tactful offices of General Marshall." *Time* carried a series of highly laudatory articles for two months culminating with the cover story on Marshall that declared that "for the first time in a major postwar issue, the power, prestige, and principles of U.S. democracy had been brought to bear in a constructive, positive fashion." The *Chicago Tribune* offered no comment.[35] *Time*'s coverage had become so positive that even the KMT was alarmed about the damage they feared might result if the initial successes gave way to failure. Premier T. V. Soong reminded Luce, "The rehabilitation of China is no less difficult than that of Europe."[36]

The ceasefire held as the KMT and the CCP attempted to iron out their own problems at the convention. Marshall returned to the United States for a month in mid-March 1946, and after the end of January coverage of China dropped from the pages of the newspapers. Only *Time* continued steady coverage. What stories and editorials did appear in newspapers dealt with fears over the continued presence of the Soviets in Manchuria.[37]

On April 15, 1946, the Soviet Union withdrew its troops from Changchun, Manchuria, and the Chinese communists attacked and captured the city. It is possible the takeover resulted from collusion between the Chinese communists and the Soviet Union, but a more likely explanation is that Mao's forces had moved quickly to fill a vacuum.

Chiang used the communist takeover of Changchun as an excuse to launch an all-out offensive in Manchuria. The communists, outflanked, withdrew from the area. Nationalist forces captured the strategic city of Ssingchieh on May 19. The generalissimo promised not to attack, but his army kept advancing and he did nothing to stop it. Within five months Marshall's initial success had been all but destroyed.

Editors and editorial writers who had lost interest in China were caught by surprise but immediately blamed the communists. The *Herald Tribune* observed, "A major share of the blame belongs to the communists. . . . [T]hey sent troops into Manchuria at the first opportunity." *Time* noted:

Not even the most efficient government could have revived China as long as Communist rebel bands lay athwart the nation's main communication lines. . . . Since the successful truce negotiations last spring, more & more Nationalist leaders, including some moderates, had reached the conclusion that a deal with the Communists would be futile because they could not be trusted. . . . If coalition was merely a dream of men of good will, the only alternative was to try to pry the Reds off China's lifeline.[38]

Perhaps because Luce did not read everything before publication or perhaps because he was open-minded enough and concerned enough about full coverage in China, correspondent William Gray had the latitude to launch a stinging attack against the KMT. He questioned their motives and added: "If the Americans cannot somehow bring a liberal revolution within the Kuomintang, then it [America] had better clear out. China's Communists are not likely to be halted in their revolutionary tracks by anything but good government."[39] Gray's remarks illustrate that he realized to some extent that both sides contributed to the end of the truce. Also, the article demonstrates that Luce, though certainly not agreeing with Gray, did not dictate *Time* editorial content in the same way that McCormick controlled the *Chicago Tribune*. Although he could be doctrinaire in his approach, Luce did not oversee every article in *Time* and did not dictate the philosophy of every story. It might be noted, though, that Gray did not praise the communists, but only allowed that the Nationalists had some housecleaning to do. John Chamberlain, who wrote editorials for *Life* at this time, recalled that Luce "blew hot and cold" on communism, but one of the pleasures of working for the Time, Inc., publisher was that Luce was an editor first and an ideologue second.[40]

But where China was concerned, the truce breakdown must have left readers of *Time* and other dailies sampled confused. Early in the year the four periodicals had left the impression that U.S. ingenuity had repaired a long-time rift in internal Chinese affairs. The U.S. war hero had gone to China, and in a few weeks U.S. know-how had shown these warring factions the way to get along. Having accepted that, the editors lost interest.

The fading interest kept these readers from understanding the real roots of the Chinese civil war and complicated news gathering. China was a story when reporters could focus on one act—the appointment of a U.S. representative. It was still a story when that one man mediated, and reporters could once again zero in on a source and quickly get a story, especially a story readers wanted to hear—that a bona fide U.S. hero had successfully negotiated a truce. But once the story widened to include the complex process of reaching a permanent settlement, the news became difficult to gather and write. It required interviews with dozens of Chinese officials and careful analysis of a wide variety of social, political, and economic factors in a foreign country. Then, the result probably would be a story about internal Chinese affairs that few Americans would be inclined to read. Rather than spend time on such subjects, editors turned to human interest stories from China or articles about Soviet activity in Manchuria. Consequently, few of the editors or readers back in the United States could comprehend what had gone wrong in the three months after the truce was declared. Hopes for a return to negotiations were soon dashed.

The two sides in the Chinese struggle began to separate. On July 7, 1946, the communists issued a manifesto that bitterly attacked U.S. mediation efforts, and the last fleeting chances for reconciliation flickered. A week later, Chiang left Nanking to direct his fighting forces in Manchuria, placing the negotiations in limbo.[41] About the same time Truman named John Leighton Stuart ambassador to China, leaving Marshall only the role of special representative. This move made it clear that Marshall's role in China was ending, and coverage dropped again. The Nationalists continued their March in Manchuria for three months. As they positioned themselves to capture the industrial city of Kalgan, they proposed a truce, which the CCP rejected. An effort by a small liberal Chinese group to negotiate a truce failed.

On December 25, 1946, the National Assembly drafted a constitution, which, according to Chiang, illustrated that he had resisted reactionary efforts to dominate the assembly. This was the only good news to come out of China in five months, and *Time* greeted it by saying, "China took a long stride toward democracy last week."[42] The three newspapers did not comment on the announcement. Actually, it was a meaningless statement, because the country had become completely polarized between the CCP and the KMT. The issue went beyond constitutions and negotiations. China would either be ruled by Chiang Kai-shek or Mao Tse-tung. There would be no coalition and no truce.

Truman announced on January 7, 1947, that Marshall would replace James F. Byrnes as secretary of state, and Marshall's role in China had ended. Truman praised Marshall for his efforts and placed Stuart in charge of mediation efforts. Clearly, the United States' first postwar effort at diplomacy had failed.

The print organizations found this fact difficult to accept. The turnaround had been too great and their assessments too wrong.

Time observed that in a practical sense Marshall had failed but his willingness to lead had been demonstrated. "In history's long-sighted eye, it [Marshall mission] might turn out to have been a success." The *Herald Tribune* added, "There is no reason to believe any other American could have done any better." The *Chronicle* noted that Truman had not issued a clear enough policy on China, and Marshall's recall dictated a need for clear enunciation of such a policy. The next day, an editorial cartoon appeared with Marshall looking at a broken bridge labeled "Chinese Unity." The caption read, "But Let's Try Again." The accompanying editorial asserted that Marshall's task had been overwhelming, but the situation in China was not hopeless, and too much was at stake for the United States not to continue industriously to resolve the impasse. The *Chicago Tribune*'s John Fisher ignored the mission in China and approved of Marshall's appointment as secretary of state. He noted Marshall was a general and would "stiffen the state department stand against Russia and . . . protect the atom bomb secrets."[43]

Fighting continued through the next two years with the communists reversing the initial Nationalist successes. By 1949 Chiang Kai-shek and his followers were driven from the mainland to the small island of Formosa, and the mainland became known as the People's Republic of China, the sworn enemy of the United States. U.S. conservatives declared that elements within the State Department had sabotaged the U.S. effort, and so China was "lost."

In truth, Marshall had little or no chance of forging a coalition government in China, especially because neither the Americans nor the Nationalists really considered the possibility of a coalition that included the communists.[44] Both Chinese antagonists merely used the early truce as a pretext to position their armies and assume public postures as willing negotiators to gain sympathetic world opinion. Twenty years of bitter division could not have easily been resolved. As *Time*'s William Gray observed, the only real hope was that Chiang could form a democratic government popular enough to provide a palatable alternative to communism for the people of China. That would have required Chiang to disavow his primary supporters, the wealthy and corrupt regional lords. Chiang was not even willing to acknowledge the need for such a step. Beal recalled that when in July 1946 he told the generalissimo that he had information that the governor of Formosa was stealing large sums of money, Chiang did not respond well. "Indulgently he informed me there was no corruption in Formosa; he knew the governor and he was a good man," Beal wrote in his memoirs.[45]

Both Truman and Marshall realized the problems that faced U.S. policy in China, and neither was fooled by the early agreements to a convention, but that message never got across to reporters. Marshall was not talking to reporters most of the time, and Truman felt it unwise to comment when Marshall was trying to bring the two sides together. In this instance it was up to the newspeople to ferret out the real story. One could not blame the diplomats for keeping tight-lipped about sensitive negotiations. Yet, placing the entire burden on the reporters under such trying circumstances was unfair. Diplomacy kept away from the probing questions of newspeople often suffers in the end.

Aside from the issue of press coverage, the experience in China set a Cold War precedent and established a pattern the United States would follow for decades to come. The United States backed a reactionary leader who had neither the sympathy nor the support of the people. The communists eventually won, because they were better soldiers and in close touch with the masses. But in the ensuing years U.S. policy leaned toward such right-wing leaders as Chiang Kai-shek, so long as they were avowed anticommunists.

At the same time the print organizations vacillated from unrealistic optimism to indifference to disappointment without analyzing China's internal problems carefully and thoroughly. The origins of the Cold War was a difficult subject to report. It spread from one end of the globe to the other and required an understanding of the Soviet Union, China, Eastern Europe, Western Europe, and any other area where fears of communist insurgency led U.S. policy. No one called a press conference to announce the origins of the Cold War, but the story needed reporting from every area and, as the China experience showed, the story rarely was completely told.

NOTES

1. Lyman P. Van Slyke, ed., *The China White Paper*, vol. 1 (Stanford, Calif.: Stanford University Press, 1949), 64.

2. Kenneth E. Shewmaker, *Americans and Chinese Communists, 1927–1945* (Ithaca, N.Y.: Cornell University Press, 1971), 238. See also in Shewmaker, *Americans and Chinese Communists*, 143, 178, 233, 247, and 336 for discussion of Soviet–U.S. relations and U.S. impressions of those relations. Also see Theodore White, *Thunder Out of China* (New York: William Sloane, 1961), 239; and Dorothy Borg and Waldo Heinrichs, eds., *Uncertain Years: Chinese-American Relations, 1947–1950* (New York: Columbia University Press, 1980), 71, 215.

3. Stephen I. Levine, "A New Look at American Mediation in the Chinese Civil War: The Marshall Mission and Manchuria," *Diplomatic History*, 3 (Fall 1979): 350. Also see especially Nancy Bernkopf Tucker, *Patterns in the Dust: Chinese-American Relations and the Recognition Controversy, 1949–50* (New York: Columbia University Press, 1983), 4–5.

4. Van Slyke, *The China White Paper*, vol. 1, 113–14. For background on the history of China and relations with the Soviet Union and the United States, see especially Oleg Borisov and B. T. Koloskov, *Soviet-Chinese Relations, 1945–1970* (Bloomington, Ind.: Indiana University Press, 1975); Conrad Brandt, *Stalin's Failure in China, 1924–1927* (Cambridge, Mass.: Harvard University Press, 1958); Herbert

Feis, *The China Tangle: The American Effort in China from Pearl Harbor to the Marshall Mission* (Princeton, N.J.: Princeton University Press, 1967); and Jerry Israel, *Progressivism and the Open Door: America and China, 1905–1921* (Pittsburgh: Pittsburgh University Press, 1971).

5. See Tucker, *Patterns in the Dust*, 28; E. J. Kahn, *The China Hands: America's Foreign Service Officers and What Befell Them* (New York: Viking, 1972), 120; and Borg and Heinrichs, eds., *Uncertain Years*, 241.

6. Van Slyke, *The China White Paper*, vol. 1, 64.

7. Harry S Truman, *Years of Trial and Hope* (New York: Doubleday, 1958), 68.

8. See especially John C. Metcalfe, "Hurley Invited To Appear at Two Inquiries," *New York Herald Tribune*, December 1, 1945, 1.

9. Van Slyke, *The China White Paper*, vol. 1, 351.

10. Tsang Tsou, *America's Failure in China*, vol. 2 (Chicago: University of Chicago Press, 1963), 355.

11. Van Slyke, *The China White Paper*, vol. 2, 694.

12. Notes on March 11, 1948, press conference, Eben A. Ayers Papers, General File, Box 4. Harry S. Truman Library, Manuscripts Division, Ayers Collection, Independence, Missouri.

13. William Stueck, Jr., *The Road to Confrontation: American Policy Toward China and Korea, 1947–1950* (Chapel Hill: University of North Carolina Press, 1981), 19. Also see Stueck, *The Road to Confrontation*, 82; and Borg and Heinrichs, eds., *Uncertain Years*, 120, for additional discussion of Eurocentrism.

14. Van Slyke, *The China White Paper*, vol. 2, 609.

15. Tucker, *Patterns in the Dust*, 134; Lester Markel et al., *Public Opinion and Foreign Policy* (New York: Harper and Brothers, 1949), 8–9, 20; and Robert A. Pollard, *Economic Security and the Origins of the Cold War, 1945–1950* (New York: Columbia University Press, 1985), 168–71.

16. Joseph Hearst, "Soviet Looters Leave Mukden an Empty Shell," *Chicago Tribune*, March 4, 1946, 1; "Reds Fear Civil War Will Rage Thru All China," *Chicago Tribune*, April 14, 1946, 2; "Marines Hunt Kidnaped Yanks by Air in China," *Chicago Tribune*, July 7, 1946, 7; "Shanghai Reds Assail Truman Policy on China," *Chicago Tribune*, December 16, 1946, 11.

17. "Japan and China," *Herald Tribune* editorial, May 22, 1946, 22; "Ambush in China," *Herald Tribune* editorial, August 3, 1946, 10; "Self-Rule in Asia," *Herald Tribune* editorial, April 3, 1946, 26; Joseph Alsop and Stewart Alsop, "Only U.S. Is Held Able to Block Russian Control of Manchuria," *Herald Tribune*, February 27, 1946, 25; "Red Army Soldiers Reported in Chinese Communist Ranks," *Herald Tribune*, May 20, 1946.

18. John Dowling, "A Report on China," *Chronicle*, September 12, 1946, 4; "Spread of Fighting Is Feared in China," *Chronicle*, July 9, 1946, 4; James D. White, "Anti-American Gestures in China," *Chronicle*, December 31, 1946, 10.

19. "Good News From China," *Chronicle* editorial, February 1, 1946, 12; "Purchasing Chinese Peace," *Chronicle* editorial, May 14, 1946, 16; "UNRRA Food in China," *Chronicle* editorial, July 11, 1946, 16.

20. Templeton Peck telephone interview with author, March 27, 1985.

21. W. A. Swanberg, *Luce and His Empire* (New York: Charles Scribner's Sons, 1972), 8.

22. Henry Luce's Chungking Diary, October 7, 1945, entry, 2, and October 11,

1945, entry, 5, John Shaw Billings Papers, Box 1. Caroliniana Library, Manuscripts Division, Billings Collection, University of South Carolina, Columbia, South Carolina.

23. Luce to senior editors memo, November 13, 1945, Billings Papers, Box 1.

24. Tucker, *Patterns in the Dust*, 83; John Chamberlain, *A Life with the Printed Word* (Chicago: Regnery Gateway, 1981), 69.

25. John Shaw Billings memo to Luce, dated "Sept. 1945," Billings Papers, Box 1; also see David Halberstam, *The Powers That Be* (New York: Knopf, 1979), 81, 88.

26. See especially Robert Coughlan to Billings confidential memo, October 2, 1945, and unidentified telegram to Billings, October 5, 1945, Billings Papers, Box 1; and Chamberlain, *A Life with the Printed Word*, 67.

27. "Edgar Snow Ejected from China," *The New York Times*, December 8, 1945, 7.

28. John Robinson Beal, *Marshall in China* (Garden City, N.Y.: Doubleday, 1970), 24.

29. Shewmaker, *Americans and Chinese Communists*, 178.

30. Beal, *Marshall in China*, 44.

31. Ross collection, Box 7, Lyle C. Wilson memo to Harry S. Truman, October 12, 1945, and Hugh Baillie memo to Wilson, October 12, 1945.

32. Beal, *Marshall in China*, 137.

33. "Policies and Principles—Marshall's Mission," *Time*, March 25, 1946, cover and 28–31.

34. For a concurring opinion, see Tucker, *Patterns in the Dust*, 82.

35. See especially "Cease Fire in China," *Herald Tribune* editorial, January 11, 1946, 22; "Good News From China," *Chronicle* editorial, February 1, 1946, 12; "Policies and Principles—Marshall's Mission," *Time*, March 25, 1946, cover and 28–31.

36. Robert T. Elson, *The World of Time, Inc.: The Intimate History of a Publishing Enterprise, 1941–1960*, vol. 2 (New York: Atheneum, 1973), 146; see also W. A. Swanberg, *Luce and His Empire* (New York: Charles Scribner's Sons, 1972), 299.

37. See especially A. T. Steele, "Russians Slow to Quit Manchuria," column on editorial page, *Herald Tribune*, February 1, 1946, 18; "Our Interest in Manchuria," *Herald Tribune* editorial, March 11, 1946, 20; "The Manchurian Impasse," *Chronicle* editorial, February 21, 1946, 14; "Stripping Manchuria," *Chronicle* editorial, February 28, 1946, 16; and Joseph Hearst, "Soviet Looters Leave Mukden An Empty Shell," *Chicago Tribune*, March 4, 1946, 1.

38. "Tragedy in China," *Herald Tribune* editorial, April 16, 1946, 28; "China—Stranglehold," *Time*, August 12, 1946, 29.

39. Bill Gray, "China—Bad Government," *Time*, June 10, 1946, 34–35.

40. Chamberlain, *A Life with the Printed Word*, 70, 134.

41. Van Slyke, *The China White Paper*, vol. 1, 171.

42. "China—New Constitution," *Time*, January 6, 1947, 30–34.

43. "National Affairs—'We Will Keep the Covenant,' " *Time*, January 20, 1947, 21; "George Marshall's Return," *Chronicle* editorial, January 7, 1947, 14; "Chinese Puzzle Calls for a New Effort," *Chronicle* editorial, January 8, 1947, 14; John Fisher, "Byrnes Job to Marshall!" *Chicago Tribune*, January 8, 1947, 1.

44. For a concurring opinion, see Tucker, *Patterns in the Dust*, 8–9. For discussion of conservative forces that influenced pro-Chiang policy, see Kahn, *The China Hands*, 101, and Stueck, *The Road to Confrontation*, 42, 126.

45. Beal, *Marshall in China*, 115.

Chapter 9
Postwar Lull

I

The term Cold War did not just enunciate a foreign policy nor did the two words merely describe a relationship between two major world powers. The phrase captured a state of mind. Leaders and peoples of the United States and the Soviet Union saw in each other aggressive intentions and hostile ideologies. The origins of the Cold War related to the perception of an all-encompassing mentality that drove countries to conquer and subdue, just as the Axis powers had attempted to forge a New Order in Europe and Asia. That is why news stories and editorials must be measured as a factor in how the Cold War came to start. In an open society foreign policy can operate untouched within the upper echelons of national government only as long as the public agrees or is acquiescent. Although news organizations argue their own philosophies and do not necessarily mirror society, they can in an indirect way reflect changes in overall attitudes.

This chapter will outline the indifference in foreign affairs coverage in the months after World War II and will show how the changing world situation set the stage for a dramatic speech by Winston Churchill. Included will be discussion of how relations between Harry Truman and the news organizations deteriorated. It will show how the Soviet Union failed to influence the news and trace how Stalin's penchant for secrecy and disdain for influencing the news organizations eventually had an effect on their editorial policies.

Clearly, historical factors worked against an accommodation between the United States and the Soviet Union. The Soviet Union, isolated for decades as the only communist country in the world, continued to harbor inner misgivings about the capitalist West. Americans, though cognizant of Soviet losses during the war, viewed communism as the antithesis of everything American. In the end the goodwill engendered during World War II did not last, and the friendly relations proved to be an aberration.

In the fall of 1945 a vacuum existed in Europe after forces that had threatened world harmony for the previous decade had been eliminated. The United States and the Soviet Union had differing ideas about how to fill that vacuum. If the two countries faced ideological barriers, so did they meet traditional hurdles erected when two dominant nations form the balance of world power. Throughout history more powerful nations have dominated weaker ones, and the strongest usually clashed with each other over world influence and control. Avoiding this traditional antagonism would require some form of understanding as to where each country's influence belonged.

To negate both the ideological and historical forces pushing each country in separate directions, several circumstances had to come to pass. First, the two leaders, President Truman and Premier Josef Stalin, had to find common interests and mutual goals. These had to be genuine, not ones used for propaganda. Second, Truman needed bipartisan support, and he obviously faced a difficult task. Pressure from the Republicans and from conservatives eventually had a telling effect. Truman believed that Stalin had men around him attempting to prevent the Soviet leader from reaching an accord, but in truth Stalin's word was rule; so he did not face a similar problem. Third, Truman had to gain popular support. The state-controlled press presented no problem for Stalin, but Truman faced a largely hostile press and an increasingly skeptical public. Finally, the two leaders had to develop long-range plans for a mutual peace plan that would gain the approval of other nations.

This need for support and communication is where the most recent Cold War historians have established a new focus. They not only assign blame for the Cold War to both sides, but take into account such factors as public perceptions. For instance, Ralph B. Levering pointed out that Stalin "did not insist upon subservient government in all of Eastern Europe" until the late 1940s, but he added that "Truman and his advisers were affected by the sharp downturn in public attitudes toward Russia in late 1945 and early 1946." Levering attributed much of the negative coverage to the fact that controversy is news. He added, "It is true that, as the Cold War developed, the administration was responding to the almost universal anti-Russian sentiment which its own anti-Soviet statements and policies had helped to solidify." Levering did not confine his arguments to public opinion effects, but incorporated historical and ideological factors. Yet, his lengthy discussion of public perceptions represented a key breakthrough in historical overview of this topic.[1]

John L. Gaddis also included the theme of U.S. public opinion into his overall analysis, but he placed more emphasis on Stalin's influence on Americans. He cited a fiery speech Stalin delivered in Moscow on February 9, 1946, as inciting hostile U.S. public reaction at a crucial time. Winston Churchill's speech at Fulton, Missouri, followed soon after, and the combination brought about a change in U.S. policy, Gaddis contended.[2]

Thomas G. Paterson generalized about foreign policy, public opinion, and the Truman administration. He noted that few Americans paid attention to foreign affairs, and Truman rarely had to follow a foreign policy he did not like because of congressional reaction.[3] As for newspapers, magazines, and radio, Paterson added, "The Truman administration happily found that the elite endorsed the president's foreign policy, further enhancing his freedom in policymaking."[4]

Perhaps the most effective and thorough discussion to date of public response following World War II came in 1977 in a piece by Walter LaFeber. Buried in an anthology published in Tokyo, LaFeber reviewed the radio and newspaper commentary of the postwar era and concluded that Truman led public opinion rather than taking cues from the public. To some extent, LaFeber was correct, but as will be seen, LaFeber did not account enough for a shifting set of perceptions within the Truman administration and the dramatic effect a few carefully orchestrated public media events had. Moods can shift even among a generally disinterested public, when security and the U.S. way of life seem in the balance.[5]

The discussion of public perceptions among these postrevisionists commonly identifies opinion makers as rubber stamps for the Truman administration. Paterson stated, "It is not surprising that the public opinion the White House and State Department heard largely matched the public opinion it worked to create."[6]

These scholars added much to the Cold War debate, rejecting both extremes in the rhetorical arguments over Cold War culpability but perhaps overemphasized how much and how easily the president led opinion. As will be seen, Truman often had doubts during this period and sometimes vacillated.

It is not the contention of this study that newspapers and magazines necessarily mirror the values and beliefs of society. Clearly, it has been shown on these pages that such publishers as Robert McCormick and Henry Luce reflected a philosophy peculiar to their own instincts and upbringings. Other factors, such as peer group philosophies, public policy debate, and personal values, often act as stronger influences.[7] Yet, the spectrum of philosophies among editors and the concurrent public opinion drift represented in this study gives an indication of an overall trend at this time. Truman's low-key press conferences and lack of outspoken statements against the Soviet Union in the twelve months after World War II suggest he did not instigate this steady drift of opinion away from the Soviet Union during this twelve-month time period. Where the editors are concerned, a more likely explanation is the predisposition to dislike communism and the absence of any Soviet influence to dissuade them from this inclination.

The four points for world cooperation as outlined at the onset of this chapter were never obtained. Yet, in late 1945 the potential for accommodation did exist. Part of the reason for failure rests with public perceptions and misconceptions and the translation of goals and deeds. The four news organizations in this study provide an indicator of such reaction and suggest a complex variation on the theme of the origins of the Cold War.

II

At this crucial time, the print organizations also underwent some changes from within. Many of these alterations involved the absorption of those returning from military service. At the *San Francisco Chronicle,* for instance, a number of reporters and editors joined the staff in late 1945 and early 1946. Editor Paul Smith was among them. Upon his return he appointed Kenneth McArdle chief editorial writer, retaining Royce Breier as editorial-page editor and as a columnist. Templeton Peck, who would later become editorial editor, became an editorial writer in February 1946, leaving his position in the Office of War Information. The news and editorial staffs increased in size, and the quality of both the editorial page and the editorials improved markedly. Editorials began to explore issues in more depth and with a more internationalist tone.[8]

Months after his return Smith decided that the functions of the revamped editorial page ought to be more familiar to readers. He asked Peck to write a house editorial explaining how opinions were formulated at the newspaper. This became a generally accepted practice after the activist 1960s, but in the 1940s it was an extraordinarily frank step and a stark contrast to the Hearst policies across town. The editorial asserted that the *Chronicle* did not take a dogmatic approach to world affairs, but carefully examined issues on their own merit. "We can live with ourselves, not in any spirit of complacency, but with the knowledge that we've called the shots to the best of our ability, and if we erred it was honestly and not maliciously," the editorial stated.[9]

Peck recalled years later that the editorial was something of an exaggeration, downplaying the newspaper's liberal, internationalist leanings and putting a modest face on Smith's role in influencing editorial policy, but it was an important editorial. It represented an earnest attempt by the newspaper to convince readers of a sincere desire to properly analyze and represent world affairs objectively.[10]

At the *Chicago Tribune,* the staff swelled with returning war veterans as well, but editorial and news management personnel and policies did not change appreciably. J. Loy Maloney remained managing editor, Leon Stolz editorial editor, and Donald Starr foreign news chief. The real force behind the newspaper editorial policy remained Robert R. McCormick, newspaper publisher and editor.[11] McCormick toured the world right after the war to observe war's residue firsthand and to expand Tribune Company operations. The publisher decided to move into other industries, acquiring hydroelectric operations, aluminum smelting plants, and heavy industrial products. McCormick pursued a controversial ideology in the pages of his newspaper, but few could deny his acumen as a businessman.[12]

When Truman took office, the *Chicago Tribune* was delighted with his tough talk toward the Soviet Union, but the delight soon changed to the newspaper's more traditional antagonism toward a Democratic president. *Chicago Tribune* reporters were directed to find negative aspects of the Truman administration and to emphasize them in their stories. The *Chicago Tribune* and the Hearst newspapers were especially known for this approach during the Truman years, according to Robert Nixon, International News Service White House correspondent at the time.[13]

Columnist Joseph Alsop joined the *Herald Tribune* in 1946 giving the editorial pages an even wider and more distinguished spectrum of opinion. Henry Luce, publisher of *Time,* had eyed Alsop for the news magazine as word spread that the columnist was considering leaving Whaley-Eaton. Frank McNaughton, *Time* Washington bureau chief, filed a confidential memo in October 1945 telling the *Time* editors of the bad news that Alsop had chosen the New York newspaper.[14]

On January 7, 1947, Ogden Reid, *Herald Tribune* editor and publisher, died of pneumonia. His thirty-three-year-old son, Whitelaw, became editor, and Ogden Reid's widow retained control of the newspaper.[15] The Reid tradition of pro-British, internationalist philosophy continued, but in the years to come the newspaper's financial situation deteriorated under the new leadership. During the period of this study, the news and editorial operations remained largely unchanged, however.

At *Time* Luce left for China in the fall of 1945 for his month's tour. The foreign staff had been somewhat demoralized by Chambers's stifling influence and the departure of both Theodore White and John Hersey. In December 1945 Chambers suffered a heart attack and took a leave of absence. When he returned months later, he did not become involved in directing the foreign-news page, but instead assumed the nominal position of adviser to Luce on communist affairs, and he worked on special projects, effectively ending Chambers's weekly influence on the foreign news. News coverage became more objective and more insightful. The quality of the writing also improved.[16]

Meanwhile, relations between Truman and the *Chicago Tribune* became untenable. The *Chicago Tribune*'s dogmatism had not changed with war's end or with the new president. Truman, possibly lulled by the kind words in the early weeks of his administration, bristled at the *Chicago Tribune*'s attacks later. At a staff meeting on August 18, 1945, the feisty president remarked that an article by correspondent Walter Trohan purporting to have uncovered secret agreements at Potsdam "was another part of the effort to raise differences between the United States and Russia."[17] About a month later, Truman received a small framed portrait of Stalin as a gift from the premier. He bitterly joked that he ought to invite McCormick and William Randolph Hearst to his office for a chat and leave the picture on his desk facing them.[18] The president delivered a radio speech on January 13, 1946, discussing a range of topics. Newspaper reaction the next day was largely negative, but Truman dismissed it as criticism one might expect from "the *Chicago Tribune* and papers of that stripe."[19]

Time inadvertently became enmeshed in the ill feelings between Truman and Luce's wife, Republican Representative Clare Boothe Luce. The president's dislike for Mrs. Luce and for Representative Adam Clayton Powell illustrate the president's deep feelings about verbal attacks, especially involving his family. Truman accused Mrs. Luce of criticizing Truman's wife, Bess, during the 1944 vice-presidential campaignn.

In March 1946 the president met with Joseph Martin, Republican House leader. Martin asked Truman why the president refused a request from Representative Luce for a meeting in the White House to discuss congressional matters. Truman responded that all members of Congress were welcome at the White House except Mrs. Luce and Powell. Truman said he would relent in Mrs. Luce's case, if she apologized to Bess Truman. Mrs. Luce wrote a letter three days later, but it apparently did not satisfy the president, and the two remained at odds.

Powell's case, though not relating to a news organization, helps to illustrate the surprising intensity of emotion Truman felt against his detractors, especially those who would criticize members of his family. Powell and his wife, singer Hazel Scott, were black. In the fall of 1945 the Daughters of the American Revolution held a convention in Washington's Constitution Hall. Mrs. Truman was invited and attended. Hazel Scott had expected to sing the national anthem, but her participation was canceled, apparently because she was black. Incensed, Powell criticized Mrs. Truman saying she should have intervened. At a White House meeting weeks later, Truman told his staff he wanted aide George F. Allen to go to New York and look up that "damn nigger preacher" and "kick him around."[20] The remarks remained private until years later, but the reporters around the White House knew that Truman could react quite negatively to criticism.

Truman continued to spend occasional weekends with selected reporters on fishing trips and in marathon poker games. The group, dubbed the Hardrock Club, was composed of reporters who had covered Truman's vice-presidential campaign. Those newsmen who accompanied the president to Potsdam were added to the group during the summer of 1945. Tom Reynolds, *Chicago Sun* correspondent, and Felix Belair of *The New York Times* were left out and complained bitterly to Eben Ayers, assistant press secretary, but to no avail. Obviously, Truman couldn't take the entire White House press contingent on outings, but his selectivity caused jealousies and antagonism, though the trips cemented good relations with those chosen to go.[21]

Truman obviously felt comfortable among the reporters, and these outings represented his inclination to spend time with the working journalist. As will be seen, the president not only resented the Republican-oriented philosophy of the publishers and editors of these news organizations, but also felt ill at ease spending time at social gatherings with them. The former haberdasher saw himself as the epitome of the democratic working man, and the more socially elite gatherings drew less enthusiasm. But even the male rituals he embarked upon with the reporters could create problems.

On one occasion an outing backfired on *Time* correspondent Ed Lockett. *Time* published an article about a Hardrock trip in June 1945. The reporters understood that the excursions were to be strictly off the record and Press Secretary Charles Ross did not take kindly to the article. He called Lockett into his office and lambasted the *Time* reporter. Lockett told Ross he had mentioned the trip in passing to one of the editors, who wrote the article, apparently not aware that Lockett had agreed not to publish such articles. This did not satisfy Ross and left a distance between Lockett and the White House.[22]

The president himself sometimes contributed unnecessarily to strained relations in his reticence to curry more influential persons. In October 1945 the *Herald Tribune* held a public forum on national affairs and invited Truman to speak. The president would naturally add prestige to the event, but such participation would also afford an opportunity for a meeting with the Reids. Both Ross and Ayers urged Truman to accept the invitation, but the president refused, using the excuse that he had already scheduled a speech in New York two weeks later, and two trips to the city in such a short time would be a waste of time.[23]

Lippmann drew the president's ire in November 1945 when the columnist devoted a piece to what he perceived as a drifting foreign policy. Truman fumed to his staff that Lippmann did not understand how much had been accomplished. His remarks were restrained but showed disappointment and surprise. The president respected Lippmann's opinion and felt betrayed by the column.[24]

Even the working reporters felt the sting of Truman's ire. Bert Andrews, the newspaper's White House correspondent, came in for a tongue lashing during a press conference in May 1946. Andrews had asked a routine question about the impending creation of a defense department, noting that James Forrestal, secretary of the Navy and the apparent choice for defense secretary, had opposed a new department. Truman derided Andrews in front of his colleagues saying the reporter was wrong and that if he would "study things more he would understand [them] better."[25]

Truman by no means contained his attacks to the newspapers and the magazine in this study. Columnist Drew Pearson drew special attention. The columnist had an unsavory reputation for gossip and inaccuracy. At a press briefing in January 1946 the two met face to face and shouted at each other in an argument over Pearson's criticism of a trip taken by the Truman family and over administration policy for release of servicemen from active duty. The intensity of the exchange surprised even the reporters present.[26]

All these incidents illustrate a declining rapport between the White House and the news organizations, a relationship that had to have an influence on the flow of news. This was especially true of the editorial policy makers. Rather than attempt to control the news, Truman had a penchant for creating an environment that made it difficult for him to get his message across. Combined with an uncertainty of Soviet motivations and dissension within the administration, the news emanating from the White House in late 1945 and 1946 was hardly aimed at guiding reporters and editors in their thinking.

Meanwhile, relations deteriorated between the Soviet government and U.S. reporters. Banned from Red Army occupied areas and restricted in the Soviet Union, the newspeople found only frustration and mutual antagonism. Even in Moscow reporters met stifling restrictions. On October 26, 1945, Craig Thompson, *Time* Moscow correspondent, filed a memo, sent by diplomatic pouch to ensure secrecy. Thompson explained that Soviet officials allowed *Time* only one reporter in Moscow and then watched him constantly. Executive editor Thomas Matthews urged John Shaw Billings, editorial director, to allow publication of an article about Soviet restrictions in Moscow. "The ensuing blow-up might very well get him [Craig] kicked out of Moscow and us exiled for a while, but it should clear the air. The only alternative, it seems to me is to continue to connive at being used as a tool by the Soviet propaganda machine," Matthews wrote.[27]

Billings denied the request, but the incident illustrates the declining relationship in Moscow. Only infrequently did Soviet leaders or diplomats attempt to project positive images in U.S. publications, an about-face from the war years.

On the other hand, the Red Army was projected in U.S. periodicals, not as the instrument of liberation, but as an ominous, occupying force dominating foreign nations. The army's image in news articles changed completely after V-J Day. Soviet soldiers were seen as obstructionists and thieves. As an example, one article in the *Chicago Tribune* even described how Soviet troops looted a bank in Korea and removed money and thousands of pounds of ginseng root, a popular Oriental tonic.[28] Newspersons were turned away from Eastern European capitals, and open elections gave way to Communist party domination.

In part, this increasingly hostile portrayal also became a function of the news. Finland's accord was not news nor was the Soviet withdrawal from Manchuria. It did not create controversy and, as Gaddis asserts, news centers on conflict, making negative Soviet moves more newsworthy than positive steps. This is not to suggest that editors did not slant coverage of Soviet affairs anyway, but the fact that it made good headline material did not hurt.

The Soviet Union's lack of influence with U.S. news reporters helps to explain why the real problems and needs of the Soviet Union often were not heard. Some revisionists, such as Kolko, Horowitz, Alperovitz, and Charles Mee, contend that Americans hoped to dominate Europe and forced the Soviet Union into a defensive posture, while only trying to protect her own security. Yet, if they are correct, they fail to acknowledge that Soviet leaders never got this message across to the U.S. public. Their heavy-handed methods and their uncompromising hold on most occupied areas greatly contributed to the rapidly declining images, especially when justifications were rarely offered.

The final and most important link between the United States and the Soviet Union in the fall of 1945 was the relationship between Stalin and Truman. At Potsdam the three countries agreed to establish a Council of Foreign Ministers, who would first meet in London in September to resolve outstanding border disputes and agree on peace terms with Axis countries in the Balkans. The council included the Big Three and representatives from Europe and Asia. Truman had hoped the council would be a mechanism for keeping friendly relations with the Soviet Union and for resolving details left unsettled at Potsdam. But the Soviet Union rejected one proposal after another, and the conference ended in failure.

Concerned, Truman suggested to his White House staff on November 19, 1945, that he wanted to send Harry Hopkins to see Stalin again. But Hopkins was ill, and none of the staff members could think of a suitable alternative. Still troubled, Truman remarked that something had to be done. "Just like during the war, Russia gets all the information about what is happening here, but we can't find out what is happening in Russia," the president said.[29] Truman had many practical fears of Soviet expansionism, and Ayers noted in his diary: "The president seemed to feel the situation is working toward the old power line-up and there was mention of the possibility of Russia attempting to grab control of the Black Sea straits. The President said Turkey would fight but it would be like the Russian-Finnish war. The president felt we must go along with Russia and seemed to feel there was not going to be any war with Russia."[30]

As the Soviet Union continued to consolidate its hold on occupied areas and to make demands in Turkey, Greece, and Iran, she forced Truman to change his attitude. He began to fear that the Potsdam Conference had been meaningless. On January 24, 1946, he met with Admiral William Leahy, Roosevelt's chief of staff and an adviser at Potsdam. Truman remarked over lunch that historians might see Potsdam as a "bad conference." Truman added, "Yet, nothing more could have been done because [we] were con-

fronted with so many accomplished facts before [we] started." Leahy disagreed, saying only the Polish situation had been established.[31] With no
contact from Stalin, Truman increasingly became suspicious of Soviet motivations, but he did not comment on his fears publicly. In fact, during this
period, only the Iranian situation and the London foreign ministers conference in the fall of 1945 commanded public attention, and Truman offered
little comment on both issues. Still, public opinion was changing.

At a staff meeting on February 24, 1946, after Stalin's speech in Moscow,
the president pulled a number of telegrams from his desk containing con-
stituent complaints about the Soviet Union. Truman observed that it appeared the United States would be going to war with the Soviet Union "or
words to that effect," Ayers wrote.[32]

Public opinion toward the Soviet Union had, indeed, begun to erode.
During and after the war, various pollsters queried the U.S. public about
Soviet–U.S. relations. Sample groups were asked, "Do you think Russia
can be trusted to cooperate with us after the war is over?" In February and
March 1942 opinion was evenly divided with 38 to 39 percent answering
"yes" and 37 to 39 percent responding "no." The remaining respondents
either did not know or had no opinion. By August 1942 half the respondents
felt the Soviet Union could be trusted and 30 percent did not. In August
1945 the favorable responses had increased to 54 percent, while negative
answers remained at 30 percent. Two months later, in October 1945, only
38 percent answered "yes" and 45 percent "no."

Had the news changed so much that Americans had become disenchanted
with the Soviet Union? To some extent, yes. As has been mentioned, Soviet
images had been altered. But just as important, immediately after the war
news of the Soviet Union had been relegated to back pages, if used at all.
Like the returning soldiers, the four news organizations had largely turned
their backs on foreign affairs. What foreign news did grab headlines came
from Japan and China, especially where the occupation drew interest, as
did a congressional investigation of Pearl Harbor. As Appendix A indicates,
the percentage of positive stories about the Soviet Union was down dramatically over March 1945, especially in the *Chronicle* and *Herald Tribune*.
But the sampling also shows that the number of articles in September was
about half that of March. At a time when mutual suspicion was growing,
unfortunately the Soviet Union was not hot copy.

But as 1945 drew to a close and Americans looked forward to their first
full year of world peace since 1938, a well of goodwill toward the Soviet
Union still existed. The well had been somewhat tapped, but no loud outcry
against the Soviet Union swept the country.

To be sure, there was concern about Eastern Europe, Greece, Turkey,
and Iran. Yugoslavia supported leftists rebels in Greece, and communist
insurgents threatened stability in Turkey. In Iran the government refused

to grant the Soviet Union oil concessions, and the Soviets supported a revolt in Northern Iran.[33]

Still, many voices urged calm. Lippmann called for another Big Three meeting.[34] Although Bert Andrews worried that the Soviet Union was drifting toward an isolationist position, *Herald Tribune* editorial writers noted that the Soviet Union had left Finland alone and made enough concessions elsewhere that Americans could view Soviet moves as concern for Soviet security.[35] The *Chronicle* observed that the Soviet Union had dispatched communist infiltrators to the United States in the past, but that period was over. "There remains no reason why we cannot look with complete detachment on Russia and its experiment, do our best to understand them and do our best to get along with them," the newspaper concluded.[36] A cover story in *Time* in December 1945 focused mainly on Iran's internal problems, mostly ignoring the Soviet Union's role there.[37]

On the whole, then, neither Truman nor the news organizations greatly stirred public opinion against the Soviet Union in the months after the war. The administration issued few antagonistic statements, and reporters seemed interested in other matters. During daily morning White House press briefings in late 1945 and early 1946, questions about the Soviet Union rarely surfaced. White House correspondents seemed more interested in a bowling alley being built in the basement of the White House for Truman than a potential Cold War.[38] Relations between Truman and White House reporters declined, but that did not become a factor in the reporting of Soviet–U.S. relations until later. The key factor in turning part of the U.S. public against the Soviet Union at the time seems to have been Soviet actions and a refusal to explain those actions clearly.

When Stalin announced on February 9, 1946, that he had set a top priority for developing military power for the next fifteen to twenty years, doubt increased. Lippmann found this to be a serious threat to Soviet–U.S. relations, "but much too serious a threat to be met by hysteria." Differences between the two countries could be resolved, he asserted. The *Herald Tribune* dismissed the Stalin harangue as "designed for domestic political effect."[39] LaFeber's emphasis on this speech and its concurrent effect on the U.S. public seems misplaced and overstated. The effect was nothing compared to the reaction to Churchill in the coming weeks.

Time still remained for compatibility, but the U.S. public, the news organizations, and the president had misgivings.

Lingering in the minds of the editors were the images of red fascism. Was the communist totalitarian menace still lurking? Wasn't Stalin's version of repression as stultifying and undemocratic as Hitler's national socialism? In February 1946 *Time* quoted a leftist militiawoman in Poland as saying of her government, "Good democratic leaders. They fight fascists." *Time* asked: "Would most Poles agree with her? . . . A year after Warsaw's liberation, in the thick of an epic and revolutionary reconstruction, Poland still struggled to define her freedom." The *Chicago Tribune* observed three months later: "Stalin has replaced Hitler as the scourge of middle Europe. Stalin's anschluss differs from Hitler's only in that it is more ruthless, more larcenous, and more unpopular."[40]

As the spring of 1946 approached, it became clear that someone would need to step forward and enunciate what course Soviet–U.S. relations should follow. One type of perception could destroy Soviet credibility in the United States. That was the concept that the valiant efforts by the Soviet people during the war were performed for self-interested leaders who harbored ambitions of world conquest while fighting Hitler only as a means to further those scurrilous aims. In March 1946 someone did step forward to stir the U.S. public, but he was neither a Russian nor an American, and the speech Winston Churchill gave would break the lull and establish that using U.S. news organizations could be a key Cold War tool.

NOTES

1. Ralph B. Levering, *The Cold War 1945–1972* (Arlington Heights, Ill.: Harlan Davidson, 1972), 16, 27–28.

2. John L. Gaddis, *The United States and the Origins of the Cold War, 1941–1947* (New York: Columbia University Press, 1972), 299–306; for a complete postrevisionist review, see John L. Gaddis, "The Emerging Post-Revisionist Synthesis on the Origins of the Cold War," *Diplomatic History*, 7 (Summer 1983): 171–204.

3. Thomas G. Paterson, *On Every Front: The Making of the Cold War* (New York: Norton, 1979): 119–20.

4. Paterson, *On Every Front*, 119–20.

5. Walter LaFeber, "American Policy-Makers, Public Opinion and the Outbreak of the Cold War, 1945–50," in *The Origins of the Cold War in Asia*, eds. Yonosuke Nagai and Akira Iriye (Tokyo: University of Tokyo Press, 1977), 43–65.

6. Paterson, *On Every Front*, 121.

7. For a discussion on public-opinion influences and the Soviet Union during this period, see M. Brewster Smith, "The Personal Setting of Public Opinions: A Study of Attitudes Toward Russia," *Public Opinion Quarterly* 11 (Winter 1947): 507–23. For discussion of public opinion and government policy, see Benjamin I. Page and Robert Y. Shapiro, "Effects of Public Opinion on Policy," *The American Political Science Review* 77 (March 1983): 175–90; and Michael Leigh, *Mobilizing Consent: Public Opinion and American Foreign Policy 1937–1945* (Westport, Conn.: Greenwood, 1976), 140–166. Polls at this time showed that Americans in late 1945 and early 1946 trusted Soviet leaders in decreasing numbers. The overwhelming support of August 1945 had declined drastically. In January 1946, 26 percent of Americans surveyed said the Soviet Union wanted to dominate the world, 12 percent said Britain did, 10 percent said Germany did, and only 6 percent said Japan did. Six weeks later, a survey found that by a 52-to–35 margin Americans did not think the Soviet Union would cooperate with the United States in world affairs. George H. Gallup, *The*

Gallup Poll: Public Opinion 1935–1971, vol. 1 (New York: Random House, 1972), 564–65.

8. Templeton Peck interview with author, March 27, 1985.

9. "The 'How' of Chronicle Editorials," *San Francisco Chronicle* editorial, July 17, 1947, 12.

10. Peck interview with author, March 27, 1985.

11. John McCutcheon telephone interview with author, April 30, 1985. McCutcheon was an editorial writer at the *Chicago Tribune* at the time.

12. Frank Waldrop, *McCormick of Chicago: An Unconventional Portrait of a Controversial Figure* (Englewood Cliffs, N.J.: Prentice-Hall, 1966), 266.

13. Robert Nixon oral history, vol. I, 223. Interview with Jerry N. Hess, archivist, Bethesda, Maryland, October 9, 1970. Interview stored in Manuscript Room, Truman Library, Independence, Missouri.

14. Frank McNaughton Memo to home office, October 29, 1945, Frank McNaughton Papers, Box 8. Harry S. Truman Library, Manuscripts Division; McNaughton Reports, Independence, Missouri.

15. "Old Hand, New Experts," *Time,* January 27, 1947, 49.

16. These conclusions are drawn from the author's review of the articles appearing at this time. A concurring opinion may be found in W. A. Swanberg, *Luce and His Empire* (New York: Charles Scribner's Sons, 1972), 238.

17. Eben A. Ayers Diary, August 18, 1945, entry, Box 16. Harry S. Truman Library, Manuscripts Division, Ayers Collection, Independence, Missouri.

18. Ayers Diary, September 14, 1945, entry, Box 16.

19. Ayers Diary, January 14, 1946, entry, Box 16.

20. Ayers Diary, March 26, 1946, and October 13, 1945 entries, Box 16.

21. Ayers Diary, December 5 and 6, 1945, entries, Box 16.

22. Ayers Diary, June 24, 1946, entry, Box 16.

23. Ayers Diary, September 26, 1945, entry, Box 16.

24. Ayers Diary, November 26, 1945, entry, Box 16. See also Lippmann column, "Today and Tomorrow," *Herald Tribune,* November 26, 1945, 29.

25. Ayers Diary, May 1, 1946, entry, Box 16.

26. Ayers Diary, January 8, 1946, entry, Box 16.

27. T. S. Matthews memo to Billings, October 26, 1945, John Shaw Billings Papers, Box 1. Caroliniana Library, Manuscripts Division, University of South Carolina, Columbia, South Carolina.

28. Arthur Veysey, "Reds Grab Tonic Worth Millions," *Chicago Tribune,* September 13, 1945, 1. For other examples of anti-Red Army articles, see "The Nations—Spasm of Aggression," *Time,* February 25, 1946, 25; "UNO Will Investigate Iran, Despite Russia," *Chronicle,* January 26, 1946, 1; "Rising Soviet-American Tension," *Chronicle,* March 2, 1945, 1; "Trends in Eastern Europe," *Herald Tribune* editorial, December 2, 1945, 10.

29. Ayers Diary, November 19, 1945, entry, Box 16.

30. Ayers Diary, November 19, 1945, entry, Box 16.

31. Ayers Diary, January 24, 1946, entry, Box 16.

32. Hadley Cantril, ed., *Public Opinion, 1935–1946* (Westport, Conn.: Greenwood Press, 1951), 370–71.

33. See especially Levering, *The Cold War, 1945–1972,* 18, 24; U.S. Department of State, undated Briefing Paper, *Foreign Relations of the United States: Conference of*

Berlin (Potsdam), vol. 1 (Washington, D.C.: U.S. Government Printing Office, 1960), 951.

34. Lippmann columns, "Today and Tomorrow," *Herald Tribune,* November 21, 1945, 27; December 11, 1945, 29.

35. Bert Andrews, "Soviet Trend to Isolationist Stand Feared," *Herald Tribune,* October 13, 1945, 1; "Trends in Eastern Europe," *Herald Tribune* editorial, December 2, 1945, 1.

36. "Twenty-eight Years," *Chronicle,* November 7, 1945, 12.

37. "Iran—The Rhythm Recurs," *Time,* December 17, 1945, cover and 28–30.

38. See Records of White House briefings, Ayers Collection, Box 13.

39. Lippmann column, "Today and Tomorrow," *Herald Tribune,* February 12, 1945, 25; "A Promise to Russia," *Herald Tribune* editorial, February 11, 1946, 20.

40. "Poland—The Peasant and the Tommy Gun," *Time,* February 11, 1946, 28–29; "The Barbarians Take Vienna," *Chicago Tribune* editorial, May 9, 1946, 18. For a lengthy discussion on the concept of red fascism, see Les K. Adler and Thomas G. Paterson, " 'Red Fascism': The Merger of Nazi Germany and Soviet Russia in the American Image of Totalitarianism, 1930s–1950s," *American Historical Review* 75 (1970): 1046–64.

Chapter 10
1946, Deepening Crisis

I

Although his country's influence waned drastically after World War II and although he no longer held office, Winston Churchill had a profound effect on the Cold War in 1946. On December 19, 1945, the White House learned that Churchill would be arriving in Florida three weeks later for a winter vacation. Churchill had accepted an invitation to speak at Westminster College in Fulton, Missouri, and to receive an honorary degree there on March 5, 1946. Truman agreed to join Churchill in Fulton, while the renowned British aristocrat delivered a speech on foreign affairs. The invitation to Churchill had been arranged through General Harry Vaughan, a Westminster alumnus and Truman's military aide. Truman had also recommended that Churchill accept. Churchill kept the Truman administration abreast of what he would say, but Truman decided not to interfere with Churchill's choice of words.[1] The two men met in Washington on March 4 and traveled by train to Fulton, just 140 miles east of Independence, the president's home town.

The next day, as more than 300 reporters penciled notes, Truman introduced Churchill, and the former prime minister told the audience in the packed gymnasium of the iron curtain that had descended across Europe. This was the same description he had given to Truman in a cable ten months earlier.

Churchill proposed that the United States and Great Britain forge an English-speaking alliance to combat Soviet aggression. "Fraternal association requires not only the growing friendship and mutual understanding between our two vast but kindred systems of society, but the continuance of the intimate relationship between our military advisors, leading to common study of potential dangers, the similarity of weapons and manuals of instructions, and to the interchange of officers and cadets at technical colleges," he said. The former prime minister also called for a strong United Nations but cautioned against the United States and Great Britain sharing atomic secrets. "It would nevertheless be wrong and imprudent to entrust the secret knowledge or experience of the atomic bomb, which the United States, Great Britain, and Canada now share, to the world organisation, while it is still in its infancy," Churchill counseled. George Kennan remembered the speech forty years later and labeled the attempt to rekindle a special British–U.S. relationship as "an empty dream." Churchill feared the end of British influence in Europe. Churchill, historian G. F. Hudson observed, would have opposed Soviet expansion whether the country were ruled by a czar or a bolshevik. Churchill's purpose was to enlist the United States in upholding British influence.[2]

Churchill had a largely sympathetic following in the United States, and reaction from all areas was swift. His oratory during the Battle of Britain in 1940 had stirred many Americans. Biographer Robert H. Pilpel wrote, "He said what the British people felt, what they would have said themselves had they possessed his powers of articulation, and he said it with a lyric majesty and an electric air of conviction that still have the capacity to thrill and inspire." At Fulton the buildup and the large number of reporters had set the stage perfectly, and the Great Orator had responded. Soviet–U.S. relations had drawn scant attention in the news in the six months since the war had ended. The London foreign ministers conference had ended in failure but did not arouse great concern. Soviet incursions in Iran had commanded more attention in the news in January and February 1946 but had not stirred blatant anti-Soviet rhetoric. Yet, in March, after Churchill spoke, the newspapers and *Time* could not write enough about Soviet affairs. Legislators publicly wrung their hands about world communism and quickly assured constituents they were fighting communism with their last breaths. Others, fewer in number, criticized Churchill for urging a return to power politics.[3] At a press conference on March 8, Truman at first refused comment on the speech except to say it was a free country and anyone could speak his mind. Then he told reporters he had confidence that differences with the Soviet Union could be worked out in the United Nations.[4] The same day Moscow radio blasted Churchill as "aggressive." Stalin waited another five days before he attacked Churchill through *Pravda*, saying Churchill had issued a "call to war." The former British leader basked in the attention, and in New York a few days after his speech, he told reporters he would not recant a single word.[5]

The news organizations mulled the rediscovered dilemma of international communism. Caught in a deadline crunch, *Time* had less to say than the newspapers. Washington correspondent Ed Lockett told Press Secretary

Charles Ross at a March 4 press briefing that *Time* had to have a copy of Churchill's speech in advance to meet an evening deadline. Ross complied.[6] The next edition of *Time* contained a detailed summary of the Churchill speech and a color story on the trip from Washington to Missouri, but little analysis. Articles in the subsequent edition dealt with reaction. A quirk of the calendar had left *Time* with no time to offer detailed comment on this most crucial speech.[7]

The *Chicago Tribune* faced no such deadline problems, and the newspaper's reaction provides insight into both McCormick's philosophy and his ideological dilemma. Chesly Manly covered the Missouri speech and wrote glowingly of "Britain's famed war-time prime minister" and "England's greatest statesman of modern times." But a *Chicago Tribune* editorial the next day more closely reflected the newspaper's russophobia and anglophobia. After praising Churchill's skills as an orator, the *Chicago Tribune* pointed out that the former prime minister had not said anything the *Chicago Tribune* had not urged for months. The editorial added, "Because we presented these obvious facts a great many people, including a large number who are going to applaud Mr. Churchill's identical description unreservedly, accused us of attempting to destroy world unity." Churchill had helped design the world of 1946 at Teheran and Yalta, the newspaper said, and yet the prime minister decried the world he created, expecting Americans to react quickly because some Americans like to "hobnob with English aristocrats."

The newspaper counseled against any British–U.S. alliance. A page-one editorial cartoon depicted Churchill pushing a reluctant bridegroom, Uncle Sam, to an ugly bride at the altar labeled "Britannia." A little boy Truman is holding Uncle Sam's coattails.[8]

For McCormick and the *Chicago Tribune* the world had become an uncomfortable place. On the one hand, growing Soviet influence presented a demonic, monolithic monster that would some day try to slosh through Lake Michigan and swallow all of Chicago. On the other hand, McCormick found it difficult to accept that isolationism was a thing of the past for the premier economic force in the world and the guardian of atomic secrets. Capitalist ideals and democratic principles had to prevail, in McCormick's estimation, but accepting entangling alliances with the likes of Great Britain presented an equally unpalatable alternative. McCormick wanted to stem communism with U.S. might without deploying the military all over the world and without entering into entangling agreements.

While recognizing the impact of Churchill's words, the *San Francisco Chronicle* worried not about what Churchill's influence might do to Americans, but about what he had not said. For the *Chronicle*, which still remained understanding of Soviet needs for security, the Churchill speech had forced Americans to rethink their positions in the world. But Churchill had not mentioned the atomic bomb, the newspaper pointed out, and that was crucial. Atomic weaponry made useless any attempts by Britain and the United States to team up against the Soviet Union. The answer lay at the bargaining table, the newspaper counseled, not in Churchill's call for politics. The *Chronicle* did take a change in tone from previous editorials by noting that the Soviet Union had not helped the situation by her "strong-headed tactics of power politics."

The newspaper took great delight in the *Chicago Tribune*'s discomfort. An accompanying editorial cartoon depicted four scenes. One was Churchill summoning George Washington as the former president rowed away in a dinghy; the second a tornado labeled "Churchill's speech" extending high above a spot labeled "Fulton" on a globe; the third a building labeled "Daily Worker" exploding—a swipe at the U.S. communist newspaper; and the fourth a heavyset man identified as McCormick with a blood pressure valve on his arm in a doctor's office. The valve was popping into the air.

After *Pravda* attacked Churchill, the *Chronicle* editorialized that Churchill's speech had been based largely on emotion. The shrill response from Stalin had just piled up more hysteria onto an already too-high emotional heap. Interestingly, the *Chronicle*, as it had done after Potsdam, advised readers that the staff would wait an extra day before commenting on the speech.[9]

Both the *Herald Tribune* and Lippmann approached the Churchill speech cautiously, downplaying Churchill's proposal for an alliance, and suggesting that he had not addressed a number of problems in Greece, Iran, and elsewhere. The real answer lay in an East–West understanding, both contended. Lippmann pointed out that a union with Great Britain would likely weaken U.S. influence in Asia, because Americans would be associated with a hated form of colonialism. Soviet aggression would be the catalyst to another war, not how the West reacted, Lippmann said.[10]

Whether he was castigated or praised, Churchill's speech had stirred editorial opinion. He had forced Stalin to react in an awkward and shrill manner. As *Time* summarized, Stalin knew that the Churchill speech, even though it was far too strong for many, would "crystallize public opinion in the democracies."[11] *Time* was correct. The newspapers and magazine changed their editorial thrusts in the months after Fulton. The *Herald Tribune* and *Chronicle* more carefully focused on Soviet moves in Europe and the Middle East, and *Time* and the *Chicago Tribune* expressed more self-assurance in their damnations of Soviet communism.

Churchill had elevated a world power struggle into an ideological crusade. He hoped to forge a stronger British–U.S. alliance, but Americans were not amenable to such alliances at the moment and focused instead on the communist danger Churchill had identified. A speech by a single man, who no longer held public office, had far greater impact on the news organizations than did the movements of millions of soldiers or hundreds of edicts in occupied parts of the world. Such was the structure of the news business and the ability of someone like Churchill to capitalize on susceptible news organizations. The Cold War in the 1940s would be a war of words and philosophies, and Churchill knew how to wage such warfare.

Churchill had damaged Truman's ability to negotiate. The ever-suspicious Stalin felt he had even more reason to fear the West, and Republicans and conservative Democrats in the United States voiced many of their heretofore unspoken objections to U.S. foreign policy. As was indicated by Lockett's request for an advance copy of the speech, administration officials knew of the content of the speech, but did not object. Truman sat onstage and applauded at times. Apparently, the president had miscalculated the potential public response. Negotiations with the Soviet Union would be seen as naïveté, and the news organizations began to play upon this theme.

The Cold War, indeed, was a largely psychological one, and Churchill had altered the states of mind of editors. His analysis had not changed from a year earlier, but the public forum and the forcefulness of his words made all the difference. Britain was through as a world power, but at Fulton the former prime minister had used words not power to narrow the common base of understanding between East and West. The impact of his speech can hardly be overstated.

II

In the months that followed Churchill's speech, a paradox developed in the United States. U.S. perceptions of Soviet aggression increased as actual Soviet hostile actions decreased. Ironically, polls indicated that Churchill's urgings did not convince many Americans of the need for an Anglo-U.S. alliance, but feelings against the Soviet Union ran high. Seventy-one percent of Americans polled ten days after the Fulton speech said they disapproved of Soviet policies in foreign affairs, and only 7 percent approved. At the same time, 40 percent of those who had heard of Churchill's speech said they did not favor continued military cooperation between Great Britain and the United States, while 22 percent did favor such a policy.[12]

In the next several months the Soviet Union ended its active opposition to the government in Iran, pulled its troops from Manchuria, and resisted incursions into unstable areas of Europe and Asia. At the same time Soviet administrators discontinued the wholesale removal of materials and machinery from Red-Army-occupied Germany. Though the Red Army maintained a tight hold on the Soviet German zone and blocked free movement into and out of the area, the situation had stabilized. In Eastern Europe only Poland remained under firm control of Soviet-sponsored communists, while elsewhere coalition governments sought to establish permanent rule. Hungary was relatively independent until 1947 and Czechoslovakia until 1948.

Increasingly, it became apparant that Soviet-style communism would eventually displace the coalitions, but 1946 did not bring overt Soviet activity.[13]

Yet, in the United States the news organizations expressed increasing alarm over the perceived threat of world communism. For instance, a month after the speech the *Chronicle* devoted most of its editorial page to what the editors saw as deteriorating Soviet–U.S. relations. The newspaper called for reasoned assessment with a historical perspective. Tweaking other newspapers, the *Chronicle* observed, "The *Chronicle* considers the 'crisis' antics of the banner-line school of journalism dangerous and unwise."[14] The newspaper resisted anti-Soviet pressure from the Churchill speech but found that most newspapers had not.

A week later, at *Time* magazine Senior Editor Max Ways sent a memo to Executive Editor T. S. Matthews suggesting that the "main business" of the international and foreign news sections ought to be to "make as much sense as possible about Russia." Because journalists in Moscow were so greatly censored, Ways urged that *Time* spend more time tapping other sources of information about the Soviet Union, such as state department officials, scholars, and "anti-Soviet publicists." In the memo Ways specified that the Soviet Union and communist parties outside the Soviet Union comprised the same world force. To his mind, the aims of the Soviet Union and international communism were the same. Ways and the editors at *Time* were also influenced by an off-the-record discussion with Secretary of State James F. Byrnes a week after the Churchill speech. With Robert T. Elson, *Time* Washington bureau chief, and several other reporters present, Byrnes had painted a dark picture of Soviet–U.S. relations. He held out hope because he said the Soviets were "horse-traders first, last, and always."[15]

Finally, Walter Lippmann looked back after the Churchill speech and sadly observed that "it is no longer a theoretical possibility that we may fail to make peace." The *Herald Tribune* columnist continued to urge recognition of spheres of influence but added that the new sense of alarm tended to obviate the patient approach needed in dealings with the Soviet Union. "It may be impossible . . . but if we are to fail, let us at least have tried for the sake of the dead," Lippmann added.[16]

By elevating the struggle to an ideological level, Churchill had made short-term events immaterial in the minds of Americans. In a 1949 study for the Council on Foreign Affairs, Lester Markel noted that Americans in 1946 knew little about foreign affairs. "Being aware of an event seems to require only exposure (e.g., through newspapers or the radio), whereas being informed requires active interest," Markel observed. Ralph Levering noted, "The great majority—the "mass public"—is almost always most interested in personal lives and careers, secondarily in friends and community, third in state and national domestic issues, and last in foreign policy issues." Both scholars concluded, therefore, that public perceptions of foreign affairs are hindrances to the conduct of foreign policy.[17] In the aftermath of a major news event, such as the Churchill speech, this problem can be even more magnified. A troubled public demands action but does not find the time to delve into the details behind the rhetoric or the practical aspects of such sweeping conclusions. News organizations, depending on their ideological leanings and the quality of their staffs, may be swept along with this uninformed tide or remain steadfast in the insistence on rational policies. In 1946 the U.S. public began to clamor for action. That no threatening steps had been taken by the Soviet Union in the immediate past was immaterial. Stalin would eventually seek to subvert governments everywhere some time. The United States no longer needed to look for an excuse for confrontation.

This uneasy mood pervaded the news pages through the summer of 1946. Unfortunately, the four news organizations began to express uninformed alarm.[18] The *Chicago Tribune*'s ideological leanings made that newspaper the worst offender. On September 9 the *Chicago Tribune* carried an editorial that contended that Stalin always viewed the United States as an enemy. Another war was in the making because the U.S. government had not opposed the "spreading infection of hostility," the *Chicago Tribune* asserted.[19] A foreign ministers meeting in Paris during the summer had produced only minor agreements on armistice terms with former Axis countries, and the situation worsened in China. At the same time the Soviet Union continued to reject U.S. proposals on U.N. control of atomic weapons. If Americans did not face a threatening army or menacing insurgents in Europe, they did face a diplomatic stalemate, probably due in part to Churchill's hostile speech.

About this time Henry Wallace, secretary of commerce and a former vice-president under Roosevelt from 1941 to 1945, addressed a Democratic fund-raising dinner in Manhattan to help kick off the 1946 congressional election campaign. In the speech he urged the United States to recognize co-spheres of influence that would allow the Soviet Union to dominate Eastern Europe and the United States to control the West. A few days earlier, Wallace had taken a copy of his speech to the White House for Truman's approval. The president quickly glanced at it and told Wallace it was acceptable but did not carefully analyze its contents.

Reporters had received advance texts of the speech, and at the press conference before the address, William Mylander of the *Minneapolis Star-Tribune* asked if Wallace's speech represented administration policy. Truman wisely sidestepped the question, saying he could not comment on a speech not yet delivered. But Mylander persisted and, while his press aides probably cringed, the president said the address did represent his views.[20] Two days after Wallace spoke, Truman told reporters he meant to say that he had approved Wallace's right to make the speech, not the context. Wallace in July had sent a letter to Truman opposing prevailing U.S. attitudes toward atomic control. After the Wallace address in September, a copy of the July letter was leaked to reporters, creating additional uproar. On September 18 Wallace resigned.[21] Wallace had advocated what was generally recognized in the United States during the war as the proper postwar course of action. But times had changed, and such feelings in 1946 created only embarrassment for Truman.

Conservatives and moderates both castigated Truman and Wallace for the fiasco. The *Chicago Tribune* carried a front-page editorial cartoon and an inside editorial claiming that Truman had two foreign policies. One was the Byrnes version—"subservience to Britain"—and the other was the Wallace line—"appeasement of Russia."[22] The *Herald Tribune*, describing Wallace as "soft-headed," also reproached Truman for his carelessness. The entire episode would probably aid the Republicans, isolate Wallace Democrats, and prevent intelligent discussion of basic foreign policy, the newspaper said.[23] In a cover story *Time* described Wallace as well-meaning but hopelessly misguided and predicted the demise of the Democrats in November.[24] The *Chronicle* asserted that it supported Byrnes's policy of "firmness and conciliation" and that Wallace did not recognize reality. However, the newspaper said that Wallace should be heard and his position would aid the country by keeping an open dialogue.[25]

Sensing victory in November, the Republicans bore in on the Truman administration, using the confusion over foreign policy positions to good advantage. Truman hoped Wallace's resignation would quell the turmoil, but he was wrong.

The Democrats lost control of both houses for the first time in fourteen years. They needed a strong single-minded front to stave off natural political changes inherent after one party has dominated for a long time, but the Wallace debacle added to the Republican momentum. On November 5 Republicans won thirteen additional seats in the Senate to take a 51 to 47 majority and picked up fifty-seven seats in the House for a 249–186 advantage. Democratic Senator J. William Fulbright of Arkansas suggested Truman appoint a Republican secretary of state and then resign to allow the Republicans to take over the presidency and avoid a legislative stalemate. Truman did not respond to Fulbright. Truman's popular appeal had waned drastically. A poll in October 1945 showed Truman, in a head-to-head sampling, ahead of Thomas Dewey in voter preference by a 58 to 30 margin. Just after the 1946 election a sampling revealed a 57 to 29 preference for Dewey.[26]

Clearly, though, foreign policy had been wrested from the hands of the president. The pressure from the Churchill speech and Wallace's mishandling of the leadership of the soft-line position had made Soviet–U.S. relations a key political issue in the United States. Republicans in 1947 would have nearly as much to say about foreign policy as Truman, if he did not alter his approach.

Truman was faced with unwanted additional pressure. Though Soviet coercion in Europe continued to wane, chances dimmed for U.S. foreign policy makers to react. The Republican Congress would be less amenable to accommodation with the Soviet Union.

III

The year 1947 ushered in the final phase of the origins of the Cold War; rising mutual suspicions pushed both the United States and the Soviet Union in opposite directions. Historian Ralph Levering wrote: "In the absence of strong and consistently conciliatory signals from Moscow, it was only natural that a beleaguered administration, already inclined toward a tougher stance, would embrace the widespread and growing anti-Soviet sentiment in the nation and try to turn it to its own political advantage."[27] Truman himself recognized a year later that he had been forced to reverse his position on foreign policy. In a speech to the American Society of Newspaper Editors in April 1948, Truman recalled: "Now everybody in this country was of the opinion that the Russians could be dealt with, and so was I. But everybody has had to deal with them . . . [has] come back shaking their heads. They can't understand that No - No - No to everything we propose."[28]

At the same time it had become obvious to Truman that James Byrnes would not be the proper vehicle for achieving a new direction in foreign policy. Byrnes had too much of a mind of his own. As has been indicated from the conversations Byrnes had with reporters, he often criticized the president and made no secret of his feelings that he, not Truman, would make the better president. Byrnes had submitted his resignation in April 1946 citing poor health, but the resignation was rejected then. In December Byrnes once again told Truman he wanted to step down, and this time the president agreed. George Marshall returned from China to replace Byrnes. Historian Robert L. Messer noted that Truman was a master at leading public opinion, and Byrnes would have stayed on had he enjoyed the support of the president, but the secretary of state knew he could not challenge Truman's popularity or appeal at the time.[29] Marshall took office on January 21, 1947.

The new secretary of state had only six weeks before he faced his first major foreign policy crisis. The financially beleaguered British government in late February announced that peacekeeping troops in Greece would be withdrawn by the end of March. Both Greek and British leaders appealed to the United States to provide aid to Greece and Turkey to keep communist insurgents at bay. Truman met with key members of Congress to establish a consensus. Despite tough talk by Republicans the previous fall, congressional leaders were not in a spending mood, and Truman learned that a limited amount of funding would be available for a specific financial request. He prepared to make such a request at a joint session of Congress on March 12.

The news from southern Europe had jolted U.S. public-opinion leaders into a crisis mentality once again. The news organizations called for immediate action. *Herald Tribune* columnist Joseph Alsop proclaimed on March 3 that the "optimistic foundation of American policy has quite literally been shattered by a series of hammer blows."[30] Truman decided to use the March 12 speech to change the emphasis of his foreign policy.

As a packed congressional chamber listened, the president told Congress a world struggle had begun between communism and democracy. Greece and Turkey would be the first battlegrounds, but there would be many more, the president counseled. The first arsenal would be $400 million in aid to the two southern European nations, but Truman made it clear that he was calling for sweeping opposition to the Soviet threat in Europe and worldwide. The Truman Doctrine, as it came to be known, called for U.S. aid and influence to spread wherever needed.[31]

British financial woes precipitated a crisis. Walter Lippmann argued just a week before the Truman Doctrine speech that there was no immediate emergency that required the British to remove their troops in a month's time, but the British could not affort the cost of maintaining the troops.[32]

For Truman and his administration the speech had the desired effect. The president had seized the initiative to stir the country. Historians, such as David Horowitz, cite opinions by columnists, including Lippmann, to indicate that Truman's speech was not well received.[33] In fact, the news organizations supported the president. The editorial writers were wholly in support of a hard line against communism.

Chicago Tribune reaction was negative, but largely because Truman made the speech. Next-morning coverage featured a banner story that emphasized that Truman had decided to draw the nation into a fighting war. An editorial the same day repeated that theme and compared the Truman Doctrine to supposed efforts by Roosevelt to drag the United States into World War II. Truman's hard line carried a price tag, and the *Chicago Tribune* resented that. But in truth, the newspaper had become virulent enemies with the president, and even a tough approach toward the Soviet Union could not please the newspaper's editorial writers.[34]

The Truman speech met with more rational discussion in *Time*, which devoted five articles to the Truman proposal in the magazine's first edition after the speech. Most of the coverage dealt objectively with the proposals and included reactions to and analyses of the speech's implications. "Despite the professed astonishment of some congressmen, the road the President indicated was a logical development of U.S. diplomacy," *Time* observed, noting that Marshall had written three fourths of the speech. The article quoted former British ambassador Joseph Kennedy as describing the Doctrine as a policy that would lead to national bankruptcy. The poor of the world would eventually have to experiment with communism, if only out of desperation, Kennedy said.[35]

More typical treatment came in the *Herald Tribune*, which lauded Truman, pointing out that the "American system offers a working alternative to the totalitarian order." The newspaper contended that the president had only recognized the obvious. Through the months after the Churchill speech, the newspaper had drifted toward a hard line, and Truman's speech had been the final blow. "When one considers the probable consequences of any other course, it is difficult to gainsay [Truman's] conclusion," the newspaper argued.[36]

Even the liberal, internationalist *Chronicle* exhibited signs of morning-after panic. The newspaper had just opened a Washington bureau and newly added staff correspondent, Carroll Kirkpatrick, wrote a favorable story about Truman. The newspaper editorial writers observed, "There can hardly be a man or woman in America this morning who doesn't have that pit-of-the-stomach awareness of impending danger." The real enemy was not communism, but poverty, the newspaper argued, but the editorial found a likelihood that the United States would indeed need to fight communism. The words of optimism from the past four years had dimmed drastically.[37]

Only Walter Lippmann held to the same power dynamics theory of coexistence that had guided his thinking since the two countries had risen to preeminent positions. Lippmann wanted to know why Truman had to take a localized problem in Greece and Turkey and turn it into a world crusade. "Everyone will read into it his own fears and hopes, and it could readily act as incitement and inducement to civil strife in countries where national cooperation of parties is delicate and precarious," Lippmann wrote.[38] At this juncture Lippmann's presence on the staff of the newspaper became crucial. The *Herald Tribune* had abandoned its support of negotiating differences. The Reid family decision to allow Lippmann to express divergent feelings would become ever important in the next few months.

The two superpowers by summer of 1947 had sunk into ideological camps of warfare from which they would not emerge for decades. The U.S. people had accepted the Cold War, and so had *Time* and two of the newspapers— the *Chronicle* would within the next few months. The foundations for the differences stretched back as far as 1917, but certainly the negative public relations campaign by the British, the failed international policies of the Truman administration, and the refusal by Soviet leaders to soothe U.S. fears contributed heavily to the perceived need for the Truman Doctrine.

The March 12 address was a beginning of outright, official ideological warfare with implications for years to come. The national policy debate was all but over. Yet, the debate had been meager indeed. Truman had not led the news organizations, nor had the reporters and editors pressured the administration. The government and its watchdogs had been merely also-rans in these most crucial foreign policy decisions.

NOTES

1. Eben A. Ayers Diary, December 19, 1945, entry, Box 16. Harry S. Truman Library, Manuscripts Division, Ayers Collection, Independence, Missouri; "Behind

the Iron Curtain Speech," *St. Louis Post-Dispatch*, March 2, 1986, F1, F9. See also Robert H. Pilpel, *Churchill in America 1895–1961: An Affectionate Portrait* (New York: Harcourt, Brace, Jovanovich, 1976), 218–21. Pilpel points out that after the speech Dean Acheson, under-secretary of state, had reconsidered whether to attend a dinner in New York with Churchill because of the furor over the speech.

2. See especially, "Text of Churchill Speech," *San Francisco Chronicle*, March 6, 1946, 4; Winston S. Churchill, "The Sinews of Peace," in *Winston S. Churchill: His Complete Speeches 1897–1963*, vol. 7, ed. Robert Rhodes James (New York: Chelsea, 1974), 7285–93; Kennan interview in *Post-Dispatch*, March 2, 1986, F9; G. F. Hudson, *The Hard and Bitter Peace: World Politics Since 1945* (New York: Praeger, 1967), 32. For further concurrence on Churchill's motives, see Joyce Kolko and Gabriel Kolko, *The Limits of Power: The World and United States Foreign Policy, 1945–1954* (New York: Harper and Row, 1972), 45; and Walter LaFeber, *America, Russia and the Cold War, 1945–1980*, 4th ed. (New York: John Wiley and Sons, 1980), 39–40.

3. Robert H. Pilpel, *Churchill in America 1895–1961*, 128; Raymond A. Callahan, *Churchill: Retreat from Empire* (Wilmington, Del.: Scholarly Resources, 1984), 73–74, 80; "Churchill's Speech," *Chronicle*, March 7, 1946, 1; James, ed., *Winston S. Churchill*, 7285–93.

4. Notes on March 8, 1946, press conference, Ayers Collection, General File; Bert Andrews, "Truman Voices Faith in Russia," *New York Herald Tribune*, March 9, 1946, 1.

5. "Moscow Radio Says Churchill Is 'Aggressive,' " *Herald Tribune*, March 8, 1946, 3; "The Nations—Stalin Takes the Stump," *Time*, March 25, 1946; "Churchill Takes the Challenge," *Time*, March 25, 1946, 27.

6. Text of March 4, 1946, press briefing, 3, Ayers Collection, Box 13.

7. "The Nation—From Mo. to O.," "Foreign Relations—This Sad & Breathless Moment," "Shoot If You Must," "The Presidency—Mr. Truman's Balloon," *Time*, March 18, 1946, 17–20. "The Presidency—No Cause for Alarm," *Time*, March 25, 1946, 18.

8. Chesly Manly, "Churchill Hits Red Peril," *Chicago Tribune*, March 6, 1946, 1; "Mr. Churchill's Plea," *Chicago Tribune* editorial, March 7, 1946, 7; editorial cartoon, *Chicago Tribune*, March 8, 1946, 1.

9. "Toward a Good Understanding," *Chronicle* editorial, March 7, 1946, 14; editorial cartoon, *Chronicle*, March 7, 1946; "Pravda Speaks Her Mind," *Chronicle* editorial, March 12, 1946, 14; *Chronicle* editor's note, March 6, 1946, 14.

10. "Fraternal Association," *Herald Tribune*, March 7, 1946, 18.

11. "The Nations—Stalin Takes the Stump," *Time*, March 25, 1946, 26.

12. George H. Gallup, *The Gallup Poll: Public Opinion 1935–1971*, vol. 1 (New York: Random House, 1972), 567. Also see similar poll results in Hadley Cantril, *Public Opinion 1935–1946* (Princeton, N.J.: Princeton University, 1951), 960–64. Polls also showed that Americans were split in their opinion about what newspapers were reporting about the Soviet Union. A survey in August 1946 found that 44 percent of Americans thought reporting of news about the Soviet Union to be fair, 31 percent did not think it was fair, and 25 percent had no opinion. A month later, 17 percent of poll survey respondents said they thought newspapers were making the Soviet Union look better than she really was, while 42 percent said worse than she was, 21 percent said the same as she was, and 20 percent did not know. See Cantril, *Public Opinion 1935–1971*, 522–23.

13. For concurrence on this point, see Ralph B. Levering, *The Cold War, 1945–1972* (Arlington Heights, Ill.: Harlan Davidson, 1982), 16; and LaFeber, *America, Russia and the Cold War*, 44.

14. "Where Has Unity Gone?" *Chronicle* editorial, April 12, 1946, 14.

15. Max Ways to T. S. Matthews memo, April 19, 1945, 1–4 John Shaw Billings Papers, Box 2. Caroliniana Library, Manuscripts Division, Billings Collection, University of South Carolina, Columbia, South Carolina; Robert T. Elson to David Hulbard, Jr., confidential memo, March 13, 1946, 1–5, Billings Papers, Box 2.

16. Walter Lippman column, "Today and Tomorrow," *Herald Tribune*, March 12, 1946, 25.

17. Ralph B. Levering, *The Public and American Foreign Policy: 1918–1978* (New York: William Morrow, 1978), 32; Lester Markel et al., *Public Opinion and Foreign Policy* (New York: Harper and Brothers, 1949), 53.

18. Articles and editorial supporting this point include "Charge Reds Loot Hungary," *Chicago Tribune*, July 27, 1946, 1; "Americans in Peril," *Chicago Tribune* editorial, May 23, 1946, 18; "Russia Exposed, But Not Britain," *Chicago Tribune* editorial, June 20, 1946, 16; Walter Lippmann column, "Today and Tomorrow," *Herald Tribune*, July 2, 1946, 25; Joseph Alsop column, "Riddle of Soviet Aims Is Topic Most Discussed at Paris Parley," *Herald Tribune*, August 2, 1946, 20; "How to Win a Peace," *Chronicle* editorial, June 19, 1946, 10; "Questions to Ask Moscow," July 10, 1946, 14; "The Nations—Destiny's Men," *Time*, July 15, 1946, 27; "Yugoslavia—The Gale of the World," *Time*, July 22, 1946, 33; John Stanton, "Deutschland Erwache," *Time*, July 22, 1946, 34. See also John L. Gaddis, *The United States and the Origins of the Cold War, 1941–1947* (New York: Columbia University Press, 1972), 319; Robert J. Donovan, *Conflict and Crisis: The Presidency of Harry S. Truman 1945–1948 (New York: W. W. Norton, 1977), 196; Robert L. Messer, The End of An Alliance: James F. Byrnes, Roosevelt, Truman, and the Origins of the Cold War* (Chapel Hill: University of North Carolina Press, 1982), 191.

19. "Stalin's Hostility," *Chicago Tribune* editorial, September 9, 1946, 20.

20. Ayers Diary, September 5, 1946, entry, Box 16; "The Presidency—What I Meant to Say . . ." *Time*, September 21, 1946, 21.

21. Ayers Diary, September 7 and 18, 1946, entries, Box 16; Bert Cochran, *Harry Truman and the Crisis Presidency* (New York: Funk & Wagnalls, 1973), 183–84; Alonzo Hamby, *Beyond the New Deal: Harry S. Truman and American Liberalism* (New York: Columbia University, 1973), 127–32.

22. "Split Personality," *Chicago Tribune* cartoon, September 14, 1946, 1; "Wallace's Speech," *Chicago Tribune* editorial, 14.

23. "Mr. Wallace Does It Again," *Herald Tribune* editorial, September 13, 1946, 6; "Not Too Little, but Too Late," *Herald Tribune* editorial, September 21, 1946, 10.

24. "The Nation—The Real Choice," *Time*, September 30, 1946, cover and 21–24.

25. "Wallace in Perspective," *Chronicle* editorial, September 21, 1946, 8.

26. "Fulbright Invites Truman to Resign," *The New York Times*, November 7, 1946, 3; Hamby, *Beyond the New Deal*, 138; Cantril, *Public Opinion 1934–1946*, 645.

27. Ralph Levering, *The Cold War, 1945–1972* (Arlington Heights, Ill.: Harland Davidson, 1982), 28–29.

28. Notes on Harry S. Truman address to American Society of Newspaper Ed-

itors, April 17, 1948, Statler Hotel, Washington, D.C., 5, Ayers Collection, Box 4.

29. Messer, *The End of An Alliance*, 174–79, 192; Ayers Diary, January 7, 1947, entry, Box 16.

30. Joseph Alsop column, "Matter of Fact," *Herald Tribune*, March 3, 1947, 17.

31. See especially "Congress Will Act Soon on Truman's Plea for Aid to Greece, Turkey," *Chronicle*, March 13, 1947, 1.

32. Walter Lippmann column, "Today and Tomorrow," *Herald Tribune*, March 4, 1947, 25.

33. David Horowitz, *Free World Colossus: A Critique of American Foreign Policy in the Cold War* (New York: Hill and Wang, 1971), 99. At the same time, public opinion polls indicate the Americans agreed with Truman too. Of those who had heard of Truman's speech, 56 percent said they approved of aid to Greece, and 32 percent disagreed. The polls also suggested that the get-tough policy had allowed the president to regain popular support. Just after the speech, Americans were asked about Truman's handling of the presidency. He received an approval rating by a margin of 60 to 23. Another survey found that Americans by a margin of 61 to 26 thought that membership in the American Communist party should have been forbidden. Gallup, *The Gallup Poll*, vol. 1, 636–67, 640.

34. " 'War Debate' in Congress," *Chicago Tribune*, March 13, 1947, 1; "Here We Go Again," *Chicago Tribune* editorial, March 13, 1947, 18.

35. "The World & Democracy," *Time*, March 24, 1947, 18–19.

36. "In Support of Our Beliefs," *Herald Tribune* editorial, March 13, 1947, 30.

37. "Congress Will Act Soon on Truman's Plea for Aid to Greece, Turkey," *Chronicle*, March 13, 1947, 1; "Only Full Reconstruction Can Save This One World," *Chronicle* editorial, March 13, 1947, 14.

38. Walter Lippmann column, "Today and Tomorrow," *Herald Tribune*, March 15, 1947, 13.

Chapter 11
Mr. X and Other Interpretations

I

After President Truman's speech to Congress in March 1947 only two key foreign policy questions remained to be decided while the United States and the Soviet Union separated into hostile camps. First, how would Stalin and his Kremlin advisers react to the Truman Doctrine? Would the speech cause them to retrench and seek compromise in the face of an obvious hardening of U.S. attitudes or would the Soviets stiffen and match the tough talk? Second, what form would the Truman Doctrine take after a time? Would the United States involve its armed forces in conflicts around the globe where communism seemed to threaten, or would the United States confine its military interest to where communist influence would do the most damage?[1]

The answer to the first question came quickly. As Truman delivered his speech, Marshall arrived in Moscow to discuss with the foreign ministers of the leading industrial nations the fates of the defeated Axis countries and their possessions. Among other things, the Council of Foreign Ministers sought to decide the long-term disposition of the then-divided Germany and to find a suitable solution to the Korean problem, where the Japanese had colonized for over forty years. Marshall learned that the Soviet Union would take a hard line. The Soviets refused compromise and insisted that the United States withdraw its military forces from Europe. Marshall and his chief adviser, John Foster Dulles, were dismayed. After six weeks the conference ended in deadlock. A cover story in *Time* noted: "At last even the dullest U.S. citizen was made to realize the exasperating difficulty and the aggravating exhaustion of dealing with the Soviet government. Now the question became: What does the U.S. do next?"[2]

In late May the communists staged a coup in Hungary and Lajos Dinnyes replaced anticommunist Premier Ferenc Nagy with the help of the Red Army. The United States cut off aid to Hungary and protested vigorously, but to no avail. U.S. claims of violations of the armistice agreement and the Yalta accord were ignored. Marshall decided the United States would have to develop a long-term policy of economic assistance in Europe to prevent further communist incursions.[3]

During a speech at Harvard University on June 5, 1947, Marshall called for a European Economic Recovery Plan that would provide U.S. assistance to Europe and feed and house some of the hungry and homeless. Dubbed the "Marshall Plan," the proposal sought to provide a pathway upward for decimated areas of Europe and cement relations with those countries.

The question of U.S. response to Soviet expansionism and world communism would be debated later in the year. U.S. leaders would have to decide whether to use confrontation, containment, or regional hegemony in dealing with expanding communism. George F. Kennan, the minister-counselor to the U.S. embassy in Moscow from 1944 to 1946, wrote an article for *Foreign Affairs* magazine, which was published without author identification in July 1947. He described Soviet leaders as aggressive dictators with expansionist aims. Kennan called for the United States to meet the Soviet threat by containing communism to certain geographical areas where the Soviet Union already had footholds. Eventually, communism would wither, Kennan postulated. He rejected Truman's call for a world struggle that would draw U.S. interests to every corner of the globe. Lippmann responded with a series of articles in the *Herald Tribune* in September that disputed Kennan's analysis and called for co-existence through recognized spheres of influence.[4] The resolution of U.S. foreign policy goals would not occur for two or three years to come, but the Kennan–Lippmann discussion set the stage for the national debate.

At the same time Marshall was planning to present his recovery plan, two separate, key developments occurred at *Time* and at the *Chronicle*. In the spring of 1947 the *Chronicle* changed its position and opposed any further accommodation with the Soviet Union. The newspaper had been drifting in that direction since the summer of 1946. One key influence on the editorial board was Kennan, who had stopped in San Francisco on his way back from Moscow to Washington. Kennan spent several hours with the editorial writers during his stopover, offering his evaluation of the Soviet regime. "We were impressed," recalled editorial writer Templeton Peck, adding that many of the editorial writers looked differently at the Soviet Union after the meeting with Kennan. Peck said agitation among guild members by communists had also turned many staff members away from the Soviet

Union. The rejection of the "Baruch Plan" for atomic controls seemed to be the final issue that caused the break in support for the Soviet Union.[5]

The *Chronicle* was the last news organization in this study to reject accommodation with the Soviet Union. Personal contact with Kennan had a great deal of impact. During this study, there were few instances of U.S. leaders directly influencing editorial policy by personal contact with editorial boards. Kennan's chance meeting with editors in San Francisco was an exception. As Appendix A indicates, news and editorial content concerning the Soviet Union was almost totally negative by September 1946, having changed drastically during the year. By late 1947 the few positive articles in any of the four publications were published in the *Herald Tribune* and *Time*, not in the *Chronicle*.

At *Time* a moderate change occurred in the relationship between the president and the magazine because of a change in staff. Edward B. Lockett, *Time* White House correspondent, resigned. Bureau Chief Robert T. Elson wrote to John S. Billings, Time, Inc., editorial director, in March 1947 that he had learned that Lockett had misled editors about the atmosphere in the White House. Elson said part of the hostility between Lockett and Truman resulted from Lockett's story in June 1946 about the Hardrock Club and Truman's excursions with reporters. Elson added that he had learned that Lockett had agitated Truman in other ways and the president would not even speak to Lockett in private, though he answered his questions at press conferences. Elson noted that much of the animosity from the White House was directed toward *Time* generally, because of the magazine's opposition to administration policies. Elson predicted that the relationship between *Time* and the president would only improve slightly, but he added that editors no longer would be misled about the extent to which Truman had severed relations with the magazine.[6]

Individual personalities did influence the news flow from the White House, but overall the magazine's philosophy brought a cold response from the White House. The president's tendency to speak forthrightly and punish his enemies while rewarding his friends continued to erode press relations throughout 1947 and into 1948. Most of the nation's newspapers and news magazines aligned against the administration and gleefully, but incorrectly, predicted a Thomas E. Dewey landslide in the 1948 presidential election. The deteriorating press relations again hindered the flow of news and reporting of foreign affairs.

Marshall still had to deal with the situation in Europe, and his recovery plan helped to soothe much of the concern in the United States over a lack of movement on the problem in Europe. Not only had Marshall created the impression that the United States stood ready to act forcefully, but he generated support and praise from European leaders, who emphasized the humanitarian aspects of the plan. Who could oppose a plan to feed and shelter the victims of war and to prop up economically unstable countries lying in the path of onrushing communism?

With the exception of the xenophobic *Chicago Tribune*, the news organizations applauded Marshall's proposals. Walter Lippmann wrote, "Such a program will not be a dole, but an investment in working capital that makes Europe self-supporting and solvent."[7] Joseph and Stewart Alsop observed that the Marshall Plan was the only way to keep communism from "wrecking the economies of Western Europe."[8] The *Herald Tribune* called the plan the "most stimulating idea in the field of international affairs since the end of the war."[9] The aim of the plan, *Time* noted, was not to continue to pour more money into Europe, but to make an investment that would allow Europeans to become self-sufficient.[10]

The magazine took care to leave the impression that the Republicans had as much to do with the Marshall Plan as the Democrats. *Time* published a two-page column written by Republican Senator Styles Bridges, of New Hampshire, the chairman of the Senate Appropriations Committee. Bridges supported the Marshall Plan. Such an extraordinary amount of space was usually reserved for the most important stories of the day.[11]

The *Chronicle*'s new policy of criticism of the Soviet Union was vented in discussion of the Marshall Plan. The newspaper observed that Soviet resistance to the proposal proved that Soviet leaders never wanted a reconstructed Europe in the first place. The Marshall Plan had "forced them to confess to it," the *Chronicle* editorialized.[12]

Chicago Tribune opposition to the Marshall Plan centered on fiscal concerns. In an editorial that carefully explained many points of concern with the concept of aid for economic recovery, the *Chicago Tribune* cited opposition by former president Herbert Hoover. Hoover wrote to Bridges urging the senator not to succumb to such an open-ended plan. The newspaper agreed saying the $6 billion in aid would be just a beginning. "It is time to tell the world to go to work. Only ruin is in it for ourselves if we try to carry them on the dole any longer," the newspaper concluded.[13] The *Chicago Tribune* wanted no part of an international plan to fight communism. The Soviet Union had to be opposed by each nation individually marshaling its own financial resources.

Marshall had not consulted with Stalin or any of the Soviet leaders in developing the Marshall Plan. Obviously, with a mandate from the president and seeing nothing but frustration at the Moscow Conference, Marshall decided that only an independent course of action would resolve the problem. The Hungarian coup only provided additional support for this conviction.[14]

In July 1947 the United States and fifteen other nations met in Paris to map strategy for implementing the Marshall Plan. The Soviet Union declined to attend, and so did the Eastern bloc countries. Czechoslovakia had announced it would participate but withdrew after Foreign Minister Jan Masaryk met with Stalin in Moscow.

Did the Marshall Plan unnecessarily drive another wedge between the United States and the Soviet Union? By this time most Americans had conceded there was little hope for accommodation with the Soviet Union.[15] But none of the news organizations even raised the question of the propriety of such an independent course of action. The well of goodwill toward the Soviet Union had run dry, and none of the opinion leaders even considered good relations with the Soviet Union as important. The Marshall Plan may have been a final blow to Soviet–U.S. relations, but that idea was not reflected in the newspapers or *Time*. To the editors, the Marshall Plan represented only a magnanimous gesture on the part of the United States. Soviet opposition clearly represented obstructionism.

II

In the months after World War II Kennan wrote often to State Department officials about what he saw as a growing Soviet menace in Europe. Kennan believed that the totalitarian nature of Soviet communism imperiled U.S. democracy merely by its presence in the world and that Soviet leaders had always harbored desires to dominate Europe. Kennan felt U.S. policy makers were not fully aware of Soviet designs. He feared Americans would awaken too late to the red tide sweeping over the world. He spoke privately with editors and reporters, as he had in San Francisco, urging opinion makers to be alert to Soviet aggression. In July his article appeared, and he was soon identified as the author. The article was republished in *Life* magazine a few weeks later.

Kennan spent much of the article explaining the historical influence that caused Marxist leaders to seek to subvert capitalism. He wrote: "Now the maintenance of this pattern of Soviet power, namely the pursuit of unlimited authority domestically, accompanied by the cultivation of the semi-myth of implacable foreign hostility, has gone far to shape the actual machinery of Soviet power as we know it today."[16] Kennan warned that U.S. efforts to influence Soviet foreign policy were useless because Marxist doctrine precluded listening to "glib persuasiveness from the outside world."[17] He concluded, "In these circumstances it is clear that the main element of any United States policy toward the Soviet Union must be that of a long-term, patient but firm vigilant containment of Russian expansive tendencies."[18]

Immediate discussion of the article focused on Kennan's warnings about Soviet conduct. Only months and years later did U.S. opinion leaders probe the policies that Kennan advocated—namely avoidance of global commitments to confront communism at every turn. Kennan advocated containing communism and allowing Soviet dominance to wither by the flaws of its own system. This philosophy would be rejected in 1949 by the Council on Foreign Affairs, a civilian advisory body with great influence on the State Department. The council's proposition received reinforcement with the invasion of South Korea in 1950. Kennan did not foresee the Korean War, but he realized Truman had set the nation on a course that would be costly and traumatizing. Often in the years that followed, Kennan spoke against interpretations that used his article as a justification for all-out military commitments to anticommunist crusades.[19]

Lippmann saw the Kennan piece as a challenge, and the New York columnist responded. In June 1947 the *Herald Tribune* announced that Lippmann would take an indefinite vacation from writing his column.[20] The long-time *Herald Tribune* columnist did not take a respite, but instead worked feverishly in his apartment crafting a response to Kennan.[21] The result was a series of fourteen columns that appeared throughout the month of September. In these writings Lippmann first coined the phrase "Cold War," a description that U.S. journalists and historians would use for decades. Lippmann told his readers that because Kennan, as director of Policy Planning in the State Department, had written the article in *Foreign Affairs*, Lippmann treated the writing as a statement of U.S. policy.

Throughout the month-long discussion, Lippmann dissected the Kennan argument and attacked its foundations through ideological arguments and practical points of view. Kennan had underestimated the Soviet Union by predicting its system would wither, Lippmann told his readers.[22] The United States could not control its imports and exports in a way that would make containment feasible, Lippmann added. He pointed out that the U.S. people would not tolerate a military commitment that would place the military in defensive positions for long periods. The proper course of action was to resist a policy that abandoned diplomatic negotiation, because the Soviet Union was a nation with historical needs for expansion. Nothing could change that. The United States had to recognize the natural course of history, Lippmann concluded.[23]

Lippmann's and Kennan's differing outlooks sparked controversy, but it is hard to discern that from copies of other publications at the time. The force of Lippmann's arguments was contained in his own prestige and the weight of his syndicated column. Other newspapers in this study did not recognize the debate, probably owing to the competitive nature of the news business and to the consensus in favor of Kennan. *Time*, which frequently commented on other media, carried an article on the Lippmann series in mid-September. Lippmann's conclusions treaded on debatable ground, *Time* argued, because the "red Army was built by Marxist rulers" and Soviet aims were not the same as in the time of Peter the Great—Marxist Russia represented a "new-fashioned force."[24]

The Lippmann–Kennan debate brought to a close the period commonly described as the origins of the Cold War. In early 1948 Jan Masaryk was killed in Czechoslovakia, and a communist government was installed there. By the end of the year the Soviets had attempted to blockade West Berlin, and U.S. pilots were forced to provide supplies by airlift to keep the western part of the city functioning. U.S. policy makers formed a North Atlantic Treaty Organization in conjunction with Western Europe. The Soviet Union responded with an Eastern bloc alliance. The communist takeover in China and the invasion of South Korea by North Korean regular army troops dragged the Cold War into Asia. But the period when differences could have been minimized came in the two years after World War II. The failure to mitigate the rising differences would leave its imprint for decades to come.

The Lippmann–Kennan debate underlined the role of the news organizations and that of public opinion. Lippmann's series illustrates that in the United States there was room and need for editorial debate over foreign policy goals. Not enough of this occurred. That is not to say that the news organizations did not follow closely unfolding world events or that they failed to comment on these daily occurrences. However, there was no vigorous clamor for the Truman administration to work toward a reasonable postwar accommodation. The news organizations too often were bogged down in domestic politics and short-term foreign affairs considerations.

Secondly, it is clear that Lippmann had not altered his feelings toward the Soviet Union since the early 1940s. He had advocated in 1947 the same policies that he had supported in his discussion in 1944 for which William Hard, *Reader's Digest* roving editor, had criticized him. Lippmann had expressed his overview in perhaps more complete and eloquent terms in the fall of 1947, but throughout the war and afterward he had consistently urged the two nations to recognize regional hegemony. Conversely, the *Chicago Tribune*'s foreign affairs position did not change either, because one man, publisher Robert R. McCormick, advocated a conservative, ethnocentric ideology that never waivered. This single-minded view provided a predictable base for debate when analyzing various opinions on foreign affairs. Americans knew where Lippmann and McCormick stood.

The changing philosophy at *Time*, depending on Henry Luce's mood of the moment or Whittaker Chambers's degree of influence, could provide a varying array of opinions. Similarly, the shifting world events in 1946 and 1947 altered the house opinions at both the *Herald Tribune* and the *Chronicle*. This flexibility provided for open discussion at editorial board meetings and the ability to change with the discovery of new information. Less dogmatism led to fewer clumsy arguments. This left fewer uncomfortable corners from which there could be no escape. But at the same time, this democratic handling of editorial opinion could, at times, allow drastic shifts based on short-term assumptions and vacillation over matters of great import.

Finally, it is clear from the Lippmann–Kennan debate that the New York columnist had spoken forcefully but not effectively. His words came too late. Forces from within and without had pushed the country toward an antagonistic posture months before the debate. By the fall of 1947 Lippmann had been cast as a voice for a small minority. Henry Wallace, as a candidate of moderation in the 1948 presidential election, barely drew a million votes. Lippmann's eloquent words provided a foundation for discussion years later but did not carry much weight in 1947.

NOTES

1. See William Appleman Williams, *The Tragedy of American Diplomacy*, 2d rev. ed. (New York: Delta, 1972), 268–70. Williams sees the Truman speech not so much as an expression of conviction, but as a way in which the president was able to marshall public support. Williams sees this as an inevitable result of U.S. policies. See also Ronald Steel, *Pax Americana* (New York: Viking, 1967), 24–25. Steel sees this anticommunist crusade as an outcropping of insecurity at home among Americans. Walter LaFeber, *America, Russia and the Cold War, 1945–1980*, 4th rev.ed. (New York: John Wiley and Sons, 1980), 50–51, argued that Truman feared communist takeovers in Western Europe through legitimate elections.

2. "The Education of the Misters," *Time*, May 12, 1947, 22. See also "Conferences—Four Men on a Horse," *Time*, April 7, 1947, 24–25; "Moscow Parley Nears End—Marshall Lays Blame for Failure on Russia," *Chicago Tribune*, April 24, 1947,1; "Failure at Moscow," *Chicago Tribune* editorial, April 26, 1947, 8; "Big Four Treaty Failure Called 'Most Depressing Development Since War,' " *San Francisco Chronicle*, April 16, 1947, 1; Walter Lippmann column, "Today and Tomorrow," *Herald Tribune*, May 1, 1947, 25; and "Big Four Fail to Lessen Gap," *Herald Tribune*, April 21, 1947, 1.

3. See especially "U.S. to Protest Soviet Coup in Hungary," *New York Herald Tribune*, June 2, 1947, 1.

4. X, "The Sources of Soviet Conduct," *Foreign Affairs*, July 1947, 566–82; Lippmann column, "Today and Tomorrow," *Herald Tribune*, articles appearing from September 2, 1947, to October 2, 1947. Also see Ronald Steel, *Walter Lippmann and the American Century* (Boston: Little, Brown, 1960). For background on the Marshall Plan, see especially John Gimbel, *The Origins of the Marshall Plan* (Stanford, Calif.: Stanford University Press, 1976); Charles L. Mee, *The Marshall Plan: The Launching of the Pax Americana* (New York: Simon and Schuster,1984); Stanley Hoffman and Charles Maier, eds., *The Marshall Plan: A Retrospective* (Boulder, Colo.: Westview Press,1984); Douglas Batting, *The Aftermath: Europe* (Alexandria, Va.: Time-Life, 1983).

5. Templeton Peck telephone interview, March 27, 1985.

6. Robert T. Elson memorandum to John S. Billings, March 15, 1947, 1–2, John Shaw Billings Papers, Box 1. Caroliniana Library, Manuscripts Division, Billings Collection, University of South Carolina, Columbia, South Carolina.

7. Lippmann column, "Today and Tomorrow," *Herald Tribune*, June 28, 1947, 13.

8. Joseph Alsop and Stewart Alsop column, "Matter of Fact," June 11, 1947, 26.

9. "The Marshall Plan Grows," *Herald Tribune* editorial, June 17, 1947, 18.

10. "Conferences—How to Use a Checkbook," *Time*, July 7, 1974, 23.

11. Styles Bridges, "What Price Peace?" *Time*, July 21, 1947, 24–25.

12. "A Blueprint for Two Worlds," *Chronicle* editorial, July 1, 1947, 18.

13. "Taxing Americans to Support Europe," *Chicago Tribune* editorial, June 18, 1947, 18.

14. For a conservative view on the Marshall Plan, see Henry W. Berger, "A Conservative Critique of Containment: Senator Taft on the Early Cold War Program," in *Containment and Revolution*, ed. David Horowitz (Boston: Beacon, 1969), 133. Many historians see the Marshall Plan as a natural outcropping of the Truman Doctrine, not as a primarily humanitarian effort. See LaFeber, *America, Russia and the Cold War*, 59; Joyce Kolko and Gabriel Kolko, *The Limits of Power: The World and United States Foreign Policy, 1945–1954* (New York: Harper and Row, 1972), 359–61; Gimbel, *The Origins of the Marshall Plan*; Williams, *The Tragedy of American Diplomacy*, 270–71.

15. A Gallup poll taken in February 1947 found that Americans surveyed wanted Marshall to be firmer with the Soviet Union than Byrnes had been. The margin was 51 to 19. In July a poll found that about half the Americans surveyed had heard of the Marshall Plan, and of those who had heard of it, the plan received an approval rating of 57 to 21. George H. Gallup, *The Gallup Poll: Public Opinion 1935–1971*, vol. 1 (New York: Random House, 1972), 628, 661.

16. X, "The Sources of Soviet Conduct," *Foreign Affairs*, July 1947, 571.

17. X, "The Sources of Soviet Conduct," 574.

18. X, "The Sources of Soviet Conduct," 575.

19. Lloyd C. Gardner contends that Kennan's article was a way of expressing his ideas so that such men as Secretary of Defense James Forrestal could understand them. The author also sees it as a way of placing the argument in a forum that the public could understand. See Lloyd C. Gardner, "Architects of Illusion," in *America and the Origins of the Cold War*, ed. James Compton (Boston: Houghton Mifflin, 1972), 120–21; also see for additional insight Williams, *The Tragedy of American Diplomacy*, 268. Williams sees the Kennan philosophy as an internalization of the Open Door policy. Also consult Ronald Steel's introduction in Walter Lippmann, *The Cold War*, rev. ed. (New York: Harper and Row, 1972), vii–xvii.

20. Lippmann column, "Today and Tomorrow," *Herald Tribune*, June 28, 1947, 13.

21. Steel, *Walter Lippmann and the American Century*, 432; "Foreign Relations—Lippmann's 'Cold War,' " *Time*, September 22, 1947, 22–23.

22. Lippmann column, "Today and Tomorrow," *Herald Tribune*, September 2, 1947, 25.

23. Lippmann column, "Today and Tomorrow," October 2, 1947, 25.

24. "Foreign Relations—Lippmann's 'Cold War,' " *Time*, September 22, 1947, 23.

Epilogue

This study points up several conclusions about the press and the origins of the Cold War. First, the evidence provides a platform that rejects the inevitability themes of such writers as William Appleman Williams, Gabriel Kolko, and Gar Alperovitz. Certain underlying historical, economic, and ideological forces were at work from 1944 to 1947 and undeniably formed the basis for the Cold War. However, examination of the four publications in this study suggests that a failure to influence writers and editors contributed to a lack of communication.

Ample editorial sympathy existed in the United States for the Soviet Union in 1944 and 1945, and Truman did not take a hard-nosed approach toward the Soviet Union upon taking office. He changed his mind after continual Soviet intransigence forced his hand. Additionally, dramatic speeches by Winston Churchill and Henry Wallace followed by a resounding defeat at the polls brought pressure from the right.

Secondly, press is a misnomer often mistakenly applied to news organizations, in general. There is no such entity as a monolithic press where foreign affairs goals and ideas are concerned. Each of the news organizations in this study dealt with the origins of the Cold War in individual ways, based on their overall philosophies, personnel, and knowledge or lack of knowledge of the inner governmental circle. It is conceivable, for instance, that the *San Francisco Chronicle* may have been less susceptible to the influence of the Truman Doctrine or George F. Kennan's personal urgings, if the newspaper had a correspondent in Washington privy to the discussions among Cabinet members and in the White House. Whittaker Chambers's position as *Time* foreign affairs editor certainly had an impact on *Time* articles at a crucial juncture.

Certain uniform responses can be assigned to the news organizations at particular times. Editors all reacted to war with horror, to national importance with pride and certain home-grown biases, to plans for peace with receptiveness, and to news blackouts with suspicion. But these collective reactions usually were short-lived and did not reflect the overall inclinations of the newspapers or news magazine, unless a long-term pattern evolved.

It would be simple to discount the shrill ideological diatribes of the *Chicago Tribune*, for instance, but much of what the *Chicago Tribune* espoused came to be U.S. policy in the late 1940s and 1950s. Conservatives always had a major forum in the *Chicago Tribune*, and the continued presence of such philosophy had to be a reinforcing mechanism for midwestern readers, especially when other factors eventually made an anti-Soviet mood popular.

If Ralph Levering, Walter LaFeber, and Lester Markel are correct and readers tend to be ignorant of foreign affairs, it is also true that they look to news organizations to watch such developments for them. When major news events occur, these images stay with readers, and repeated exposure to conservative or liberal philosophies as espoused in newspapers and news magazines can have lasting subliminal effects as well. Kolko's dismissal of public opinion as a factor and LaFeber's and Levering's arguments that Truman led popular opinion during the 1945 and 1947 period are only partly true. Kolko places too little emphasis on the weight of popular sentiment in an open society, and Levering and LaFeber generalize too much about the Truman administration. As was noted in Chapters 9 and 10, LaFeber's and Levering's observations are correct for the period after March 1947, but a different climate existed prior to the Truman Doctrine.

Thirdly, it would seem from examination of the newspapers and magazine in this study that the editors and reporters reacted after foreign policy goals had been established. They were not on the cutting edge of foreign policy decisions. Largely, this was a reflection of their uncertainties and puzzlement over Soviet attitudes. They reacted with surprise, consternation, and then angry resolution. Only the *Chicago Tribune* could claim steady opposition to any Soviet–U.S. accord.

During the first few years after World War II, opinion makers added up the events around them and, as the negative evidence mounted, decided that the world had divided into two camps. How these opinion leaders obtained their evidence varied from staff to staff, but certainly part of the problem was that neither government provided all the evidence needed.

The news organizations, then, did not directly influence the origins of the Cold War and, by implication, neither did news organizations across the country. Indirectly, they did. By devoting attention to failures of diplomacy—the Moscow Conference in 1947, the London Ministers Conference in the fall of 1945, and the San Francisco Conference of the spring of 1945—and Soviet incursions into Iran and Greece, they fueled a negative image. These were stories, but so were the suffering of the Soviet people and the positive effects of a restrained Soviet approach in 1946. A strong outpouring of editorial support for moderate policies could have created doubts at the policy-making level. Certainly, on the other hand, the paucity of such editorial discussion had the opposite effect.

What were the factors that contributed to this rapid shift and subsequent loss of goodwill between the United States and the Soviet Union? Why would Eddie Gilmore's charade at a Seattle nightclub have brought jeers and shouts in 1947, instead of the applause and cheers in 1943? Two nations were unable even to communicate their goals and find common solutions, and that communication could have made a difference.

The Soviet Union captured headlines throughout the war by virtue of the acts and deeds of its soldiers. When the war ended, the images changed and so did the perceptions of U.S. readers. The occupation of Germany, for instance, created negative headlines, where the defeat of Germany had stirred fervent support. It was the same Germany and the same Red Army, but Nazism had been vanquished and losses sustained by the conquerors were diminished by reinterpretations of the aims of Soviet leaders. This suggests the news organizations felt empathy for actions, not people, for reasons of self-interest. Three of the news organizations believed that the Soviet Union could be a friendly partner in the postwar world, but obviously with little conviction.

Because the news organizations in this study were controlled by wealthy entrepreneurs, it is likely that they would have found communism at least as reprehensible as did the man on the street. Such distaste had its origins decades before the Cold War and stood as a natural barrier to mutual accommodation. In the same vein, it would seem natural that U.S. editors and reporters primarily would see the U.S. point of view. With the two countries clearly rising as the most powerful forces on earth, it would seem natural that mutual antagonism would develop.

But the reflections in the newspapers and magazine were not that simple. With the exception of the *Chicago Tribune*, they looked beyond those natural barriers and in 1944 and 1945 hoped for mutual understanding. The *Herald Tribune* and *Chronicle* particularly held out for some kind of accommodation, carefully analyzing every occurrence as another bit of evidence.

Truman found little time for editors and publishers. The president rejected even minimal courtesies, refusing to press his point of view, except in official statements and in discussion with working reporters. His administration did not carefully lead news organizations in the months after World War II as LaFeber contends, but instead waited for diplomacy to take its course.

Stalin and his Kremlin advisers remained silent, unless provoked to issue propaganda statements through official sources in Moscow. The Soviets knew how to influence U.S. public opinion and had worked hard to do so during the war, when Soviet leaders desperately wanted Western Allies to open a second front in Europe. Once the war had ended, Stalin and his advisers pulled into a shell of suspicion and propaganda, acting with indifference and disdain toward the U.S. news organizations. *Tass* reporters attacked in print the Western press soon after the war ended. Even a minor event such as a visit by Soviet war hero, Marshall Zhukov, to New York in the fall of 1945 was canceled for no apparent reason. Soviet leaders had no interest in influencing U.S. opinion.

This refusal to cultivate U.S. periodicals and their readers became more of a factor in 1946 when a restrained Soviet foreign policy received no acclaim in U.S. newspapers and magazines. Truman's brusque approach to news reporters and Stalin's distrust left nothing but negative images with U.S. readers. The differences between the two countries were not nearly so insurmountable as readers were led to believe.

Finally, the news organizations came to accept the inevitability of the Cold War because right-wing elements in the United States had a stronger case to make and made their case better. The British also seized upon U.S. bewilderment to push the United States away from the Soviet Union. Churchill's speech at Fulton was a brilliant piece of rhetoric, which galvanized the country. The Henry Wallace debacle and the Republicans' ability to capitalize on the confusion shifted public opinion further and cornered Truman. The announced British pullout in Greece forced the president's hand.

U.S. news institutions are powerful vehicles of public opinion. How those organizations are influenced and how they perceive foreign developments can have an effect on policy in open societies. The direction of foreign affairs can often ebb and flow depending on the perceptions of opinion leaders and their abilities to seek out and understand daily occurrences. What elements affect news organizations both from within and without can be a complexity in itself, and no single person, no one speech, and no individual incident can be a deciding factor. It is not the intention here to make definitive statements about all of the reporting in the United States at this time. This study was confined to four specific news groups. However, the findings here do suggest that opinion makers and images in print played a greater role than most historians of this era have conceded. A voluminous study of several hundred periodicals in an encyclopedic gathering of information would likely demonstrate even more the power of news organizations in foreign affairs at this time. What this examination shows is that the origins of the Cold War came from a variety of complex historical and political factors, but dialogue concerning these factors often was negligible or tardy. The Cold War resulted from failed policy, but at the same time, these four news organizations failed to encourage an agenda for discussion.

Appendix

Dates	S.F. Chronicle NEWS pro	NEWS con	EDIT pro	EDIT con	N.Y. Herald Tribune NEWS pro	NEWS con	EDIT pro	EDIT con	Chicago Tribune NEWS pro	NEWS con	EDIT pro	EDIT con	Time NEWS pro	NEWS con
3/44	52	0	12	0	48	16	8	0	31	9	2	6	7	3
9/44	36	1	5	1	46	12	4	0	30	5	0	4	4	0
3/45	27	0	5	1	36	3	9	0	31	23	0	10	4	4
9/45	8	7	0	2	9	19	3	3	4	20	0	4	0	6
3/46	23	67	4	6	27	90	0	18	0	64	0	4	3	10
9/46	1	22	0	12	12	69	3	18	1	32	0	6	1	8
3/47	6	46	2	8	9	42	2	12	2	42	0	10	1	6
9/47	0	31	0	8	6	28	2	17	0	24	0	6	2	9
TOTALS	153	174	28	38	193	279	31	68	99	219	2	50	22	46

The following chart lists sample articles that appeared in the three newspapers and the news magazine in this study in connection with the Soviet Union during the years 1944 through 1947. The news items are catalogued as to whether they were substantially favorable or unfavorable to the Soviet Union and as to whether they were news or editorial in content.

154

Selected Bibliography

ARTICLES

Abelson, Robert. "Computers, Polls and Public Opinion—Some Puzzles and Paradoxes." *Transaction* 5 (September 1968): 20–27.

Adler, Les K., and Thomas G. Paterson. " 'Red Fascism': The Merger of Nazi Germany and Soviet Russia in the American Image of Totalitarianism, 1930s–1950s." *American Historical Review* 75 (1970): 1046–64.

Ambrose, Stephen. "Some Like It Cold." *New York Review* 17 (November 18, 1971): 41–43.

Angell, R. C.; V. S. Durham; and J. D. Singer. "Social Values and Foreign Policy Attitudes of Soviet and American Elites." *Journal of Conflict Resolution* 8 (1964): 329–41.

Bagdikian, Ben. "The Chronicle Chronicles." *San Francisco Magazine* (May 1982): 64–72.

Blankenburg, William, and Ruth Walden. "Objectivity, Interpretation and Economy in Reporting." *Journalism Quarterly* 54 (Autumn 1977): 591–95.

Boyer, John H. "How Editors View Objectivity." *Journalism Quarterly* 58 (Spring 1981): 24–28.

Carynnyk, Marco. "The Famine the *Times* Couldn't Find." *Commentary* 77 (November 1983): 356–58.

Cashman, Greg, and Arthur N. Gilbert. "Some Analytical Approaches to the Cold War Debate." *History Teacher* 10 (February 1977): 263–80.

"Characteristics of the Reading Audiences of *Newsweek, Time,* and *U.S. News and World Report.*" *Advertising Age* 31 (February 15, 1960): 36.

Eduard, Mark. " 'Today Has Been a Historical One': Harry S. Truman's Diary of the Potsdam Conference," *Diplomatic History* 4 (1980): 317–26.

Erskine, Hazel G. "The Cold War: Report from the Polls." *Public Opinion Quarterly* 25 (Summer 1961): 300–15.

Fedler, Fred; Mike Meeske; and Joe Hall. "*Time* Magazine Revisited: Presidential Stereotypes Persist." *Journalism Quarterly* 56 (Summer 1979): 353–59.

Feis, Herbert. "The Secret that Traveled to Potsdam." *Foreign Affairs* 38 (1960): 300–17.

Ferrell, Robert H. "Truman at Potsdam." *American Heritage* 31 (1980): 36–47.

Fuller, Daniel J., and T. Michael Ruddy. "Myth in Progress: Harry Truman and the Meeting at Potsdam." *American Studies* 18 (1977): 99–106.

Gaddis, John L. "Was the Truman Doctrine a Real Turning Point?" *Foreign Affairs* 52 (January 1974): 386–402.

———. "Containment: A Reassessment." *Foreign Affairs* 55 (July 1977): 873–87.

Gamson, William A., and Andre Modigliani. "Knowledge and Foreign Policy Opinions: Some Models for Consideration." *Public Opinion Quarterly* 30 (Summer 1966): 187–99.

Glazer, Renina Migdal. "From the Old Left to the New: Radical Criticism in the 1940s." *American Quarterly* 24 (December 1972): 584–603.

Hopkins, George E. "Bombing and the American Conscience during World War II." *Historian* 28 (May 1966): 451–73.

Jiggs, Gardner. "*Time*, the Weekly Fiction Magazine." *Nation* 189 (August 15,1959): 65–67.

Kennan, George F. "The Sources of Soviet Conduct." *Foreign Affairs* 25 (July 1947): 566–67.

Kriesberg, Martin. "Soviet News in the *New York Times*." *Public Opinion Quarterly* 10 (1946): 540–63.

———. "Cross Pressure and Attitudes: A Study of the Influence of Conflicting Propaganda Opinions Regarding American-Soviet Relations." *Public Opinion Quarterly* 13 (Spring 1949): 5–16.

Ledeen, Michael. "Public Opinion, Press Opinion, and Foreign Policy." *Public Opinion Quarterly* 7 (August/September 1984): 5–7.

Leigh, Michael. "Is There a Revisionist Theory on the Origins of the Cold War?" *Political Science Quarterly* 89 (March 1974): 101–16.

Maddox, Robert J. "Harry S. Truman's Early Months in the White House." *American History Illustrated* 7 (1972): 12–22.

Maddux, Thomas R. "American News Media and Soviet Diplomacy, 1934–41." *Journalism Quarterly* 58 (Spring 1981): 29–37.

Mee, Charles L.; W. Averell Harriman; and Elie Abel. "Who Started the Cold War?" *American Heritage* 28 (August 1, 1977): 8–23.

Merrill, John C. "How *Time* Stereotyped Three U.S. Presidents." *Journalism Quarterly* 42 (Autumn 1965): 563–70.

Nagorski, Zygmunt. "The Potsdam Conference: Two Viewpoints." *Polish Review* 6 (1961): 108–16.

Page, Benjamin I., and Robert Y. Shapiro. "Effects of Public Opinion on Policy." *American Political Science Review* 77 (March 1983): 175–90.

Paterson, Thomas G. "Potsdam, the Atomic Bomb, and the Cold War: A Discussion with James P. Byrnes." *Pacific History Review* 42 (1972): 225–30.

Patterson, David S. "Recent Literature on Cold War Origins: An Essay Review." *Wisconsin Magazine of History* 60 (Summer 1972): 320–29.

Perkins, Bradford. "The Tragedy of American Diplomacy: Twenty-five Years After." *Reviews in American History* 14 (March 1984): 1–15.

Quester, George H. "Origins of the Cold War: Some Clues from Public Opinion." *Political Science Quarterly* 93 (Winter 1978–79): 647–63.

"Recollections of Henry R.Luce." *Fortune,* 75: 4 (April 1967).

Reinhardt, Richard. "Doesn't Everybody Hate the Chronicle?" *Columbia Journalism Review* 20 (January–February 1982): 25–32.

Rogers, William C.; Barbara Stuhler; and Donald Koenig. "A Comparison of Informed and General Public Opinion on U.S. Foreign Policy." *Public Opinion Quarterly* 31 (Summer 1967): 242–52.

Schlesinger, Arthur, M., Jr. "Letters." *New York Review* 7 (October 20, 1966): 22–25.

———. "The Origins of the Cold War." *Foreign Affairs* 46 (October 1967): 23–56.

Shaplen, Robert. "Denson's Revolution at the *Herald Tribune.*" *Saturday Review.* 44 (July 8, 1961): 36–38.

Simmons, George E. "The 'Cold War' in Large City Dailies of the U.S." *Journalism Quarterly* 25 (December 1948): 354–59, 400.

Smith, M. Brewster. "The Personal Setting of Public Opinions: A Study of Attitudes toward Russia." *Public Opinion Quarterly* 11 (Winter 1947): 507–23.

Steel, Ronald. "Did Anyone Start the Cold War?" *New York Review* 17 (September 2, 1971): 23–28.

———. "The Power and Old Glory." *New York Review* 20 (May 31, 1973): 29–34.

———. "The Good Old Days." *New York Review* 20 (June 19, 1973): 33–36.

Villa, Brian. "The U.S. Army, Unconditional Surrender, and the Potsdam Proclamation." *Journal of American History* 63 (June 1976): 66–92.

Wagner, R. Harrison. "The Decision to Divide Germany and the Origins of the Cold War." *International Studies Quarterly* 24 (June 1980): 155–90.

Walsh, Warren B. "What the American People Think of Russia." *Public Opinion Quarterly* 8 (1944): 513–22.

Warner, Geoffrey. "The United States and the Origins of the Cold War." *International Affairs* 46 (1970): 529–44.

White, Ralph K. "Hitler, Roosevelt, and the Nature of War Propaganda." *Journal of Abnormal Psychology* 44 (April 1949): 157–74.

Wooley, Wesley T., Jr. "The Quest for Permanent Peace—American Supernationalism, 1945–47." *Historian* 35 (November 1972): 18–31.

Yavenditti, Michael J. "John Hersey and the American Conscience: The Reception of 'Hiroshima.' " *Pacific Historical Review* 43 (1974): 24–79.

———. "The American People and the Use of Atomic Bombs on Japan," *Historian* 36 (February 1974): 224–47.

BOOKS

Adler, Ruth, ed. *The Working Press: Special to the New York Times.* New York: Harper and Row, 1949.

Adorno, Theodore W. *The Authoritative Personality.* New York: Harper and Row, 1950.

Agar, Herbert. *The Price of Power: America Since 1945.* Chicago: University of Chicago Press, 1957.

Almond, Gabriel A. *The American People and Foreign Policy.* New York: Harcourt Brace, 1950.

Alperovitz, Gar. *Cold War Essays.* Garden City, N.J.: Anchor, 1970.

Alsop, Joseph, and Stewart Alsop. *The Reporter's Trade.* New York: Reynal, 1958.

Ambrose, Stephen E. *Rise to Globalism: American Foreign Policy, 1938–1976*, rev. ed. New York: Penguin, 1976.

Anderson, Terry H. *The United States, Great Britain and the Cold War, 1944–1947.* Columbia, Mo.: University of Missouri Press, 1984.

Aronson, James. *The Press and the Cold War.* Indianapolis: Bobbs-Merrill, 1970.

Bagby, William. *The Road to Normalcy.* Baltimore: The Johns Hopkins University Press, 1962.

Bailey, Thomas A. *The Marshall Plan Summer: An Eyewitness Report on Europe and the Russians in 1947.* Stanford: Hoover Institution Press, 1977.

Balfour, Michael L. G. *The Adversaries: America, Russia and the Open World, 1941– 62.* Boston: Routlege, 1981.

Barland, Harriet. *Soviet Literary Theory and Practice during the First Five-Year Plan, 1928–1932.* New York: Greenwood Press, 1969.

Beal, John R. *Marshall in China.* Garden City, N.J.: Doubleday, 1970.

Berger, Meyer. *The Story of the New York Times, 1851–1951.* New York: Simon and Schuster, 1970.

Bernstein, Barton, and Allen Matusow, eds. *The Truman Administration: A Documentary History.* New York: Harper and Row, 1966.

Best, James F. *Public Opinion: Micro and Macro.* Homewood, Ill.: Dorsey, 1973.

Borg, Dorothy, and Waldo Heinrichs, eds. *Uncertain Years: Chinese-American Relations, 1947–1950.* New York: Columbia University Press, 1980.

Borisov, O. B., and B. T. Koloskov. *Soviet-Chinese Relations, 1945–1970.* Bloomington: Indiana University Press, 1974.

Botting, Douglas. *The Aftermath: Europe.* Alexandria, Va.: Time-Life, 1983.

Brandt, Conrad. *Stalin's Failure in China, 1924–1927.* Cambridge, Mass.: Harvard University, 1958.

Brehm, J. W., and Arthur R. Cohen. *Explorations in Cognitive Dissonance.* New York: John Wiley and Sons, 1962.

Brockriede, Wayne, and Robert L. Scott. *Moments in the Rhetoric of the Cold War.* New York: Random House, 1970.

Byrnes, James F. *Speaking Frankly.* New York: Harper and Brothers, 1947.

———. *All in One Lifetime.* New York: Harper and Brothers, 1958.

Calvocoressi, Peter. *World Politics Since 1945.* London: Longman, 1982.

Callahan, Raymond A. *Churchill: Retreat from Empire.* Wilmington, Del.: Scholarly Resources, 1984.

Cantril, Hadley. *Gauging Public Opinion.* Princeton, N.J.: Princeton University Press, 1944.

———. *Soviet Leaders and Mastery over Man.* New Brunswick, N.J.: Rutgers University Press, 1960.

———. *Public Opinion 1935–1946.* Princeton, N.J.: Princeton University Press, 1951.

Cary, Francine Curro. *The Influence of War on Walter Lippmann, 1914–1944.* Madison: University of Wisconsin Press, 1967.

Chamberlain, John. *A Life with the Printed Word.* Chicago: Regnery Gateway, 1982.

Chambers, Whittaker. *Witness.* New York: Random House, 1952.

Churchill, Winston S. *Triumph and Tragedy.* Boston: Houghton Mifflin, 1953.

Clemens, Diane Shaver. *Yalta.* New York: Oxford University Press, 1970.

Cochran, Bert. *Harry Truman and the Crisis Presidency.* New York: Funk and Wagnalls, 1973.

Cohen, Bernard C. *The Press and Foreign Policy.* Princeton, N.J.: Princeton University Press, 1963.

Cole, Hugh Marshall. *The Ardennes: Battle of the Bulge.* Washington, D.C.: U.S. Government Printing Office, 1965.

Collier, Richard. *The Freedom Road, 1944–45.* New York: Atheneum, 1984.

Combs, Jerald A., ed. *Nationalist, Realist and Radical: Three Views of American Diplomacy.* New York: Harper and Row, 1972.

Compton, James V. *America and the Origins of the Cold War.* Boston: Houghton Mifflin, 1972.

Cornwell, Elmer E., Jr. *Presidential Leadership of Public Opinion.* Bloomington: Indiana University Press, 1956.

Crabb, Cecil V. *American Foreign Policy in the Nuclear Age.* New York: Harper and Row, 1983.

Crowl, James William. *Angels in Stalin's Paradise: Western Reporters in Soviet Russia, 1917 to 1937, A Case Study of Louis Fischer and Walter Duranty.* Washington, D.C.: University Press of America, 1982.

Culbert, David H. *News for Everyman: Radio and Foreign Affairs in Thirties America.* Westport, Conn.: Greenwood Press, 1976.

Czistrom, Daniel. *Media and the American Mind: From Morse to McLuhan.* Chapel Hill: University of North Carolina Press, 1982.

Davies, Joseph E. *Mission to Moscow.* New York: Simon and Schuster, 1941.

Dean, Vera Micheles. *The Four Cornerstones of Peace.* New York: McGraw Hill, 1946.

Desmond, Robert W. *The Press and World Affairs.* New York: Arno, 1972.

Dinerstein, Herbert S. *Fifty Years of Soviet Foreign Policy.* Baltimore: The Johns Hopkins University Press, 1968.

Dinsmore, Herman H. *All the News That Fits: A Critical Analysis of the News and Editorial Contents of the New York Times.* New Rochelle, N Y,: Arlington House, 1969.

Divine, Robert A. *The Reluctant Belligerent: America's Entry into World War II.* New York: John Wiley and Sons, 1965.

———. *Foreign Policy and U.S. Presidential Elections, 1940–1948.* New York: New Viewpoints, 1974.

Doenecke, Justus D. *The Literature of Isolationism: A Guide to Non-Interventionist Scholarship, 1930–1972.* Colorado Springs: Ralph Myles, 1972.

Donnelly, Desmond. *Struggles for the World: The Cold War and Its Causes.* London: Collins, 1965.

Donovan, Robert J. *Conflict and Crisis: The Presidency of Harry S. Truman 1945–1948.* New York: W. W. Norton, 1977.

Druks, Herbert. *Truman and the Russians.* New York: Robert Speller and Sons, 1981.

Edwards, Jerome E. *The Foreign Policy of Col. McCormick's Tribune, 1929–1941.* Reno: University of Nevada Press, 1971.

Ekrich, Arthur A., Jr. *The Decline of American Liberalism.* New York: Atheneum, 1967.

Elson, Robert T. *Time, Inc.: The Intimate History of a Publishing Enterprise,* vols. 1 and 2. New York: Atheneum, 1968, 1973.

Emery, Edwin, and Michael Emery. *The Press and America: An Interpretative History of the Mass Media*, 4th ed. Englewood Cliffs, N.J.: Prentice-Hall, 1978.

Farrar, Ronald T. *Reluctant Servant: The Story of Charles G. Ross*. Columbia: University of Missouri Press, 1969.

Feis, Herbert. *Between War and Peace: The Potsdam Conference*. Princeton, N.J.: Princeton University Press, 1957.

———. *Churchill, Roosevelt, Stalin: The War They Waged and the Peace They Sought*. Princeton, N.J.: Princeton University Press, 1957.

———. *The China Tangle: The American Effort in China from Pearl Harbor to the Marshall Mission*. Princeton, N.J.: Princeton University Press, 1967.

———. *From Trust to Terror: The Onset of the Cold War*. Princeton, N.J.: Princeton University Press, 1970.

Ferrell, Robert H., ed. *The Autobiography of Harry S. Truman*. Boulder: Colorado Associated University Press, 1980.

Filene, Peter G., ed. *American Views of Soviet Russia, 1917–1965*. Homewood, Ill.: Dorsey Press, 1957.

Fleming, D. F. *The Cold War and Its Origins, 1917–1960*. Garden City, N.J.: Doubleday, 1961.

Fontaine, Andre. *The History of the Cold War*. New York: Pantheon, 1968.

Ford, Edwin H., and Edwin Emery. *Highlights in the History of the American Press*. Minneapolis: University of Minnesota Press, 1954.

Free, Lloyd A., and Hadley Cantril. *The Political Beliefs of Americans: A Study of Public Opinion*. New Brunswick, N.J.: Rutgers University Press, 1968.

Freeland, Richard M. *Foreign Policy, Domestic Politics and Internal Security 1946–1948*. New York: Knopf, 1972.

Gaddis, John L. *The United States and the Origins of the Cold War, 1941–1947*. New York: Columbia University Press, 1972.

———. *Strategies of Containment: A Critical Appraisal of Postwar American National Security Policy*. New York: Oxford University Press, 1982.

Gallagher, Matthew P. *The Soviet History of World War II*. New York: Praeger, 1963.

Gallup, George H. *The Gallup Poll: Public Opinion 1935–1971*, vol. 1. New York: Random House, 1972.

Gardner, Lloyd C. *Architects of Illusion: Men and Ideas in American Foreign Policy 1941–1949*. Chicago: Quadrangle, 1970.

———. Arthur Schlesinger, Jr.; and Hans J. Morgenthau. *The Origins of the Cold War*. Lexington, Mass.: Xerox, 1970.

Garraty, John A., and Edward T. James, eds. *Dictionary of American Biography Supplement IV, 1946–1950*. New York: Charles Scribner's Sons, 1951.

Gilmore, Eddy. *Me and My Russian Wife*. New York: Greenwood Press, 1968.

Goolrick, William K. *Battle of the Bulge*. Alexandria, Va.: Time-Life, 1979.

Greene, Felix. *A Curtain of Ignorance: How the American Public Has Been Misinformed about China*. New York: Doubleday, 1964.

Griffith, William E. *The Superpowers and Regional Tensions: The USSR, the United States and Europe*. Lexington, Mass.: Lexington Books, 1982.

Grossman, Michael Baruch. *Portraying the President: The White House and the News Media*. Baltimore: The Johns Hopkins University Press, 1981.

Halberstam, David. *The Powers That Be*. New York: Knopf, 1979.

Halliday, Ernest Milton. *The Ignorant Armies: The Anglo-American Archangel Expedition, 1918–1919*. London: Weidenfeld and Nicolson, 1961.

Hamby, Alonzo. *Beyond the New Deal: Harry S. Truman*. New York: Columbia University Press, 1973.

Hammond, Paul. *The Cold War Years: American Foreign Policy Since 1945*. New York: Harcourt, Brace, Jovanovich, 1969.

Hammond, Thomas T. *Witnesses to the Origins of the Cold War*. Seattle: University of Washington Press, 1982.

Hastings, Paul. *The Cold War, 1945–1969*. London: Benn, 1969.

Herken, Gregg. *The Winning Weapon: The Atomic Bomb in the Cold War, 1945–1950*. New York: Knopf, 1980.

Herring, George C., Jr. *Aid to Russia, 1941–1946: Strategy, Diplomacy and the Origins of the Cold War*. New York: Columbia University Press, 1973.

Herz, Martin F., ed. *George Kennan and His Critics*. Washington, D.C.: Georgetown University Press, 1978.

Hilderbrand, Robert C. *Power and the People: Executive Management of Public Opinion in Foreign Affairs, 1897–1921*. Chapel Hill: University of North Carolina Press, 1981.

Hill, John E. C. *Lenin and the Russian Revolution*. New York: Penguin, 1971.

Hoffman, Stanley, and Charles Maier, eds. *The Marshall Plan: A Retrospective*. Boulder, Colo.: Westview Press, 1984.

Hohenberg, John. *Foreign Correspondence: The Great Reporters and Their Times*. New York: Columbia University Press, 1964.

———. *Free Press, Free People*. New York: Columbia University Press, 1971.

Hollander, Paul. *Soviet and American Society: A Comparison*. New York: Oxford University Press, 1973.

Horowitz, David, ed. *Containment and Revolution*. Boston: Beacon, 1967.

———. *The Free World Colossus: A Critique of American Foreign Policy in the Cold War*. New York: Hill and Wang, 1971.

Houghton, Neal D., ed. *Struggle Against History: U.S. Foreign Policy in an Age of Revolution*. New York: Washington Square, 1968.

Hovland, C. I., and I. L. Janis, eds. *Personality and Persuasibility*. New Haven, Conn.: Yale University Press, 1959.

Hovland, C. I., and H. H. Kellog, eds. *Communication and Persuasion: Psychological Studies of Opinion Change*. New Haven, Conn.: Yale University Press, 1953.

Howe, Quincy. *Ashes of Victory: World War II and Its Aftermath*. New York: Simon and Schuster, 1972.

Hudson, G. F. *The Hard and Bitter Peace: World Politics Since 1945*. New York: Frederick A. Praeger, 1967.

Israel, Jerry. *Progressivism and the Open Door: America and China, 1905–1921*. Pittsburgh: Pittsburgh University Press, 1971.

James, Robert Rhodes. *Winston S. Churchill: His Complete Speeches 1897–1963*, vol. 7. New York: Chelsea, 1974.

Jessup, John K., ed. *The Ideas of Henry Luce*. New York: Atheneum, 1969.

Johnson, Christopher. *Superpower: Comparing American and Soviet Foreign Policy*. New York: St. Martin's, 1984.

Juergens, George. *News from the White House: The Presidential Press Relationship in the Progressive Era*. Chicago: Rand McNally, 1981.

Kahn, E. J., Jr. *The China Hands: America's Foreign Service Officers and What Befell Them.* New York: Viking, 1972.

Kaltenborn, Hans V. *Fifty Fabulous Years 1900–1950.* New York: G. P. Putnam's Sons, 1950.

Kaplan, Stephen S. *Diplomacy of Power: Soviet Armed Forces as a Political Instrument.* Washington, D.C.: Brookings Institute, 1981.

Katz, Elihu, and Paul F. Lazarsfeld. *Personal Influence.* New York: Free Press, 1955.

Kennan, George F. *American Diplomacy 1900–1950.* Chicago: University of Chicago Press, 1951.

———. *Memoirs 1925–1950.* Boston: Little, Brown, 1960.

Kern, Montague; Patricia W. Levering; and Ralph B. Levering. *The Kennedy Crises: The Presidency and Foreign Policy.* Chapel Hill: University of North Carolina Press, 1984.

Kirkendall, Richard S., ed. *The Truman Period as a Research Field.* Columbia, Mo.: University of Missouri Press, 1967.

Kluger, Richard. *The Paper: The Life and Death of the New York Herald Tribune.* New York: Knopf, 1986.

Kobler, John. *Luce: His Time, Life, and Fortune.* Garden City, N.J.: Doubleday, 1968.

Kolko, Gabriel. *The Politics of War: The World and United States Foreign Policy, 1943–1945.* New York: Random House, 1968.

Kolko, Gabriel, and Joyce Kolko. *The Limits of Power: The World and United States Foreign Policy, 1945–1954.* New York: Harper and Row, 1972.

Kubek, Anthony. *How the Far East Was Lost: American Policy and the Creation of Communist China, 1941–1949.* Chicago: H. Regnery, 1963.

LaFeber, Walter. *America, Russia, and the Cold War, 1945–1980,* 4th ed. New York: John Wiley and Sons, 1980.

———. ed. *America in the Cold War: Twenty Years of Revolutions and Response, 1947–1967.* New York: Cornell University Press, 1969.

Larson, Thomas B. *Soviet-American Rivalry.* New York: W. W. Norton, 1978.

Lasch, Christopher. *American Liberals and the Russian Revolution.* New York: Knopf, 1962.

Leigh, Michael. *Mobilizing Consent: Public Opinion and Foreign Policy 1937–1947.* Westport, Conn.: Greenwood Press, 1976.

Levering, Ralph B. *American Opinion and the Russian Alliance, 1939–1945.* Chapel Hill: University of North Carolina Press, 1976.

———. *The Cold War, 1945–1972.* Arlington Heights, Ill.: Harlan Davidson, 1982.

Liang, Chin-Tung. *General Stilwell in China, 1942–1944: The Full Story.* Jamaica, N.Y.: St. John's University Press, 1972.

Liebling, A. J. *Mink and Red Herring: The Wayward Pressman's Casebook.* New York: Doubleday, 1949.

Lippmann, Walter. *The Cold War: A Study in U.S. Foreign Policy.* New York: Harper and Row, 1947.

Lowenstein, Meno. *American Opinion of Soviet Russia 1917–1933.* Washington, D.C.: Council on Public Affairs, 1941.

McLane, Charles B. *Soviet Policy and the Chinese Communists, 1931–1946.* New York: Columbia University Press, 1958.

McLane, Marshall. *Understanding Media.* New York: McGraw-Hill, 1964.

McPhaul, John J. *Deadlines & Monkeyshines: The Fabled World of Chicago Journalism.*
Englewood Cliffs, N.J.: Prentice-Hall, 1962.

Maddox, Robert. *The New Left and the Origins of the Cold War.* Princeton, N.J.:
Princeton University Press, 1973.

Mandelbaum, Michael. *The Nuclear Revolution: International Politics Before and After
Hiroshima.* New York: Cambridge University Press, 1981.

Markel, Lester. *Public Opinion and Foreign Policy.* New York: Harper and Brothers,
1949.

Markowitz, Norman D. *The Rise and Fall of the People's Century.* New York: Free
Press, 1973.

May, Ernest R. *The Truman Administration and China, 1945–1949.* Philadelphia:
Lippincott, 1975.

May, Gary. *China Scapegoat: The Diplomatic Ordeal of John Carter Vincent.* Washington, D.C.: New Republic, 1979.

Mayer, Arno. *Wilson vs. Lenin: Political Origins of the New Diplomacy, 1917–1918.*
Cleveland: Meridian, 1959.

Mee, Charles L., Jr. *Meeting at Potsdam.* New York: M. Evans, 1975.

———. *The Marshall Plan: The Launching of Pax Americana.* New York: Simon and
Schuster, 1984.

Messer, Robert L. *The End of an Alliance: James F. Byrnes, Roosevelt, Truman, and
the Origins of the Cold War.* Chapel Hill: University of North Carolina Press,
1982.

Michael, Henri. *The Second World War.* New York: Praeger, 1975.

Miller, Lynn H., and Ronald W. Preussen, eds. *Reflections on the Cold War: A Quarter
Century of American Foreign Policy.* Philadelphia: Temple, 1974.

Neumann, William L. *After Victory: Churchill, Roosevelt, Stalin and the Making of
Peace.* New York: Harper and Row, 1967.

Oglesby, Carl, and Richard Schaull. *Containment and Change.* London: MacMillan,
1967.

O'Neill, William L. *The Great Schism: Stalinism and the American Intellectuals, A Better
World.* New York: Simon and Schuster, 1982.

Pacher, Henry. "Revisionist Historians and the Cold War." In *Beyond the New Left,*
ed. Irving Howe. New York: McCall, 1970.

Paterson, Thomas G. *Soviet-American Confrontation: Postwar Reconstruction and the
Origins of the Cold War.* Baltimore: The Johns Hopkins University Press,
1973.

———. *On Every Front: The Making of the Cold War.* New York: Norton, 1979.

Perkins, Dexter. *The Diplomacy of a New Age: Major Issues in U.S. Policy Since 1945.*
Bloomington, Ind.: Indiana University Press, 1967.

Peterson, Theodore. *Magazines in the Twentieth Century.* Urbana, Ill.: University of
Illinois Press, 1956.

Phillips, Cabell. *The Truman Presidency: The History of a Triumphant Succession.* New
York: Macmillan, 1966.

Pilpel, Robert H. *Churchill in America 1895–1961.* New York: Harcourt, Brace,
Jovanovich, 1976.

Poen, Monte, ed. *Strictly Personal and Confidential: The Letters Harry Truman Never
Mailed.* Boston: Little, Brown, 1982.

Pogue, Forest C. *The Supreme Command.* Washington, D.C.: Office of the Chief of Military History, 1954.

———. *George Marshall: Education of a General, 1880–1939.* New York: Viking, 1963.

———. *George C. Marshall: Ordeal and Hope, 1939–1942.* New York: Viking, 1966.

———. *George C. Marshall: Organizer of Victory, 1943–1945.* New York: Viking,1973.

Pollard, Robert A. *Economic Security and the Origins of the Cold War 1945–1950.* New York: Columbia University Press, 1985.

Reardon-Anderson, James. *Yenan and the Great Powers: The Origins of Chinese Communist Foreign Policy 1944–1946.* New York: Columbia University Press, 1980.

Roosevelt, Nicholas. *A Front Row Seat.* Norman: University of Oklahoma Press, 1953.

Rose, Lisle Abbott. *After Yalta.* New York: Scribner, 1973.

Rosenau, James N. *Public Opinion and Foreign Policy.* New York: Oxford University Press, 1967.

Rosenberg, Emily S. *Spreading the American Dream: American Economic and Cultural Expansion, 1890–1945.* New York: Hill and Wang, 1982.

Salisbury, Harrison E. *A Journey for Our Times.* New York: Harper and Row, 1983.

Schuman, Frederick L. *The Cold War: Retrospect and Prospect.* Baton Rouge: Louisiana State University Press, 1967.

Schwartz, Morton. *Soviet Perceptions of the United States.* Berkeley: University of California Press, 1978.

Seabury, Paul. *The Rise and Decline of the Cold War.* New York: Basic, 1967.

Sears, Stephen W. *Battle of the Bulge.* New York: American Heritage, 1969.

Service, John S. *Lost Chance in China: The World War II Dispatches of John S. Service.* New York: Random House, 1974.

Shadegg, Stephen. *Clare Booth Luce.* New York: Simon and Schuster, 1970.

Shirer, William L. *Berlin Diary: The Journal of a Foreign Correspondent, 1934–1941.* New York: Wiley, 1944.

Simons, Gerald. *Victory in Europe.* Alexandria, Va.: Time-Life, 1982.

Small, Melvin, ed. *Public Opinion and Historians: Interdisciplinary Perspectives.* Detroit: Wayne State University Press, 1970.

Smith, A. Merriman. *Thank You, Mr. President: A White House Notebook.* New York: Harper and Brothers, 1946.

———. *A President Is Many Men.* New York: Harper and Brothers, 1948.

———. *A President's Odyssey.* New York: Harper and Brothers, 1961.

———. *The Good News Day.* Indianapolis: Bobbs-Merrill, 1962.

Smith, Timothy G. *Merriman Smith's Book of Presidents: A White House Memoir.* New York: W. W. Norton, 1972.

Snell, John L., ed. *The Meaning of Yalta: Big Three Diplomacy and the New Balance of Power.* Baton Rouge: Louisiana State University Press, 1956.

Steel, Ronald. *Pax Americana.* New York: Viking, 1967.

———. *Walter Lippmann and the American Century.* Boston: Little, Brown, 1980.

Stettinius, Edward R., Jr. *Roosevelt and the Russians: The Yalta Conference.* Garden City, N.J.: Doubleday, 1949.

Stueck, William Whitney, Jr. *The Road to Confrontation: American Policy Toward*

China and Korea, 1947–1970. Chapel Hill: University of North Carolina Press, 1981.

Sulzberger, Cyrus L. *The Coldest War: Russia's Game in China.* New York: Harcourt, Brace, Jovanovich, 1974.

Summers, Harrison B. *A Thirty Year History of Programs Carried on National Radio Networks in the United States 1926–1956.* Columbus: Ohio State University Press, 1958.

Swanberg, W. A. *Luce and His Empire.* New York: Charles Scribner's Sons, 1972.

Talese, Gay. *The Kingdom and the Power.* New York: World Publishing, 1969.

Thoharis, Athan. *The Yalta Myths: An Issue in U.S. Politics, 1945–1955.* Columbia, Mo.: University of Missouri Press, 1970.

———. *Seeds of Repression: Harry S. Truman and the Origins of McCarthyism.* Chicago: Quadrangle, 1971.

Toland, John. *Battle: The Story of the Bulge.* New York: New American Library, 1960.

———. *The Last 100 Days.* New York: Random House, 1966.

Treadgold, Donald W. *The Development of the U.S.S.R.: An Exchange of Views.* Seattle: University of Washington Press, 1964.

Truman, Harry S. *Year of Decisions.* New York: Doubleday, 1955.

Truman, Margaret. *Harry S. Truman.* New York: Morrow, 1972.

Tsou, Tang. *America's Failure in China, 1941–1950.* Chicago: University of Chicago Press, 1963.

Tuchman, Barbara. *Stilwell and the American Experience in China, 1911–45.* New York: Macmillan, 1970.

Tucker, Nancy Bernkopf. *Patterns in the Dust: Chinese-American Relations and the Recognition Controversy, 1949–1950.* New York: Columbia University Press, 1983.

Ulam, Adam. *The Rivals: America and Russia Since World War I.* New York: Viking, 1971.

Varg, Paul A. *The Closing of the Door: Sino-American Relations, 1936–1946.* East Lansing: Michigan State University Press, 1973.

Wagner, Richard V., and John Sherwood, eds. *The Study of Attitude Change.* Belmont, Calif.: Wadsworth, 1969.

Waldrop, Frank C. *McCormick of Chicago: An Unconventional Portrait of a Controversial Figure.* Englewoods Cliffs, N.J.: Prentice-Hall, 1966.

Wendt, Lloyd. *Chicago Tribune: The Rise of a Great American Newspaper.* Chicago: Rand McNally, 1979.

Wexler, Imanuel. *The Marshall Plan Revisited: The European Recovery Program in Economic Perspective.* Westport, Conn.: Greenwood Press, 1983.

White, Graham. *FDR and the Press.* Chicago: University of Chicago Press, 1981.

White, Theodore Harold. *Thunder Out of China.* New York: William Sloane, 1946.

Williams, William Appleman. *The Tragedy of American Diplomacy.* Chicago: Rand McNally, 1959.

GOVERNMENT DOCUMENTS

Commission for the Publication of Diplomatic Documents under the Ministry of Foreign Affairs of the U.S.S.R. *Stalin's Correspondence with Churchill, Attlee, Roosevelt, and Truman, 1941–45,* New York: E. P. Dutton, 1958.

U.S. Department of State. *Foreign Relations of the United States, 1944*, vols. 3 and 4; 1946, vols. 2–10; 1947, vols. 3–7. Washington, D.C.: U.S. Government Printing Office, 1968–1972.

MANUSCRIPTS

Ayers, Eben A. (assistant press secretary to Truman and Franklin D. Roosevelt). Diary, Boxes 1–16. Harry S. Truman Library, Manuscripts Division, Ayers Collection, Independence, Missouri.

Billings, John Shaw (associate editor of *Time* magazine). Diary, vols. 20–26. Caroliniana Library, Manuscripts Division, University of South Carolina, Columbia, South Carolina.

————. Papers, Boxes 1–2. Caroliniana Library, Manuscripts Division, Billings Collection, University of South Carolina, Columbia, South Carolina.

Hightower, John M. (Associated Press State Department correspondent). Papers, U.S. Mss 43 AF, Box 2. State Historical Society of Wisconsin, Manuscripts Division, Madison, Wisconsin.

Kaltenborn, Hans V. (radio foreign affairs commentator). Papers, U.S. Mss 1 AF, Boxes 172–78. State Historical Society of Wisconsin, Manuscripts Division, Madison, Wisconsin.

————. Correspondence, U.S. Mss 1 AF, Boxes 102–10. State Historical Society of Wisconsin, Manuscripts Division, Madison, Wisconsin.

Lochner, Louis (Associated Press correspondent in Germany, radio commentator). Papers, U.S. Mss 21 AF, Boxes 24–28. State Historical Society of Wisconsin, Manuscripts Division, Madison, Wisconsin.

McNaughton, Frank (Washington correspondent for *Time* magazine). Papers, Boxes 1–8. Harry S. Truman Library, Manuscripts Division, McNaughton Reports, Independence, Missouri.

Oakes, John (editorial editor, *The New York Times*). Papers, Micro 96, 728, Reels 1–6. State Historical Society of Wisconsin, Microfilm Division, Madison, Wisconsin.

Ross, Charles G. (Truman's press secretary). Papers, Boxes 1–9. Harry S. Truman Library, Manuscripts Division, Ross Collection, Independence, Missouri.

Smith, A. Merriman (United Press White House correspondent). Papers, U.S. Mss 72 AF, Boxes 1–4. State Historical Society of Wisconsin, Manuscripts Division, Madison, Wisconsin.

Swing, Raymond Gram (radio commentator). Papers, U.S. Mss 63 AF, Boxes 1–2. State Historical Society of Wisconsin, Manuscripts Division, Madison, Wisconsin.

Truman, Harry S. Papers, Boxes 144, 162, 190, 589. Harry S. Truman Library, Manuscripts Division, Secretary's files, 1945–1953, Independence, Missouri.

ORAL HISTORIES, MISCELLANEOUS DOCUMENTS

Hightower, John M. Letter of February 23, 1983, to author.

McCutcheon, John. Telephone interview of April 30, 1985.

"Making History, Day by Day for Over a Century." *San Francisco Chronicle* inhouse historical brochure, 1984.

Nixon, Robert. Oral history, vol. 1. Interview with Jerry Hess, archivist, Bethesda, Md., October 9, 1970. Interview stored in Manuscript Room, Harry S. Truman Library, Independence, Missouri.
Peck, Templeton. Telephone interviews of December 12, 1984, and Martch 27, 1985.

Index

About the Author

LOUIS LIEBOVICH, an assistant professor of journalism at the University of Illinois, Urbana-Champaign, brings both a professional and academic background to this work. He received his Ph.D. in mass communication at the University of Wisconsin, Madison, and currently teaches courses in journalism history, reporting, and news editing at Illinois. Liebovich has written and published articles on the press and the presidency and the role of the press in foreign affairs. He was a newsman between 1971 and 1980 at three newspapers in the Midwest. He was a general-assignment and then full-time investigative reporter for the *Milwaukee Sentinel* between 1976 and 1980. He won or shared nine writing awards as a reporter, including five for investigative reporting. This is his first book.